INFLATION, SAVING AND GROWTH IN DEVELOPING ECONOMIES

INFLATION, SAVING AND GROWTH IN DEVELOPING ECONOMIES

A. P. THIRLWALL

Reader in Economics, University of Kent

St. Martin's Press   New York

AFFILIATED PUBLISHERS: Macmillan Limited, London—
also at Bombay, Calcutta, Madras and Melbourne

Text set in 10/12 pt. Monotype Baskerville, printed by letterpress,
and bound in Great Britain at The Pitman Press, Bath

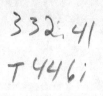

To Lorenzo and Alessandra
and their generation

Contents

Preface

The purpose of this book is to consider the theory and empirical evidence, such as it is, in support of the view that inflationary finance, and the process of inflation itself, can, within limits, accelerate the development process so that countries may achieve tolerable living standards, as measured by real per capita income, sooner than would otherwise be the case. It redresses the bias against inflationary finance found in most traditional textbooks. The book is not intended to be a tight theoretical exposition of money and inflation in growth models. It is intended as a contribution to the development debate, presenting in general terms, with occasional theoretical backing, a case for more expansionary policies in developing economies which may involve inflation. The term inflation is used here in the formal sense of a rise in the general price level whatever its cause; on the other hand, particular attention will be centred on the term in its traditional sense of governments using monetary means to finance expenditure. Strictly speaking, monetary expansion need not necessarily involve a rise in the price level if supply can match increases in monetary demand, but in situations where capital and consumer goods are in short supply it normally will – at least in the short run. There is also a distinction to be made between demand inflation and other types of inflation. The argument for inflation is essentially an argument for demand inflation. Other types of inflation, including cost inflation and structural inflation, are best considered as the price of growth rather than a stimulus.

This is not a subject which has received systematic treatment in the development literature at a level appropriate for undergraduate students. Yet the subject is important because of the issues it raises for development strategy which at some stage must be faced by the economist and policy maker alike. What is the most appropriate rate of monetary expansion? What is the 'optimum' rate of inflation? What proportion of investment resources should be bid away by governments to enable them to invest resources more 'profitably' on society's behalf? These are not questions that can be lightly pushed

aside. They must be considered alongside tax policy, choice of technology, foreign trade policy, and so on.

As will become clear throughout the course of the book the case for inflationary policies, leading to rising prices, which some people might call the Keynesian approach to development, is not clear cut theoretically, and the empirical evidence is equivocal. From studying the inflationary experience of the developing countries outside Latin America, however, it is difficult not to be struck by the apparent caution and conservatism that seems to have prevailed in the majority of countries, at least until the recent past. To some extent this can be seen from the statistics on inflation for these countries, which show for most of the post-war period rates of inflation averaging not more than 3 to 4 per cent per year. Admittedly some of the sting of excess monetary demand is typically taken out of the developing economies by imports, and inflation rates may also be under-recorded for obvious political reasons, but the impression remains that capital accumulation and employment growth may have been sacrificed for the sake of financial stability. With these background observations in mind the book is written with a bias in favour of more expansionist government policies.

It is only fair to warn the reader in advance, however, that the empirical evidence to support the assertion that inflation is strongly conducive to higher rates of per capita income growth is hard to come by. The results in Chapter 9, which examine the relation between inflation and the savings ratio, are very disappointing. As we remarked earlier, however, there is a distinction to be made between inflationary finance and the process of inflation, and also between types of inflation, some of which are conducive to growth and others not. In a way, the more 'successful' inflationary finance is in financing projects which raise output, the weaker the relation between output growth and rising prices is likely to be. Unfortunately the relation between demand expansion and growth is not directly observable. Only the relation between price rises and growth is directly observable. Furthermore, it is impossible to say how much observed inflation is attributable to one cause or another. The relation between demand inflation and growth could easily be distorted by varying degrees of other types of inflation. These difficulties should be borne in mind in interpreting and evaluating the empirical results, especially in Chapter 9.

The book turns out to be a cross between a textbook and a mild

polemic. Textbooks and polemics are not always comfortable bed-fellows. If this book suffers as a result, I apologise in advance. I am hopeful, however, that the general argument, the theoretical exposition and the mixture of old and new empirical evidence will be of interest and use to students in the sense of providing a systematic treatment of a relatively neglected topic in traditional textbooks (including my own![1]).

The polemical side of the book I am less sanguine about. It takes a particular view of the development process that many people may react against. In particular, there is heavy emphasis on the role of capital accumulation in the development process; on the role and responsibility of governments in promoting development, and on the necessity to invest in excess of plans to save to forcibly release re-sources for the development effort. The stress on combining infla-tionary policies with the development of the agricultural sector, however, and on changing factor proportions in favour of more labour intensive techniques, will I hope meet with wide support.

I am conscious, of course, that since embarking on this book, inflation in almost every country in the world has become a common fact of life. Events have caught up with me, so to speak! I am not so alarmed by this occurrence as some of my colleagues. Indeed, I take the recent bout of inflation as support for the polemical position taken. It coincides with unprecedented rates of growth of output in the greater part of the world economy.

The book was embarked on while I was Research Associate in the Industrial Relations Section, Princeton University, 1971–2. I shall be eternally grateful to the Section for its hospitality and support, not to mention the constant stimulus of my colleagues, especially Orley Ashenfelter, Dan Hamermesh, Jim Hefner, Al Rees and my research assistant, Hal White. The book was completed at the University of Kent. My colleagues Bob Dixon (now at the University of Papua New Guinea), Roger Hill, Homa Katouzian and Charles Kennedy all read the complete manuscript, and I am deeply grateful for their constructive criticisms and advice for improvement even though it has not always been heeded. My secretary, Marilyn Spice, typed successive drafts of the book. To her, for the help and under-standing over the years, I am also deeply grateful.

[1] *Growth and Development with Special Reference to Developing Economies* (London: Macmillan, 1972).

'It is worse, in an impoverished world, to provoke unemployment than to disappoint the rentier.'

J. M. Keynes

'Inflation which is due to the creation of money for the purpose of accelerating capital formation results in accelerated capital formation.'   A. Lewis

I

Inflation, Saving and Growth

Introduction

One of the primary aims of development policy in developing economies is to raise the rate of growth of output in order to raise current levels of consumption and to provide resources for investment and future consumption. A country's long-run growth rate depends on the rate of growth of its labour force (l) and the rate of growth of the productivity of labour (t). The latter depends, in turn, on capital accumulation and technical progress in the widest sense, including improvements in the quality of labour and capital and methods of organising production. The growth of the labour force (the employed and the unemployed) plus the growth rate of labour productivity can be referred to as the growth rate of effective labour or, alternatively, the natural rate of growth (G_n).[1] Hence

$$G_n = l + t \tag{1.1}$$

The natural rate of growth in any society sets the upper limit to growth in the long run. It measures a society's growth of productive potential. Growth in this sense is a supply phenomenon. It measures the ability or capacity to produce.

Whether a country can grow at its natural rate, however, depends on the quantity of investible resources it has at its disposal and on how it deploys those resources. Suppose that at an acceptable rate of profit it takes three extra units of capital to produce an additional unit of output and that the ratio of the increment of capital to national output (the investment ratio) is 9 per cent, the rate of growth permitted by these conditions is given by the division of the two ratios

$$\frac{\Delta Y}{Y} = \frac{\Delta K}{Y} \bigg/ \frac{\Delta K}{\Delta Y} = 9\,\%/3 = 3\,\% \tag{1.2}$$

[1] R. Harrod, *Towards a Dynamic Economics* (London: Macmillan, 1948).

where $\Delta Y/Y$ is the growth rate of output,
    $\Delta K/Y = I/Y$ is the investment ratio
and $\Delta K/\Delta Y = I/\Delta Y$ is the incremental capital–output ratio.

The natural rate of growth may lie substantially above this rate but it cannot be achieved unless the ratio of investible resources to output rises or capital required per unit of additional output falls. Suppose, for example, that the labour force is growing at the rate of 4 per cent per annum ($l = 4$ per cent) and that the productivity of labour is growing at the rate of 2 per cent per annum ($t = 2$ per cent). $G_n = 6$ per cent in equation (1.1). According to equation (1.2), however, to achieve a growth rate of 6 per cent requires that capital also grows at the rate of 6 per cent, which, in turn, would require an investment ratio of 18 per cent. But the investment ratio is only 9 per cent, which means that there will be a 3 percentage point gap between the actual and potential rates of growth. There will also be a gap between the growth of the labour force and the growth of employment opportunities. Given the capital–output ratio, the capital–labour ratio must rise at the same rate as the productivity of labour, which means that the growth of employment will be uniquely determined by the difference between the rate of growth of capital and the rate of growth of productivity. If productivity is growing at 2 per cent per annum and the capital stock at 3 per cent per annum, employment (the demand for labour) must be growing at 1 per cent per annum. Since the labour force is growing at 4 per cent per annum there will be a 3 percentage point gap between the rate of growth of the labour force and the rate of growth of employment. This formulation of the employment problem gives an alternative expression for the actual growth rate of

$$\frac{\Delta Y}{Y} = e + t = 3\ \% \tag{1.3}$$

where e is the rate of growth of employment

and t is the rate of growth of labour productivity.

In short, if the incremental capital–output ratio is fixed, a situation in which the natural rate of growth exceeds the attainable rate of growth can be clearly seen to represent a chronic shortage of capital. It also implies growing unemployment of the 'structural' variety because the growth of effective labour exceeds the growth of capital.

With a fixed capital–output ratio, implying fixed production coefficients, there is no way for the surplus labour to be absorbed. An economy in which the natural growth rate exceeds the attainable rate may be characterised, therefore, by inflation arising from excess demand on the one hand, and by unemployment, stemming from a shortage of capital and rigid technical coefficients of production, on the other.

Excess demand arises from the fact that if the natural rate of growth lies above the attainable rate of growth there must be profitable investment opportunities for saving in excess of the saving currently being undertaken. For example, if the natural growth rate is 6 per cent and the 'profitable' capital–output ratio is 3, there would be profitable investment opportunities for a savings ratio of 18 per cent, yet the actual savings ratio is only 9 per cent. Consumers and investors will be competing for limited resources. Planned investment will exceed planned saving causing aggregate demand to exceed aggregate supply. The inflation induced in these circumstances may produce tendencies towards equilibrium through favourable effects of inflation on saving, but the time it takes for the saving ratio to rise to permit growth at the natural rate may be extremely long.

In the context of capital-scarce countries, like most developing economies, the significance of the growth rate set by the propensity to save (call it the warranted growth rate[1]) is that it sets a limit to the actual real growth rate that can be achieved at any point in time. If capital is fully utilised because it is scarce there is little or no scope for reducing capital requirements per unit of output which, given the savings ratio, is the only way in which the actual growth rate could exceed the warranted rate determined by plans to save. Of course, if inflation makes *ex post* (actual) saving greater than *ex ante* (planned) saving, the actual growth rate can exceed the warranted rate in a definitional sense, but real saving remains the effective constraint on growth. This is so whether the classical view is taken that prior saving is necessary for investment or whether the Keynesian view is taken that investment spending can generate its own saving. A country cannot grow faster than the willingness of the community to accumulate real capital. It is of little consequence whether the warranted rate is thought of as constraining the actual growth rate, or vice versa.

---

[1] The term coined by Harrod, *Towards a Dynamic Economics*. See Chapter 4 of this book for further discussion.

At any growth rate below the natural growth rate, the actual and warranted growth rates will move together.

This book addresses itself to the question of the role of monetary expansion and inflation in raising the attainable growth rate of countries in circumstances where the warranted and actual growth rates lie below the natural rate. There are both direct and indirect effects to consider. If the savings ratio can be raised by inflationary (monetary) means, the attainable growth rate may be raised not only in the short term but also in the long term if the savings ratio is positively related to the growth rate and to the level of per capita income, both of which will rise in the initial stages of monetary expansion.

When the warranted rate has risen to the natural rate, a second set of questions arise. First, in the long-run steady state, when the warranted and natural growth rates are equal, can the characteristics of the steady state growth path be altered by monetary means? In particular, can the degree of capital intensity, on which output per head and consumption per head largely depend, be raised? Second, can a rise in the warranted rate of growth itself induce tendencies to raise the natural rate of growth to expand further the long-run output and consumption prospects of developing countries? These are important questions, but subsidiary ones in this analysis for two reasons. First, contemplation of the long-run steady state is fanciful in the context of developing economies at the present time. For reasons to be outlined shortly it is fairly evident that in most developing countries the actual growth rate falls short of the growth of productive potential owing to a shortage and misuse of capital. Second, because it is possible to take several different views of money, and its role in the economy, monetary growth models can have different and conflicting steady state solutions. Monetary growth theory is largely inconclusive and irrelevant for the analysis of growth in developing economies. All that will be done here will be to draw attention to the main issues. The major emphasis is on the means of raising the warranted and actual growth rates on the assumption that they lie below the natural rate.

The Growth of Output and Living Standards

The growth of output is not a sufficient condition for a rise in general living standards. Living standards in developing countries can only

be raised by a rise in the average level of income per head of the population. By definition, income per head of the population can only rise if the growth of total income exceeds the growth of total population. In most developing countries over the last twenty years at least there has, in fact, been a steady rise in the level of per capita income but, overall, the rise has been slower than in the more developed nations. There is a school of thought which argues that it is the more rapid growth of population in the developing countries which is to blame, which has added more to the numbers to be supported than to output or income. The cross-section evidence for this assertion, however, is weak.[1] It appears from the evidence that the relation between population growth and output growth is positive and virtually equi-proportional, so that population growth exerts a more or less neutral effect on the growth of income per head. The relatively poor performance of the developing countries seems more likely to be accounted for by low rates of capital accumulation and technical progress for which population growth is not to blame either. On the contrary, the evidence suggests that technical progress and population growth are positively related and that capital accumulation and technical progress are heavily dependent on each other.

Capital Accumulation

There is no satisfactory counter-argument to the proposition that capital accumulation, broadly defined, is central to the development process. Capital accumulation, which is broadly defined to include expenditure not just on physical assets but the purchase of all types of goods and services which enhance the productivity of labour and the flow of goods in the future, is a necessary condition for growth. In particular, capital accumulation may be necessary for the embodiment of technical progress. Time series studies for individual countries and cross-section studies between countries reveal the importance of capital accumulation for growth, especially in developing countries. For example: Correa estimates a contribution of capital to growth of the order of 4 per cent in Argentina and Mexico, 30 to 35 per cent in

[1] See my paper 'A Cross-Section Study of Population Growth and the Growth of Output and Per Capita Income in a Production Function Framework', *Manchester School of Economic and Social Studies* (December 1972) and other references cited therein.

Israel and 35 per cent in Greece.[1] Maddison, taking 22 developing countries over the period 1950–65, estimates an overall contribution of capital accumulation to growth of 55 per cent.[2] In cross-section work by the present author a close association was found between the rate of growth of output and the growth of gross domestic fixed capital formation taking a 40 country sample over the period 1950 to 1966, and a separate 23 country sample of developing countries.[3] The estimated production function taking 40 countries is

$$\frac{\Delta Y}{Y} = 2\cdot346 + \underset{(0\cdot069)}{0\cdot253} \left(\frac{\Delta K}{K}\right) + \underset{(0\cdot175)}{0\cdot521} \left(\frac{\Delta N}{N}\right) \qquad r^2 = 0\cdot43$$

where $\Delta Y/Y$ is the rate of growth of output,

$\Delta K/K$ is the rate of growth of the capital stock

and $\Delta N/N$ is population growth.

A strong association between capital accumulation and growth is also reported by Pesmazoglu taking a 43 country sample over the period 1957–68.[4] His coefficients on the growth of capital variable are very significant and very close to my own estimates. Pesmazoglu's estimated 'production function' for 43 countries is

$$\frac{\Delta Y}{Y} = 2\cdot42 + \underset{(0\cdot05)}{0\cdot28} \left(\frac{\Delta K}{K}\right) + \underset{(0\cdot04)}{0\cdot05} \left(\frac{I}{Y}\right) \qquad r^2 = 0\cdot50$$

where I/Y is the investment ratio.

$\Delta K/K$ and I/Y are included in the function as separate variables to distinguish the influence of the overall savings effect on growth (I/Y) from the technical progress-carrying effects of investment as measured by the rate of growth of fixed investment $(\Delta K/K)$.

Pesmazoglu also works with several sub-samples of countries classified according to the level of per capita income. While the variable $\Delta K/K$ is consistently significant, it is interesting to note that

---

[1] H. Correa, 'Sources of Economic Growth in Latin America 1950–62', *Southern Economic Journal* (July 1970).

[2] A. Maddison, *Economic Progress and Policy in Developing Countries* (London: Allen & Unwin, 1970).

[3] A. P. Thirlwall, 'A Cross-Section Study of Population Growth'.

[4] J. Pesmazoglu, 'Growth, Investment and Saving Ratios: Some Long and Medium Term Associations by Groups of Countries', *Bulletin of the Oxford University Institute of Economics and Statistics* (November 1972).

in very poor countries the responsiveness of output growth to capital accumulation is less than in countries at an intermediate stage of development. This can be rationalised in terms of differences in the quality of capital accumulated in the two sets of countries and differences in the quality of co-operating factors of production.

The notion of capital accumulation as a source of growth, which is as old as economics itself, fell into disrepute following Solow's dramatic finding in 1957 that only 10 per cent of the growth of output per man in the American economy over the previous half century could be accounted for by the growth of capital per man, the remaining 90 per cent being due to technical progress.[1] Early production function studies of the contribution of capital to growth, however, including Solow's, suffer from serious limitations, and even today they often fail to capture the interdependencies that exist between capital accumulation and other growth-inducing forces dependent on capital accumulation. Particularly serious in the early studies were the assumptions that technical progress is independent of the rate of capital accumulation; that capital accumulation consists exclusively of investment in plant and machinery in manufacturing industry, and that perfectly competitive equilibrium prevails in the economy (i.e. factors receive the value of their marginal product) such that the elasticity of output with respect to capital can be equated with capital's share of national income.[2]

It must also be borne in mind that even if it is the case that capital accumulation properly defined is relatively unimportant for growth in developed countries there may be a fundamental difference between countries that already have large endowments of capital per head and those which do not. In countries where there is little by way of specialisation and the division of labour, there is enormous scope for capital accumulation to permit more efficient and roundabout

---

[1] R. Solow, 'Technical Change and the Aggregate Production Function', *Review of Economics and Statistics* (August 1957). (The estimates reported above are as corrected by Hogan in *Review of Economics and Statistics*, November 1958.)

[2] Denote the elasticity of output with respect to capital as

$$\frac{\Delta Y}{\Delta K} \cdot \frac{K}{Y},$$

where $\Delta Y/\Delta K$ is the marginal product of capital. If capital is paid its marginal product then $\Delta Y/\Delta K = r$, where r is the 'price' of capital. rK/Y is capital's share of income.

methods of production. Technologically backward countries also have, by definition, a backlog of technology to make up. In these circumstances the rate of capital accumulation needed to absorb new technology is likely to be greater than in countries already developed. As Hicks has remarked, 'it is very wrong to give the impression to a poor country which is very far from equilibrium even on past technology that capital accumulation is a matter of minor importance.'[1]

Capital accumulation requires investment and ultimately a level of real saving to match it. It has already been suggested that there is reason to believe that many developing economies at the present time are not achieving their growth potential because of a shortage of investible resources. The evidence is not hard to find. Foreign capital still finds it profitable to flow into developing countries in spite of political instability and economic uncertainty. Interest rates outside the organised money markets reach levels in excess of 100 per cent, and borrowers are willing to pay the price. There is also growing unemployment in the urban sectors of developing countries which it would be difficult, if not ironic, to classify as due to deficient aggregate demand. On the average, domestic saving ratios in developing countries are some 5 to 10 percentage points below the domestic savings ratios in developing countries where capital needs are not so pressing. Whereas the ratio of gross domestic saving to income in developed countries averages approximately 22 per cent, in developing countries the ratio is approximately 15 per cent. Details for several individual countries are given in Appendix 1. A summary by 'continents' is given in Table 1.1.

The discrepancy in investible resources between developed and developing countries is narrowed somewhat by net capital flows from developed to developing countries, but the broad characterisation of developing countries as capital-scarce is correct given the needs of these countries and the low ratios of capital to labour prevailing in a wide range of activities.

Growth and the Savings Ratio

From knowledge of the production function studies reported earlier we should expect to find a positive relation between the saving/investment ratio and the rate of growth of output and per capita income,

---

[1] J. Hicks, *Capital and Growth* (Oxford University Press, 1965).

provided that the capital–output ratio is fairly uniform across countries. For a given capital–output ratio, the higher the investment ratio is, the higher will be the rate of capital accumulation and the higher the growth rate. In Table 1.2 four equations are reported for three samples of countries showing the relation between the growth of

TABLE 1.1

Saving and Investment as a % of G.N.P.
(Average 1960–7)

	Domestic saving	Gross investment
Africa	13·1	16·7
South Asia	11·3	13·9
East Asia	11·0	15·6
South Europe	21·5	24·9
Latin America	16·3	17·7
Middle East	14·8	19·8
Developing countries	15·0	17·8
Developed countries	21·7	21·2

Source: Pearson Report, *Partners in Development* (London: Pall Mall Press, 1969), p. 31.

income and the savings ratio; the growth of income and the investment ratio; the growth of per capita income and the savings ratio; and the growth of per capita income and the investment ratio. Since output growth is positively related to population growth, which grows at different rates between countries, and investment is not confined to domestic saving, the strongest association is to be expected between the rate of growth of income adjusted for population growth and the investment ratio. The evidence bears this out except in the case of the developed countries where there is a stronger association between the growth of total income and the investment ratio than between the growth of per capita income and the investment ratio.

Taking all sixty-eight observations in Appendix 1, the mixed sample of developed and developing countries gives a very weak positive relation between the growth of income and the savings ratio. The relation is slightly stronger when the growth of income is related

TABLE 1.2

Income Growth and the Savings/Investment Ratio

All Observations (68)

The growth of income

$$\frac{\Delta Y}{Y} = \quad 4 \cdot 422 + \underset{(0 \cdot 0317)}{0 \cdot 0339} \frac{S}{Y} \qquad r^2 = 0 \cdot 017$$

$$\frac{\Delta Y}{Y} = \quad 2 \cdot 221 + \underset{(0 \cdot 0351)}{0 \cdot 1405} \frac{I}{Y} \qquad r^2 = 0 \cdot 195$$

The growth of per capita income

$$\frac{\Delta Y_N}{Y_N} = \quad 1 \cdot 315 + \underset{(0 \cdot 0324)}{0 \cdot 0920} \frac{S}{Y} \qquad r^2 = 0 \cdot 108$$

$$\frac{\Delta Y_N}{Y_N} = \quad -0 \cdot 887 + \underset{(0 \cdot 0332)}{0 \cdot 1912} \frac{I}{Y} \qquad r^2 = 0 \cdot 338$$

Developing Countries (48)

The growth of income

$$\frac{\Delta Y}{Y} = \quad 4 \cdot 353 + \underset{(0 \cdot 0527)}{0 \cdot 0409} \frac{S}{Y} \qquad r^2 = 0 \cdot 013$$

$$\frac{\Delta Y}{Y} = \quad 1 \cdot 903 + \underset{(0 \cdot 0496)}{0 \cdot 1698} \frac{I}{Y} \qquad r^2 = 0 \cdot 203$$

The growth of per capita income

$$\frac{\Delta Y_N}{Y_N} = \quad 2 \cdot 095 + \underset{(0 \cdot 0542)}{0 \cdot 0248} \frac{S}{Y} \qquad r^2 = 0 \cdot 005$$

$$\frac{\Delta Y_N}{Y_N} = \quad -0 \cdot 721 + \underset{(0 \cdot 0477)}{0 \cdot 1799} \frac{I}{Y} \qquad r^2 = 0 \cdot 236$$

TABLE 1.2 (*contd.*)

Developed Countries (20)

The growth of income

$$\frac{\Delta Y}{Y} = \quad 4\cdot124 + \underset{(0\cdot0723)}{0\cdot0436} \frac{S}{Y} \qquad r^2 = 0\cdot020$$

$$\frac{\Delta Y}{Y} = -0\cdot680 + \underset{(0\cdot072)}{0\cdot240} \frac{I}{Y} \qquad r^2 = 0\cdot377$$

The growth of per capita income

$$\frac{\Delta Y_N}{Y_N} = \quad 1\cdot300 + \underset{(0\cdot0659)}{0\cdot1081} \frac{S}{Y} \qquad r^2 = 0\cdot130$$

$$\frac{\Delta Y_N}{Y_N} = -1\cdot012 + \underset{(0\cdot0757)}{0\cdot1994} \frac{I}{Y} \qquad r^2 = 0\cdot278$$

Notes: Bracketed terms are the standard errors of the regression co-efficients.
For data and data sources see Appendix 1.
S/Y is the savings ratio; I/Y is the investment ratio.

to the investment ratio, but a really strong significant relation only emerges when the growth of per capita income is related to the investment ratio.

The same pattern of results is evident taking a sample of forty-eight developing countries.

In the sample of twenty developed countries, however, while the investment ratio is a more important determinant of the growth of income and per capita income than the savings ratio, the relation between the growth of income and the investment ratio is stronger than the relation between the growth of per capita income and the invest-ment ratio. There are a number of possible explanations for this result including the possibility that the use of capital is dependent on the availability of labour; a dependence not present in developing countries. A similar result was obtained by T. P. Hill taking a sample of six developed countries over the period 1954–62 with the ratio of fixed investment to national income as the independent variable.[1]

[1] T. P. Hill, 'Growth and Investment According to International Com-parisons', *Economic Journal* (June 1964).

Relating the growth of income (G) to the fixed investment ratio (I) he obtained the equation $G = -6 \cdot 11 + 0 \cdot 58 \, I \, (r^2 = 0 \cdot 96)$. Relating the growth of per capita income (g) to the fixed investment ratio he obtained the equation $g = -3 \cdot 57 + 0 \cdot 38 \, I \, (r^2 = 0 \cdot 67)$.

Adding twelve other countries to the sample of six reduced the degree of association of both relationships but Hill concluded that investment is clearly a necessary condition for growth. No country with a high growth rate had a low investment ratio. Some countries with high investment ratios had low growth, however, which can be attributed to the structure of investment; in particular, to a low proportion of investment in machinery and equipment.

Modigliani's work also shows a strong relation between output growth and the proportion of a country's income invested.[1] Taking a mixed sample of developed and developing countries, he obtains the regression equation

$$G = 0 \cdot 52 + 0 \cdot 265 \, I$$
$$(0 \cdot 042)$$

where the bracketed term is the standard error of the regression coefficient.

The Role of Inflationary Finance

The central purpose of the present study is to consider the role of deficit spending, financed by inflationary means, in raising the ratio of saving and investment to national income and hence the growth rate of developing economies. This topic has not received the attention it deserves in the development literature partly, I suspect, because of a general antipathy towards inflation and partly due to a belief that there are easier and less harmful ways for governments to raise the level of saving and investment. Taxation and reliance on foreign capital inflows are two obvious possibilities. As developing countries have discovered by experience, however, tax revenue can be extremely inelastic with respect to the growth of income, and foreign capital inflows cannot always be relied on. In these circumstances the price of monetary conservatism can easily be stagnation.

[1] F. Modigliani, 'The Life Cycle Hypothesis of Saving and Intercountry Differences in the Savings Ratio' in *Induction, Trade and Growth: Essays in Honour of Sir Roy Harrod*, ed. W. A. Eltis, M. F. G. Scott and N. J. Wolfe (Oxford University Press, 1970).

Yet monetary and fiscal conservatism is widely practised and preached. Bangs concludes in his study of fiscal policy for emerging nations that because Keynesian deficit finance will not work efficiently in most developing economies, owing to supply inelasticities, 'greater conservatism should therefore characterise the fiscal policies of poorer countries than those of nations with higher levels of income'.[1] Two comments can be made on this type of argument. First, if monetary expansion is accompanied by investment in quick and high yielding projects, supply can be almost as elastic as if resources are unemployed. Second, the statement implies an aversion to inflation which may not be justified given a country's preference curve between the discommodity, inflation, on the one hand, and the desire for growth on the other.

In contrast to monetary stagnation, which can act as an impediment to growth, monetary expansion can force saving by redistributing income to profit earners and the government; it can be used to alter favourably the structure of capital to yield more output per unit of capital invested, and through an expansion of monetary assets it can encourage the process of voluntary saving. More important still, the very stimulus that monetary expansion may give to the growth rate and to the level of per capita income may set off a cumulative train of expansion if the savings ratio is positively related to the level or growth of per capita income, as a good deal of saving theory and empirical evidence suggests (see Chapter 7).

The interdependence between growth, saving and per capita income gives rise to the possibility of cumulative expansion initiated by inflationary finance. While growth depends on saving, there are equally good reasons for expecting the savings ratio to be dependent on the growth rate and per capita income. The dependence of saving on the growth of income (or on the growth of per capita income if population is not in balanced growth) is the prediction of the life-cycle hypothesis of saving which will be examined in Chapter 7. The dependence of the savings ratio on the level of per capita income is the Keynesian absolute-income hypothesis which will also be examined later in Chapter 7.

Given the mutual dependence between the savings ratio on the one hand and the growth of income and the level of per capita income on the other, neither relation can be strictly identified. But this is not

[1] R. B. Bangs, *Financing Economic Development, Fiscal Policy in Emerging Countries* (University of Chicago Press, 1968).

important for the present purpose. What we want to stress is the interdependence between growth, saving and per capita income, which together form a virtuous circle. The interdependence between these three variables forms the heart of a model of cumulative development and sustained expansion of living standards. The key variable is saving generated by investment. Breaking into the virtuous circle at this point offers the most hope of success and the most hope for sustained expansion.

In the absence of an increase in voluntary saving, government-induced saving is not only an attractive alternative; it may be the only alternative. In the case of Nigeria it has been remarked that 'given the problems associated with tapping rather small individual savings where the banking habit is still in the initial stages of development, the choice of deficit financing may in fact reflect a choice between orthodox monetary policy with stagnation on the one hand and economic development financed by credit creation, even at the risk of inflation'.[1] Ignoring compulsory saving by taxation there are five main ways of financing a budget deficit: the issue of new currency; net borrowing from the central bank; net borrowing from the commerical banks; net borrowing from the public; and running down foreign exchange reserves or borrowing from abroad. What effects these different methods of borrowing have depend on whether the funds represent transfers of current saving or an increase in the money supply and/or its velocity of circulation. The issue of new currency and borrowing from the central bank are normally regarded as the most inflationary, followed by borrowing from the commercial banks. Borrowing from the public is assumed to be the least inflationary. In fact, borrowing from the public can be just as inflationary as borrowing from the banks if it merely activates idle money and does not cut down the current consumption of the public.

Typically, a combination of financing methods is resorted to. As an illustration, the methods of financing public sector investment in a selection of Asian and Far Eastern countries is shown in Table 1.3. Contrary, perhaps, to popular opinion, bank borrowing has not been a major source of finance, although it is a much more important source of finance than in developed countries where public sector investment tends to be financed largely by government saving.

[1] T. Ademola Oyejide, 'Deficit Financing, Inflation and Capital Formation: An Analysis of the Nigerian Experience 1957–70', *Nigerian Journal of Economic and Social Studies* (March 1972).

The finance of investment expenditure in developing countries by monetary expansion has a number of attractive features provided inflation is not excessive. First, it provides an obvious supplement to tax revenue. Second, it can reduce dependence on external capital which has disadvantages for a country as well as advantages. It can be seen from Table 1.3 that a substantial amount of public sector

TABLE 1.3

Methods of Financing Public Investment

	Gross public investment as % of total investment	Per cent of public sector investment financed by:		
		Government saving	Domestic borrowing		External aid and other
			Bank	Non-bank	
India	63·7	20·0	16·0	29·8	34·2
Pakistan	43·0	15·1	9·7	17·0	58·2
Ceylon	46·1	8·3	26·2	48·9	16·6
Burma	46·0	—	—	—	—
Malaysia	37·7	32·0	44·8		23·2
Thailand	26·9	44·9	9·0	26·9	19·2
Philippines	—	12·4	40·7	6·4	40·5
Taiwan	44·4	—	—	—	—
South Korea	31·9	—	—	—	—

Source: ECAFE, *Economic Bulletin* (September 1968) pp. 10–28.

investment in some of the countries listed has been financed by external assistance. Third, financing expenditure by monetary means can contribute to the development of financial institutions, and introduce the public to the holding of wealth in the form of financial assets as a substitute for physical assets which may absorb society's real resources. The very act of financing expenditure by monetary means may itself increase the volume of voluntary saving available for use in productive enterprise.

The hypothesis developed in this book is that there is a positively sloped trade-off relation between growth and inflation for mild rates of inflation, but that the 'steepness' of the policy maker's preference

curve relating growth and inflation has typically been such that growth and employment have been sacrificed for the sake of price stability. Consider Fig. 1.1 below.

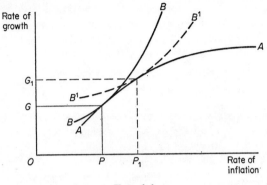

FIG. 1.1

AA represents the trade-off between output growth and the rate of inflation which is empirically determined. BB represents a policy maker's preference curve relating growth and inflation with a strong aversion to inflation built in such that the 'optimum' rate of inflation is OP. Assuming AA is fixed, a more growth-orientated policy must require a change in the shape of the policy maker's preference curve, say to B^1B^1, giving a higher rate of inflation OP_1 but a higher growth rate OG_1. The rate of inflation settled on by most developing countries in the period since the Second World War has been no more than 3 per cent per annum.

If the warranted rate of growth lies below the natural rate of growth, and profitable investment opportunities exist for, say, double the level of savings currently undertaken, a 3 per cent annual rate of inflation appears remarkably mild. One would also expect interest rates to be higher than they typically are in the organised money markets of developing countries. From the evidence it must be concluded either that planned investment is not greatly in excess of planned saving because of risk and inertia, or that governments themselves have been using deflationary policies and interest rate subsidisation to thwart the natural adjustment mechanisms of inflation and rising interest rates which otherwise would tend to raise the warranted growth rate towards the natural rate. In either case, the role of government is clear. If the first explanation is correct, it is

to reduce risks to private entrepreneurs and, by spreading risks, to invest itself on society's behalf which will act as partial compensation for private inertia. If the latter conjecture is correct, at least a more tolerant attitude towards inflation (if not higher interest rates) would seem to be called for, which would permit governments to indulge in more monetary expansion themselves. If it is true that growth might have been faster in the developing countries had they been willing to pursue slightly more expansionist policies, there is no reason in principle why it should be more difficult for monetary and fiscal policy to maintain, say, a 6 per cent rate of inflation than a 3 per cent rate of inflation.

Throughout the book arguments are supported, and empirical evidence is presented, using a sample of sixty-eight countries consisting of both developed and developing economies. A detailed description of the main data series is given in Appendix 1. Most of the data relate to average values of the variables for the period 1958–68.

2

The Case For and Against
Inflationary Finance

The Doctrine of Forced Saving

The case for inflationary finance has a long and distinguished ancestry. One of the earliest advocates of inflation-induced growth was the English eighteenth-century economist David Hume, who argued the case for persistent mild inflation on the grounds that it gives rise to continual opportunities for profit:

> The good policy of the magistrate consists only in keeping it [money], if possible, still increasing; because, by that means, he keeps a spirit of industry alive in the nation, and increases the stock of labour, wherein consists all real power and riches. A nation, whose money decreases, is actually, at that time, much weaker and more miserable than another nation, who possesses no more money, but is on the increasing hand. This will be easily accounted for, if we consider, that the alterations in the quantity of money, either on the one side or the other, are not immediately attended with proportional alterations in the prices of commodities. There is always an interval before matters be adjusted to their new situation; and this interval is as pernicious to industry, when gold and silver are diminishing, as it is advantageous, when these metals are increasing. . . . When any quantity of money is imported into a nation, it is not at first dispersed into many hands; but is confined to the coffers of a few persons, who immediately seek to employ it to the best advantage. Here are a set of manufacturers or merchants, we shall suppose . . . [who] are thereby enabled to employ more workmen than formerly, who never dream of demanding

higher wages, but who are glad of employment from such good paymasters.[1]

The doctrine of forced saving can also be found in the writings of many of the nineteenth-century classical economists. Hayek has traced the classical version of the doctrine back to Bentham, Malthus and Thornton.[2] Bentham described forced saving as 'forced frugality':

. . . the effect of forced frugality is also produced by the creating of paper money by individuals. In this case, the effect is produced by a species of indirect taxation which has hitherto passed almost unnoticed.[3]

And Thornton wrote:

It must be admitted that, provided we assume an excessive issue of paper to lift up, as it may for a time, the costs of goods tho' not the price of labour, some augmentation of stock [i.e. capital] will be the consequence; for the labourer . . . may be forced . . . to consume fewer articles. But this saving . . . will be attended with a proportional injustice and hardship.[4]

Sir Dennis Robertson revived the doctrine in 1922, advocating a progressive rise in the price level as a stimulus to the production of goods:

So long as the control of production is in the hands of a minority, rewarded by means of a fluctuating profit, it is not impossible that a gently rising price level will in fact produce the best attainable results not only for them [the controllers of industry] but the community as a whole. And it is tolerably certain that a price level continually falling, even for the best of reasons, would prove deficient in those stimuli upon which modern society, whether wisely or not, has hitherto chiefly relied for keeping its members in full employment and getting its work done.[5]

[1] D. Hume, 'Of Money', in *Political Discourses* (Edinburgh: Fleming, 1752).
[2] F. A. Hayek, 'A Note on the Development of the Doctrine of Forced Saving', *Quarterly Journal of Economics* (November 1932).
[3] Cited ibid. p. 124.
[4] Cited ibid. p. 127.
[5] D. Robertson, *Money* (London: Nisbet, 1922).

Kaldor expressed the same sentiments in *Memoranda of Evidence* to the Radcliffe Committee 1958,[1] and in two lectures at the London School of Economics in 1959:

> . . . a slow and steady rate of inflation provides a most powerful aid to the attainment of a steady rate of economic progress . . . price stability is only consistent with steady growth when the rate of [growth of] productivity and/or the working population is sufficiently large to give a relatively high rate of growth to the total national product. In a weakly growing economy price stability will mean stagnation unless the propensity to consume is raised sufficiently to offset the effect of a lower rate of growth of profits.[2]

In Kaldor's model the money rate of profit depends on the rate of inflation. Kaldor sees inflation as important for maintaining a high rate of profit and hence for maintaining a high level of investment. The profit rate (P/K) is equal to the rate of growth of money income $(\Delta Y/Y)$ divided by the proportion of profits saved (Sp/P).[3] Thus, if the rate of growth of money national income is 7·5 per cent per annum and the proportion of profits saved is 50 per cent, the average profit rate will be $7·5/0·5 = 15$ per cent. With a slow rate of real growth the importance of inflation in keeping the rate of profit in excess of the interest rate to sustain investment is clear. Kaldor concludes, in fact, that if faster growth is an objective of policy, it would be unwise for a country with a low rate of real growth to aim for price stability.

At the empirical level Hamilton has claimed that inflation has been a powerful stimulant to growth in a wide number of historical

[1] N. Kaldor, 'Monetary Policy, Economic Stability and Growth' in *Memoranda of Evidence, Radcliffe Committee on the Workings of the Monetary System* (H.M.S.O., 1958).

[2] N. Kaldor, 'Economic Growth and the Problem of Inflation', *Economica* (August and November 1959). At the same time Kaldor presented a theory of wage-push inflation based on the existence of high profits earned in inflationary periods, which provided an alternative explanation of the inverse relation between the rate of increase in money wages and the level of unemployment.

[3] For the derivation of the formula for the profit rate see Kaldor, 'A Model of Economic Growth', *Economic Journal* (December 1957). The assumptions are that all savings are invested; all saving comes from profits; and the average and marginal capital–output ratios are equal. Hence:

$$\frac{P}{K} = \frac{\Delta Y/Y}{Sp/P} = \frac{\Delta K/K}{Sp/P} = \frac{I/K}{Sp/P} = \frac{P}{K}$$

contexts. In a series of papers he has presented a vast array of evidence in support of the view that inflation was a powerful promoter of industrial growth in England and France during the price revolution of the sixteenth and seventeenth centuries and at the start of the industrial revolution in England in the latter half of the eighteenth century.[1] Hamilton's thesis is very simple. During long periods of inflation, he argues, prices tend to outrun wages, resulting in profit inflation which gives rise to a much higher rate of capital accumulation than would otherwise have occurred. Price inflation which concentrates income in the hands of the rich is in turn a stimulus to the use of saving for investment. In short, rising prices and lagging wages provide capital, and give a strong incentive to use it capitalistically. Hamilton concludes his historical studies by saying:

> that if prices and wages had not behaved as they did, or in similar fashion, it is doubtful that industrial progress would have been rapid, pervasive, or persistent enough to appear revolutionary to succeeding generations.

Rostow has also claimed that inflation has been important for several industrial 'take-offs':

> In Britain in the 1790s, the U.S. of the 1850s and Japan of the 1870s, capital formation was aided by price inflation which shifted resources from consumption to profits.[2]

Keynes claimed to have been struck by the extraordinary correspondence in history between periods of profit inflation and profit deflation, respectively, with national rise and decline. He conjectures rhetorically:

> in what degree [did] the greatness of Athens [depend] on the silver mines of Laurium – not because the monetary metals are more truly wealth than other things, but because by their effect on prices they supply the spur of profit?; . . . [was it] coincidence that the decline and fall of Rome was contemporaneous with the most prolonged and drastic deflation yet recorded?; and whether if

[1] See, E. Hamilton, 'American Treasure and the Rise of Capitalism', *Economica* (November 1929); 'Profit Inflation and the Industrial Revolution', *Quarterly Journal of Economics* (February 1942), and for a concise summary of his views: 'Prices as a Factor in Business Growth: Prices and Progress', *Journal of Economic History* (Fall 1952).

[2] 'Rostow on Growth', *The Economist* (15 August 1959).

the long stagnation of the Middle Ages may not have been more surely and inevitably caused by Europe's meagre supply of the monetary metals than by monasticism or Gothic frenzy?[1]

The Keynesian and Quantity Theory Approaches to Inflationary Finance

Keynes was certainly more predisposed to inflation than to deflation. He once described inflation as unjust and deflation as inexpedient, but of the two inflation is to be preferred because:

> it is worse, in an impoverished world, to provoke unemployment than to disappoint the rentier.[2]

He was not referring specifically to developing economies but the message is clear. Likewise in the *Treatise on Money* Keynes claimed that although inflation to increase saving has regressive distributional consequences, the long-term gains can outweigh the short-term losses:

> the working class may benefit far more in the long run from the forced abstinence which a profit inflation imposes on them than they lose in the first instance in the shape of diminished consumption . . . so long as wealth and its fruits are not consumed by the nominal owner but are accumulated.[3]

The Keynesian approach to the finance of development by inflationary means stresses that inflation can stimulate investment by raising the nominal rate of return on investment and by reducing the real rate of interest, and that investment can generate its own saving by keeping aggregate demand buoyant and by redistributing income from wage earners with a low propensity to save to profit-earners with a higher propensity to save.

A mild demand inflation keeps resources fully employed and therefore maintains a high level of saving for investment if saving is a function of income. The pressure of demand upon capacity encourages manufacturers to maintain production at the full capacity level and to refrain from cutting back output for fear of deficient demand which would reduce real growth. The existence of unemployed resources due to a deficiency of aggregate demand pro-

---

[1] J. M. Keynes, *Treatise on Money*, vol. 2 (Macmillan, 1930) p. 150.
[2] J. M. Keynes, *Essays in Persuasion* (Macmillan, 1931).
[3] J. M. Keynes, *Treatise on Money*.

vides, of course, the classic Keynesian case for inflationary deficit finance to raise the level of investment and saving. Whether the *ratio* of saving and investment to income rises, however, as distinct from the *level* of saving and investment, depends on the form of the savings function. If the savings ratio is dependent on the level of per capita income, as has already been suggested and will be demonstrated later, the savings ratio, as well as the level of saving, is likely to be affected favourably by inflationary finance and the maintenance of full employment. The simple condition for the savings ratio to rise with the level of per capita income is that the marginal propensity to save should exceed the average propensity.

It is often argued, however, that unemployment in developing economies is not of the Keynesian variety. The finance of investment by an expansion of output is therefore impossible, at least without severe inflation before the capacity-creating effects of investment become apparent. The absence of demand-deficient unemployment in developing economies is probably a reasonable assumption, and it was implicit in the characterisation of developing countries given in Chapter 1. It does not follow, however, that selective policies of deficit finance which open up particular sectors of the economy or geographic areas cannot generate saving to match the investment expenditure. In dual economies with large reserves of under-employed labour in the rural sector, and unemployed labour in the urban sector, there is a great deal of scope for demand expansion on a project by project basis which will not only create new jobs but which will also increase supply capacity quickly such that inflationary tendencies in the economy at large are moderated. Moreover, if the projects are labour-intensive with a high yield per unit of labour employed, the capital–output ratio in the economy will fall. Keynesian theory can be usefully applied not only to situations in which capital is abundant and labour is unemployed because demand is deficient but also to situations in which capital is scarce and labour is structurally unemployed.

But whether or not there is full employment, and whether or not it is of the Keynesian variety, inflation inevitably tends to redistribute income because contracts regulating wages and financial arrangements between creditors and debtors are fixed in money terms. Two main forms of redistribution can be expected to take place which will be favourable to saving and investment. First, there will be redistribution within the private sector of the economy: from the personal

sector to the corporate sector, from wages to profits. Second, there will be redistribution from the private sector to the government sector.

Income redistribution to government comes about because inflation represents a tax on money holdings, the revenue from which accrues to the beneficiaries of the increase in the money supply – namely the issuers of money.[1] Inflation as a tax on money holdings can reduce real consumption and divert resources for investment purposes – resources just as real as those obtained by more conventional means of taxation. In the simple case where all money is non-interest bearing, the real yield from the tax is equal to the real value of the new money issued, and the rate of tax is equal to the rate of inflation. Inflation as a tax on money holdings is illustrated in Fig. 2.1 below.

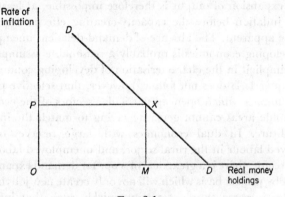

FIG. 2.1

DD represents the demand for real money holdings at different rates of inflation. With price stability the level of real money holdings demanded is OD. At inflation rate OP, which is expected to continue, the demand for real balances falls to OM. The area OPXM therefore represents the amount of real income that holders of real money balances must substitute for money balances in order to keep real balances intact. The inflation tax is equivalent to the real income foregone to maintain real balances intact in the face of inflation. Since money balances must be accumulated (and real income for-

[1] If inflation is not the result of monetary expansion but is cost-induced, the inflation tax accrues to the monetary authorities to the extent that the government validates the inflation by expanding demand to maintain full employment. If resources are left under-utilised the potential tax revenue is lost.

gone) at the same rate as the rate of inflation, the rate of tax is equal to the rate of inflation.[1] Inflation as a tax on money redistributes resources from the private sector to the government sector which can be used to finance real investment. The stress on inflation as a tax on real money balances is the essence of the so-called Quantity Theory approach to the finance of development by inflation.[2] Keynes was fully aware of this aspect of inflation. In his *Tract on Monetary Reform* he described inflation as 'a form of taxation that the public finds hard to evade and even the weakest government can enforce when it can enforce nothing else'.[3] In the Keynesian approach to development, however, inflation as a tax on money is of subsidiary interest to the role of inflation in stimulating enterprise through its effect on profits.

It should also be added that inflation tends to produce a situation in which conventional tax revenue to governments automatically rises faster than government expenditures, providing an additional source of government saving which can be used for investment purposes. Despite the general inelasticity of tax revenue with respect to income, the responsiveness of taxes to increases in money income is generally greater than the elasticity of expenditure with respect to the growth of money income.

Given a positive rate of growth of productivity, a sufficient condition for income redistribution within the private sector, from wage-earners to profit-earners, is that prices rise faster than wages. The savings ratio will rise if the propensity to save out of profits is higher than the propensity to save out of wages. This is the assumption of most growth models. In a good deal of growth theory, in fact, the extreme assumption is made that the propensity to save out of profits is unity and the propensity to save out of wages is zero. There is a lot of evidence from both developed and developing economies that wage changes lag behind price changes in the short run, and that even in the long run the regression coefficient relating the rate of increase in wages to the rate of increase in prices is less than unity.[4]

---

[1] See Chapter 6 for further discussion of inflation as a tax on money.

[2] See H. G. Johnson, *Essays in Monetary Economics* (London: Allen & Unwin, 1967).

[3] J. M. Keynes, *A Tract on Monetary Reform* (London: Macmillan, 1923).

[4] See, e.g. R. S. Koot, 'Wage Changes, Unemployment and Inflation in Chile', *Industrial and Labour Relations Review* (July 1969); M. L. Treadgold, 'Inflation, Real Wages and the Rate of Saving in the Philippines', *The Developing Economies* (September 1970); R. Solow, *Price Expectations and the Behaviour of the Price Level* (Manchester University Press, 1969).

This does not mean, of course, that it is necessary for the real wage to fall for there to be a redistribution of income in favour of profits, or that the real wage will necessarily fall if the regression coefficient relating the change in wages to a change in prices is less than unity. In a growing economy the share of profits in income will rise if the rate of productivity growth exceeds the rise in the real wage. And the real wage can rise even if the wage–price coefficient is less than unity if the rate of growth of wages that occurs independently of the rate of change of prices exceeds the loss of real earnings due to inflation. These propositions can be illustrated with the aid of the following model. Let Z be labour's share of income, so that

$$Z = \frac{wL}{PO} = \frac{w}{Pr} \qquad (2.1)$$

where w is wages per man (the wage rate)

      P is price per unit of output

      O is output

      L is the quantity of labour

and r is output per man (O/L)

Hence,

$$\frac{dZ}{Z} = \left(\frac{dw}{w} - \frac{dP}{P}\right) - \frac{dr}{r} \qquad (2.2)$$

First, equation (2.2) shows that for any given positive growth of productivity, labour's share will fall if $dw/w < dP/P$. Second, however, a rise in the real wage $(dw/w > dP/P)$ is quite compatible with a fall in labour's share (and a rise in profit's share) if $(dw/w - dP/P) < dr/r$. Prices rising faster than wages are not necessary to redistribute income to profits. The share of profits in income will rise as long as the growth in the real wage is less than the growth of labour productivity.

We may note also that if the wage–price coefficient is less than unity the real wage can still rise if there is a sufficient positive autonomous rate of growth of wages independent of price increases. Consider the equation $dw/w = a + \alpha(dP/P)$, where a is the autonomous rate of change of wages and α is the wage–price coefficient. The condition for the real wage to rise is that $(dw/w - dP/P) > 0$, or, on substitution:

$$[a + \alpha(dP/P)] - dP/P > 0$$

so that the real wage rises if

$$a + dP/P(\alpha - 1) > 0.$$

Suppose $dP/P = 6 \cdot 0$ per cent; $a = 3 \cdot 0$ per cent and $\alpha = 0 \cdot 9$. The rise in the real wage is $2 \cdot 4$ per cent. Inflation would have to exceed 30 per cent for real wages not to rise in this example. Despite the rise in the real wage, labour's share of income will fall if $a + dP/P$ $(\alpha - 1) < r$. Suppose productivity is growing at the same rate as autonomous wage growth (i.e. 3 per cent). Real wages are growing slower than productivity so that labour's share will fall and the share of profits rise. It is interesting to note that productivity-based wage bargaining, or wage policies that link wage-rate increases to productivity increases, are bound to redistribute income to profits provided the rate of inflation is positive and the wage–price coefficient (α) is less than unity.

It can also be shown using equation (2.2) that, on classical savings assumptions, the change in labour's share will be equal to minus the change in the community's savings ratio. Making the classical assumptions that all wages are spent on consumption, and that all profits are saved, equation (2.2) may be written as

$$\frac{dZ}{Z} = \frac{dc}{c} - \frac{dr}{r} \qquad (2.3)$$

where c is real consumption per worker

so that

$$\frac{dZ}{Z} = \frac{dC}{C} - \frac{dO}{O} \qquad (2.4)$$

where C is aggregate real consumption

and O is aggregate real output

or

$$\frac{dZ}{Z} = \frac{d(C/O)}{(C/O)} \qquad (2.5)$$

where C/O is the consumption–output ratio.

If the rate of growth of real consumption is less than the rate of growth of output, the consumption ratio will fall and the savings ratio will

rise. The increase in the savings ratio is identically equal to the decrease in labour's share.

There is a good deal of evidence that the propensity to save out of wage income is virtually zero and certainly less than out of non-wage income. In a cross-section study of personal saving taking twenty-eight countries Houthakker found that the short-run propensity to save out of employment income was 0·04 compared with 0·49 out of non-labour income. The long-run propensities to save were 0·02 and 0·24 respectively.[1] Williamson obtained similar short-run propensities for a cross-section of Asian countries: 0·05 for labour income and 0·68 for non-labour income.[2] What is more relevant, Houthakker found that taking *private* saving (corporate plus personal saving) in relation to *private* disposable income gave the non-proportional saving function $S = -3·08 + 0·117Y$, in contrast to a strictly proportional relation (i.e. containing no significant intercept term) between *personal* saving and *personal* income. Houthakker interprets the difference to imply that corporate saving must be proportionately more important in richer countries, which could result from a combination of a larger corporate sector in richer countries and a higher propensity to save out of corporate profits than out of wages which form the bulk of personal income.

In addition to the boost to profits from inflation which is conducive to saving and investment, the propensity to save out of profits may be expected to rise with the rate of inflation if inflation raises the rate of profit which acts as an encouragement to manufacturers to invest.

Differences in the propensity to save between the public and the private sector may not be so marked as within the private sector itself, but the evidence suggests that they exist with the government possessing a higher propensity to save than the private sector taken as a whole. Houthakker found in his study that the propensity to save of governments was higher than the weighted average of the long-run propensities to save out of wage and non-wage income in the private sector. The regression equation relating government saving per capita (S_g) to government revenue per capita (R_g) was estimated as

[1] H. S. Houthakker, 'On Some Determinants of Saving in Developed and Under-Developed Countries', in *Problems in Economic Development*, ed. E. A. G. Robinson (London: Macmillan, 1965).

[2] J. G. Williamson, 'Personal Saving in Developing Nations: An Intertemporal Cross Section From Asia', *Economic Record* (June 1968).

$S_g = 0.107\ R_g$. The estimated propensity to save of 0·107 is highly significant with a standard error of 0·014.[1]

Also suggesting that governments may have a higher propensity to save than the private sector is a study by Morss which finds a positive relation between the domestic savings ratio and the tax ratio across forty-six countries. This suggests that to meet their tax liabilities individuals cut consumption by more than governments increase consumption out of tax yields.[2]

To achieve real growth through inflation, investment must accompany the increase in saving. This is taken for granted in the Keynesian approach to inflationary finance. Inflation results from plans to invest exceeding plans to save, and inflation is the equilibrating mechanism which generates sufficient real saving to finance the investment.

In the Quantity Theory approach to inflationary finance, investment is not guaranteed, but if governments decide to redistribute resources to themselves by taxing money it is fairly safe to assume that the resources will be used for productive purposes of a capital or current nature. At least, the potential is there.

If inflation is not initiated by excess investment demand in the private or public sector, inflation can still encourage the use of saving for investment in physical assets by maintaining the profitability of investment in physical assets relative to money assets and hoarding. During inflations, the nominal rate of return on investment tends to rise relative to the rate of interest, and the real rate of interest tends to fall. Interest rates are generally slow to adjust to inflation, and enterprise benefits at the expense of rentiers. Mundell has shown (see Chapter 4) that even if inflation is fully anticipated a fall in the real interest rate can be predicted because of the effect of inflation on the real value of money balances. Under certain conditions the effect of inflation on real money balances (the so-called real balance effect) can also be a source of additional saving. This matter is discussed later in Chapter 4. In Keynesian theory the real interest rate falls if real output increases. If inflation elicits a supply response, the real interest rate will therefore fall even in the absence of initially unemployed resources.

---

[1] Houthakker, 'On Some Determinants of Saving'.
[2] E. R. Morss, 'Fiscal Policy, Savings and Economic Growth in Developing Countries: An Empirical Study' (I.M.F. DM/68/43).

The Dangers of Inflation

In discussing the gains from inflation no *explicit* distinction has yet been made between the origins, or types, of inflation,[1] and no mention has been made of the potential dangers and costs of pursuing an inflationary policy. Before proceeding further we need to make the distinction between demand inflation and other types of inflation, and to make the obvious point that inflation-induced development is not a painless and costless policy.

If not stated explicitly it should be clear from what has been said that the major advantages of inflation come mainly from inflation emanating from demand expansion, not from inflation emanating from increases in supply price (costs). It is true that the real interest rate will tend to fall and that the burden of debt will be reduced whether inflation is demand-induced or cost-induced, but the redistribution of income to profits, which is the main feature of demand inflation, will not occur. On the contrary, a cost inflation resulting from wages rising in excess of productivity will tend to increase consumption, reduce profits and reduce saving. Merely to restore the share of profits and saving in national income, let alone to increase it, a demand inflation would have to be superimposed on the cost inflation already prevailing. To maintain a full-employment level of demand would not be sufficient. The same argument applies to structural inflation to the extent that it emanates in the factor market and not in the product market. To attempt to control a cost or structural inflation by damping demand will tend to produce a negative relation between inflation and growth. The view that inflation is damaging to growth owes much to the experience of countries which have tried to control cost inflation by curbing aggregate demand.

The existence of types of inflation other than demand inflation raises serious problems in interpreting the empirical evidence of the relation between inflation and growth. An observed inflation rate will reflect a composite of various inflationary forces, and yet the impact of each inflationary force will differ; some forces will be favourable to growth while others will be detrimental. If the origins of inflation in a particular country change over time, or the primary impetus to inflation differs between countries, the normal statistical techniques of time series and cross-section analysis of the relation

[1] See Chapter 3 for a discussion of the different 'types' of inflation.

between inflation and growth may be expected to yield very disappointing results. The problem is insuperable. All that can reasonably be done is to bear the problem in mind in interpreting the empirical results.

There are also certain dangers and costs involved in pursuing a deliberate inflationary policy to stimulate development, which need to be borne in mind. The most serious threats to growth from inflation come from the balance of payments if foreign exchange is a scarce resource, and from the possibility that inflation may discourage voluntary saving, productive investment and the use of money as a medium of exchange if inflation becomes excessive. What rate of inflation should be regarded as excessive is very difficult to determine independently of its consequences; but clearly an independent definition is required to prevent arguments about excessive inflation from becoming circular. For the present purposes it is perhaps best to think of excessive inflation as inflation that cannot easily be adjusted to, either because it represents a sudden jump in the rate or because it is literally so high that adjustment is impractical. Either way, we are talking for all practical purposes of rates of inflation in excess of 10 per cent per annum.

As far as the balance of payments is concerned, if one country inflates at a faster rate than others its balance of payments may suffer severely, necessitating import substitution policies and exchange controls leading to inefficiency in resource allocation. This assumes, of course, that countries which are inflating are unable to finance deficits by capital imports. To the extent that external assistance is available the case for inflationary finance remains unimpaired as long as the productivity of capital exceeds the rate of interest payable on external assistance and some of the extra resources made available can be converted into foreign exchange. The argument also assumes a lack of exchange-rate flexibility which need not exist in practice with the adoption of more enlightened exchange rate policies. Exchange rate flexibility could theoretically free the domestic economy from an external constraint, allowing the economy to be run at any inflation rate chosen. In practice, however, such a policy might be dangerous if exports were price inelastic in demand and/or if speculation was destabilising.

As far as investment is concerned, if inflation becomes excessive, investment in physical plant and equipment may become unattractive relative to speculative investments in inventories, overseas assets,

property and artefacts which absorb a society's real resources. If the real rate of interest becomes negative, it may even become attractive to claim real resources and not to use them. If the price of an asset rises at 10 per cent per annum and it costs only 8 per cent by way of interest charges to acquire the asset, it becomes profitable to acquire the asset whether it is used or not. New ventures become 'profitable' in inflationary times even though they may be wholly uneconomic to operate.

Inflation clearly reduces the purchasing power of money. If inflation becomes excessive, not only may voluntary saving be discouraged, but the use of money as a medium of exchange may be discouraged involving society in real resource costs and welfare losses. Since inflation reduces the purchasing power of money, holders may be expected to avoid the loss by cutting down their holdings of money for transactions purposes. The cost of inflation arises from the fact that cash balances yield utility and contribute to production. When people decide to hold less in cash balances they do so by substituting other real resources for cash in making transactions. For example, the frequency of trips to the bank may increase, which absorbs labour time. Credit mechanisms may be resorted to, which absorb society's resources. Energy, time and resources are devoted to minimising the use of cash balances which are costless to produce. There is no consensus on how this welfare loss should be measured. One way is to assume that the interest rate measures the services provided by money and that the opportunity cost of holding money is the nominal rate of interest foregone. The welfare loss from a tax on money would therefore be the area under the Keynesian liquidity preference (demand for money) curve, which can be measured if the bond rate is assumed to rise with the inflation rate and the interest elasticity of demand for money is known. In Fig. 2.2 below, suppose that the nominal interest rate r_0 corresponds to a zero rate of inflation, and that an increase in the interest rate from r_0 to r_1 reflects a rise in the inflation rate from zero to 5 per cent. The welfare loss of a 5 per cent rate of inflation is then represented by the shaded area, $m_1 x_1 x m_0$.

If the nominal rate of interest rises by less than the increase in the rate of inflation, as in the theories of Keynes and Mundell (see Chapter 4), the welfare loss will be less than the shaded area. It should also be remembered that the alternative to inflation to finance development is some other form of financing which would have its

own costs and distortions. Conventional taxation involves collection costs, and attempts to avoid conventional taxes also absorb society's resources and reduce saving. The costs of any policy of development finance must be compared with alternatives. Judged by this criterion, inflation as a tax may not compare badly.

The different considerations above suggest that any statistical relation between saving and inflation, and between growth and

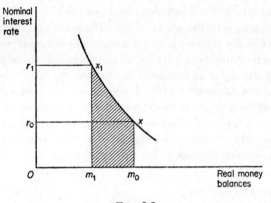

FIG. 2.2

inflation, is likely to be a quadratic of the form $Y = \alpha + \beta_1 X + \beta_2 X^2$, where X is the inflation rate, and with the expectation that $\beta_1 > 0$ and $\beta_2 < 0$. That is, the savings ratio and the growth rate reach a maximum at some 'optimum' rate of inflation, beyond which saving and growth are impaired. One of the tasks of the empirical work later will be to see whether an optimum rate of inflation can be discerned from the international cross-section data on inflation, saving, and growth.

The distributional consequences of inflation, which are often uppermost in people's minds and which constitute one of the main arguments against inflation in developed countries, are hard to assess. The consequences depend on so many characteristics of the individual and are so widely diffused that it is difficult to make a firm judgement on whether inflation increases income inequality or not; let alone to say whether the distribution is 'better' or 'worse'. The evidence is equivocal. All that can be said with some confidence is: debtors benefit at the expense of creditors; profit-earners gain at the expense of wage-earners in times of demand inflation and lose at the

expense of wage-earners in times of wage inflation; real asset holders probably gain relative to money asset holders; the strong (in a bargaining sense) probably gain relative to the weak, and the young gain relative to the old who tend to live on fixed contractual incomes. On some grounds an individual might gain from inflation; on others, lose. The net result may be zero. It cannot be assumed that the existing rich will necessarily get richer, and the poor poorer. In the context of developing countries the possible inegalitarian distributional consequences of demand inflation should not be allowed to constitute an argument against the use of mildly inflationary policies, if one of the objects of the policies is to create additional employment. The old, who suffer the most from inflation in developed countries, are frequently cared for in extended family systems in the developing countries, and large numbers of people in self-employment and farming are in a position to defend or insulate themselves against market trends. The major beneficiaries of inflationary finance should be the unemployed and under-employed, which represents a move towards a more egalitarian structure of incomes.

The Inflationary Experience

Having warned about the dangers of excessive inflation, the fact is that the inflationary experience of most developed and developing countries has been extremely mild during the greater part of recent history. It may surprise some to learn that prices in England in 1933 were no higher than the level prevailing in 1660.[1] The experience of the developed and developing countries over the period 1958–68 is given in Appendix 1. By historical standards the rates may be high but by no stretch of the imagination could they be considered high in an absolute sense. The exceptional countries are the countries of Latin America, about which more will be said later. Moreover, outside the countries of Latin America it is clearly a myth that developing countries experience higher rates of inflation than developed countries. It may be that developing countries absorb more of their inflationary pressure by running large balance-of-payments deficits, and that because of aversion to inflation and policies of subsidisation and price control the recorded inflation rate is somewhat less than would be observed if the price mechanism was allowed to work freely and the statistics remained undistorted.

[1] R. Harrod, *Economic Dynamics* (London: Macmillan, 1972) p. 83.

Nevertheless the broad picture remains the same; the recorded rates of price increase are indisputably low. Out of our sample of 48 developing countries, 38 recorded average rates of inflation of less than 6 per cent per annum over the period 1958–68. Argentina, Brazil, Chile, Colombia, Indonesia, Uruguay and South Vietnam experienced rates in excess of 10 per cent, and Bolivia, Ghana and Turkey experienced rates of between 6 per cent and 10 per cent. Except for Iceland, all countries in the developed country sample had inflation rates of less than 6 per cent, but the average rate was slightly higher than for the 38 developing countries with inflation rates of less than 6 per cent.

Other authors have also remarked on the similarity of inflationary experience across countries, and the great gulf that exists between the vast mass of countries which have experienced mild inflation and the small number of countries which have experienced perpetual chronic inflation, with few countries in between.

Adekunle took a sample of countries over the period 1949–65 and found an average rate of inflation of 3·63 per cent for 24 developing countries compared with over 4·0 per cent for a sample of 23 more developed countries.[1] He, too, disposes of the rather widespread belief that inflation has been typical and rampant in developing economies. There is, however, evidence of greater price instability in developing than developed countries as measured by the coefficient of variation of the annual rate of inflation.

In a more recent study, Jackson, Turner and Wilkinson also point to the mild, and broadly uniform, inflationary experience of most developing countries outside Latin America.[2] Two distinct groupings or distributions are observed: one around a mean rate of inflation of 3 per cent per annum, the other around a mean rate of 30 per cent per annum, with only a very small group in between. The mean rates experienced by samples of countries in different continents over five-year cycles between 1948 and 1969 are shown in Table 2.1.

Jackson, Turner and Wilkinson suggest that the vast mass of countries are linked together through external trading relations and fixed exchange rates; hence the uniform inflationary experience. The high inflation countries have escaped the regulator on internal

[1] J. Adekunle, 'Rates of Inflation in Industrial, Other Developed and Less Developed Countries, 1949–1965', *I.M.F. Staff Papers* (November 1968).

[2] D. Jackson, H. Turner and F. Wilkinson, *Do Trade Unions Cause Inflation?* (Cambridge University Press, 1972).

36   INFLATION, SAVING AND GROWTH

price movements, which are imposed by external trade, by repeated devaluations. If the fixed exchange-rate system has been the effective constraint, the general move towards floating exchange rates in the world economy may perhaps be expected to lead to higher rates of

TABLE 2.1

Average Rates of Inflation by Continent

	1948/53	1953/8	1958/63	1963/8
Industrialised countries (19)	6·0	2·7	2·5	4·0
Africa (18)	8·9	2·9	2·1	3·8
Asia (12)	3·0	1·7	1·7	3·2
Mediterranean (9)	4·7	4·9	3·4	3·8
Latin America (22) (including Caribbean)	11·3	11·7	9·0	11·1
Latin America (16) (excluding Bolivia, Brazil, Chile, Argentina, Paraguay and Uruguay)	4·8	2·6	2·6	3·3

Source: Jackson, Turner and Wilkinson, *Do Trade Unions Cause Inflation?*

world inflation in the future. An alternative hypothesis accounting for the mild and broadly similar inflationary experience is that developing countries have all been equally cautious in financing development by inflationary means.

3

Types of Inflation

The focus of this book is on demand inflation. Demand inflation can be defined as rising prices due to generalised excess demand in the product market associated with plans to invest in excess of plans to save. We have argued that excess demand in this sense is likely to be a typical characteristic of developing economies. Excess demand is not the only cause of inflation, however. Inflation may emanate from a number of different sources other than excess demand in the product market. In particular: prices may rise because prices are based on costs of production and costs rise; prices may rise because of shifts in demand from one sector of the economy to another and prices are more flexible in the upward direction than in the downward direction; and prices may rise in a self-reinforcing way because of a loss of confidence in money and the development of a wage–price spiral.

The stimulus to development from mild inflation will depend to an important extent on the origin of the inflation. Rising prices may 'force' saving and reduce real interest rates whether inflation emanates from excess demand or rising production costs, but there is an important difference between demand inflation and cost inflation with respect to the effect on profits, and saving out of profits. Whereas a demand inflation may be expected to redistribute real income to profit-earners to provide the additional saving for investment to exceed planned saving, a cost inflation will redistribute income away from profit-earners if prices do not adjust fully to match the increase in costs. Rising labour costs may encourage the adoption of more capital–intensive techniques of production which raise the productivity of labour, but if there is no change in the ratio of saving and investment to income, this can only mean more unemployment. Before analysing more closely the relation between inflation, saving and growth, it will be useful to formalise the various models of the inflationary process.

For pedagogic purposes, five major categories, or models, of inflation can be distinguished to describe the inflationary process: pure demand models; pure cost models; hybrid models containing demand and cost elements; structural models; and expectations models. In practice, of course, it may be difficult to discriminate between these different models of inflation in analysing any particular inflationary experience. Most inflations, at least once they are under way, are likely to be a combination of several forces, interacting with one another. Cost and expectations models merge; demand and cost models certainly merge. The difficulty of diagnosing cost-push and demand-pull has been colourfully described by Sir Dennis Robertson:[1]

> When the economic stalactite of inflated demand has met a sociological stalagmite of upthrusting claims; and when stalactite and stalagmite meet and fuse in an icy kiss . . . nobody on earth can be quite sure just where the one ends and the other begins.

In the event of a government wishing to restrain an inflation already under way, it is vital for policy to distinguish between the initiating causes of an inflation and its propagation mechanisms. Inappropriate policies based on faulty diagnosis of the initiating causes can lead to consequences worse than the disease itself.

Pure Demand Models

Pure demand models of the inflationary process ascribe rising prices to excess demand in the goods market. Prices rise because the demands on a society's resources from investors and consumers in money terms exceed the economy's real productive potential. A warranted growth rate which is less than the natural rate, with plans to invest in excess of plans to save, represents precisely this situation. In pure demand models, prices are assumed not to rise before the full employment level of resources is reached, denying the possibility that prices may be based on factor costs which may rise before the full-employment level of resource utilisation is reached. The essential features of the pure demand model are illustrated in Fig. 3.1 below. The successive aggregate demand curves (D_0D_0 etc.) are drawn downward sloping from left to right showing prices falling as real income

[1] D. Robertson, 'Thoughts on Inflation', in *Lectures on Economic Principles*, vol. III (London: Staples Press, 1959).

increases, other things remaining the same. The supply curve, SS, is drawn perfectly elastic up to the point of full-employment real income, Y_F, after which it is drawn infinitely inelastic, indicating zero supply response to increases in demand, by definition. Prices remain unchanged as aggregate demand expands towards the full-employment level of supply, Y_F, after which prices rise with further increases in aggregate demand, say from D_1D_1 to D_2D_2. If the price

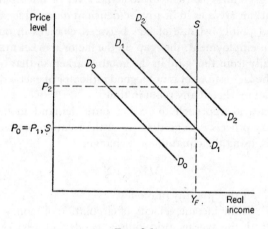

FIG. 3.1

level increases at the same rate as the expansion of demand, the *ad hoc* assumption can be made that the rate of inflation will be proportional to the proportional degree of excess demand:

$$dP/P = \gamma[(D - S)/S].$$

Changes in the supply and demand for money must play a crucial role in a pure demand explanation of the inflationary process. Plans to invest in excess of plans to save require financing for their realisation. If governments plan to invest more than is saved on the current account of the budget, the difference must be financed by some form of monetary expansion. If firms plan to invest more than is saved privately, some form of credit is required to bridge the gap. The practical difficulty in testing the pure demand hypothesis of inflation is to obtain a direct measure of the pressure of demand in the product market. Excess demand in the product market is not directly observable. One possibility is to take the level of unemployment in the

labour market as a proxy measure of the pressure of demand in the product market. This indirect approach suffers from a number of deficiencies, however. It not only assumes that unemployment has one prime cause, namely deficient demand for goods, but also that the pressure of demand in the labour market is related contemporaneously to the pressure of demand in the goods market. Both assumptions are unrealistic. On the first point, it would be absurd in the developing country context to take the level of unemployment in rural or urban areas as indicative of deficient demand for goods. On the second point, because of lags between changes in output and changes in employment, the 'gap' in the factor market may diverge substantially from the 'gap' in the goods market, so that unemployment in the factor market is not a good indicator of excess demand in the product market at any point in time.

The classical approach to testing pure demand models of the inflationary process is to go directly to the relation between money and prices, using the equation of exchange:

$$MV = PY \qquad (3.1)$$

where M is the quantity of money
        V is the income velocity of circulation of money
        P is the average price of final goods and services
and Y is real income.

The classical equation of exchange is turned into a theory of aggregate price determination by assuming that V and Y are constant or change predictably through time. The classical quantity theory of money and prices is the purest of the pure demand models of the inflationary process, predicting a direct and proportional relationship between increases in the money supply and increases in the general price level, with monetary expansion playing the initiating role. The assumption of a fixed or predictable Y is based on the classical prediction that economies tend automatically towards full employment so that the volume of real output is fixed in the short period and will grow smoothly over time according to the rate of growth of productive potential of the economy. The assumption that V is constant is equivalent to the assumption that the demand to hold money in relation to income (K_d) is constant i.e. $K_d = M/PY$, where $K_d = 1/V$. The assumption of a stable demand function for money had some logic and practical relevance in classical theory which was formulated at a

time when the purchase of goods was the main outlet for money and when the main motive for holding money was for transactions purposes. It is fairly natural that if money is only required for transactions purposes, the demand for it should be in some fixed proportion to the value of commodities turned over within an accounting period. It was the growth of a securities market that led to full recognition of money as an asset that could be held for speculative purposes and hence subject to changes in demand according to changes in the rate of interest. It was the recognition of money as an asset that led to the neo-classical reformulation of the classical equation of exchange, laying stress on the determinants of the demand for money. The neo-classical approach on which Keynes built is particularly relevant in the context of developing countries which are not fully monetised, and in which the range of financial assets is continually expanding.

The neo-classical reformulation of the quantity theory of money may be written:

$$M = K_d PY \tag{3.2}$$

Putting the equation of exchange in this form highlights the fact that the supply of money must equal the demand for money in equilibrium, and that if M increases equilibrium can be restored either by a change in K_d or PY. If K_d and Y are fixed then prices must rise to restore equilibrium. If K_d and Y are not fixed then clearly there cannot be a direct equi-proportional relation between changes in the money supply and changes in the price level. There cannot be a predictable relation either unless movements in K_d and Y are themselves predictable as the money supply expands. A monetarist interpretation of inflation must assume that K_d and Y are fixed in the short term and predictable in the long run.

A monetary theory of inflation must also convince that it is monetary expansion which is the independent variable in the system, and that the money supply is not merely responding to 'exogenous' changes in the price level to prevent real income from falling. It is easily seen from equation (3.2) that if P rises, while M and K_d remain the same, Y must fall to restore equilibrium. In any empirical test of the monetary explanation of inflation, the identification problem of whether it is M causing changes in P or changes in P causing changes in M must be solved. One factor which may cause P to change, independently of changes in M, is labour unions bidding for higher

wages irrespective of the pressure of demand (which pure demand models of the inflationary process deny or ignore). If wage (cost) increases are to be conceded without causing unemployment, there must be sufficient aggregate demand to buy up the goods produced at a higher level of prices. This can only come about through monetary expansion. In a modern capitalist economy with powerful trade unions, coupled with a government commitment to the maintenance of full employment and stable interest rates, it may be very difficult to distinguish what is cause and what is effect. The argument applies equally to the modern sector of developing countries where trade unions are well entrenched and powerful, and where governments are prone to granting exorbitant wage increases in the public sector with no more economic justification than to maintain parity with wages in private industry, or to enhance the status of public employment.

The classical and neo-classical equations of exchange provide a useful framework for considering the nature and origins of hyper-inflation. Up to now it has been assumed that the demand to hold money is independent of the rate of inflation. In reality, since inflation reduces the real value of money holdings, the demand to hold money in relation to income is likely to be inversely related to the rate of inflation. If rising prices reduce K_d (raise V), the effect of monetary expansion on the rate of inflation is compounded.

If hyperinflation is defined as an accelerating rate of inflation which leads to a high absolute rate of inflation, a sufficient condition for hyperinflation to occur is that the elasticity of the demand for money relation to income with respect to the rate of inflation exceeds unity in in absolute value. The following simple model is enough to illustrate the point. Taking rates of change of the variables in equation (3.2) and rearranging gives

$$\left(\frac{dP}{P}\right)_t = \left(\frac{dM}{M}\right)_t - \left(\frac{dK_d}{K_d}\right)_t - \left(\frac{dY}{Y}\right)_t \quad (3.3)$$

Now let

$$\left(\frac{dK_d}{K_d}\right)_t = \gamma_o \left(\frac{dP}{P}\right)_t^e \quad (3.4)$$

where $(dP/P)_t^e$ is the expected rate of change of prices equal to the past rate of change of prices $(dP/P)_{t-1}$,

and dM/M and dY/Y are exogenously given.

Substituting (3.4) into (3.3) gives

$$\left(\frac{dP}{P}\right)_t + \gamma_o \left(\frac{dP}{P}\right)_{t-1} = \frac{dM}{M} - \frac{dY}{Y} \qquad (3.5)$$

If $\gamma_o > |1|$, inflation will accelerate through time. If the government expands the money supply to maintain the real value of its revenues, the rate of acceleration will be even higher.

In the real world, hyperinflations are rare, and it is interesting to speculate why. One explanation is that inflation rarely becomes so severe in the first place for people to lose confidence in money such that the demand for money declines more than in proportion to the increase in the price level. Confidence in money is maintained presumably in the belief that excessive inflation will be brought under control by the responsible authorities. In other words, money is retained as a medium of exchange, which imposes a limit on the degree to which K_d falls. Brown has observed that the historical experience suggests that a marked flight from cash does not usually begin unless prices are doubling at least every six months.[1] Apparently the public is willing to pay a very high price for the convenience of holding cash balances. In his classic study of seven hyperinflations Cagan also refers to the public's lingering confidence in the future value of money despite the experience of inflation.[2] According to Cagan hyperinflations have resulted more from monetary irresponsibility than from increases in the velocity of circulation of money. Typically what has happened is that governments have issued more and more money to maintain the real value of their revenues in the face of rapidly rising prices. Cagan doubts whether, in the absence of continuing monetary expansion, hyperinflations would proceed very far.

Another factor contributing to stability is that when money balance holdings are cut, the excess money balances are not all spent in the goods market. In addition, they are used to purchase 'hedges' against inflation such as land, real estate, inventories, precious metals, foreign exchange and the like. The prices of these assets rise, but not necessarily the prices of final goods and services. Thus the reduction in the demand for money following the initial inflation need not

[1] A. J. Brown, *The Great Inflation 1939–51* (Oxford University Press, 1955).
[2] P. Cagan, 'The Monetary Dynamics of Hyperinflation' in *Studies in the Quantity Theory of Money*, ed. M. Friedman (University of Chicago Press, 1956).

exacerbate inflation and generate the conditions for a cumulative inflationary spiral which is the essence of a hyperinflation. Inflation is damped and the motive for reducing money holdings diminishes. The interdependence between inflation and changes in the demand for money is just one of a range of models of hyperinflation. Another model will be considered later in which accelerating inflation is produced by workers bidding for wage increases in anticipation of future price increases. First, however, let us consider pure cost models of the inflationary process, which go to the other extreme to pure demand models and ignore demand as the initiating cause of inflation.

Pure Cost Models

Pure cost models of the inflationary process ascribe inflation to the activities of monopolistic groups in the labour market (trade unions), and imperfectly competitive producers, who are claimed to be able to bid up wages and profits, respectively, independently of the pressure of demand in the factor or product market. Wage increases are transmitted into price increases through a mark-up of prices on wage costs per unit of output; and profits-push inflation results from an increase in the mark-up itself. According to the mark-up hypothesis

$$P = \frac{w}{(O/L)} (1 + \pi) = \frac{W}{O} (1 + \pi) \qquad (3.6)$$

where P is the price per unit of output
        w is the wage rate
      O/L is the productivity of labour
      W/O is wage costs per unit of output
and π is the percentage mark-up on wage costs.

It follows from equation (3.6) that

$$\frac{dP}{P} = \frac{dw}{w} - \frac{d(O/L)}{(O/L)} + \frac{d\pi}{(1 + \pi)} \qquad (3.7)$$

In words, the rate of change in prices is equal to the rate of change of wages minus the rate of change in labour productivity plus the rate of change of $(1 + \pi)$. A change in the mark-up by imperfectly competitive producers can raise prices. If the mark-up is fixed the rate of inflation is simply the difference between the rate of wage

inflation and the growth of labour productivity. What determines the rate of wage inflation is an open question. The degree of monopoly power in the labour market is one possibility. Another possibility is that wage rate increases are based on the rate of productivity advance in the fastest growing sector of the economy. The main features of the pure cost model are represented diagrammatically in Fig. 3.2.

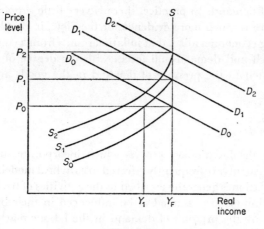

FIG. 3.2

In an environment of strong trade unions, supply curves of output are assumed to shift to the left by a constant amount, irrespective of the pressure of demand (represented by supply curves moving leftwards equidistant from each other). Or, to put it another way, the level of real income associated with stable prices continually falls because rising costs (wages) price factors of production (labour) out of the market. This can be seen in Fig. 3.2 from points at which the successive supply curves S_0, S_1 and S_2 cut the stable price line, P_0. Full-employment real income, Y_F, can only be maintained at rising price levels, P_0, P_1, P_2 etc. The cost of maintaining prices at the level P_0, in the event of a shift in the supply curve from S_0 to S_1, would be unemployment equivalent to a loss of real income Y_1Y_F. If a government is committed to full employment it must expand demand – in this case from D_0D_0 to D_1D_1 – to maintain the full-employment level of income, Y_F, given the new supply curve S_1S. This is where the role of money becomes important, and which leads to the expectation of a correlation between rising prices and increases in the money supply.

In pure cost models of the inflationary process, however, money is assumed to be endogenous to the system and to propagate inflation rather than initiate it.

To support the dynamic version of the pure cost theory of inflation the empirical evidence would have to show a constant rate of wage or price inflation irrespective of the pressure of demand. In pure cost models there is no trade-off between the rate of inflation and the pressure of demand. In practice, there is very little support for this view. There is much more evidence for the view, in developed and developing economies alike, that inflation results from a combination of cost-push and demand-pull forces with the degree of cost-push being related to the pressure of demand in the goods and labour markets.

Hybrid Models

Models of the inflationary process which incorporate supply and demand elements are frequently referred to as hybrid models. In these models inflation is generally ascribed to the activities of trade unions, but trade unions are assumed to be influenced in their bargaining behaviour by the pressure of demand in the labour market. If the market is tight, labour is assumed to bargain for higher wage rate increases than if the market is slack. Employers are assumed to be weaker in their resistance to wage claims in buoyant conditions because cost increases can be more easily passed on in the form of higher prices, and profits are likely to be healthy. The constant mark-up assumption of the pure cost models is retained so that wage increases are transmitted directly into price increases. In hybrid models of the inflationary process, therefore, shifts in the supply curve of output are assumed to be positively related to the closeness of the economy to the full-employment level of output, as shown in Fig. 3.3 below; that is, the vertical distance between the supply curves increases the closer the economy is to Y_F.

To maintain price stability (at P_0 for example) in the event of shifts in supply requires more unemployment the closer the economy is to full employment. Hybrid models are often called dilemma models because they highlight very clearly the clash between full employment and price stability, and the fact that one discommodity (unemployment) must be traded for another (inflation). In the short run (and in the long run as well, provided wage-earners do not fully anticipate

price increases) the cost of containing inflation may mean substantial under-utilisation of resources which neither developed nor developing countries committed to growth can afford to tolerate.

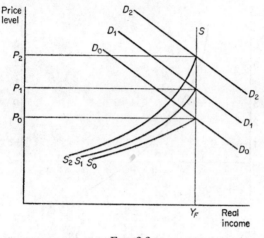

FIG. 3.3

The most familiar hybrid model of inflation is epitomised by the Phillips curve[1] which relates the percentage rate of change of money wages (dw/w), or the percentage rate of change of prices (dP/P), to the percentage level of unemployment as a measure of the pressure of demand, as shown in Fig. 3.4. The difference between dw/w and dP/P at any level of unemployment is equal to the rate of growth of labour productivity, assumed to be 3 per cent in Fig. 3.4.

An inverse relation between the level of unemployment and the rate of inflation is not an isolated phenomena observed only in modern capitalistic economies during the recent past. It has been observed in many different contexts over long periods of time. Of course, there have been deviations from the long period estimated relation, but generalisations about economic and social phenomenon based on careful analysis of the historical data are not made defunct by short-term aberrations. The long view must be taken if any sense at all is to be made of economic behaviour.

One plausible set of hypotheses to generate a Phillips curve relation

[1] A. W. Phillips, 'The Relation Between Unemployment and the Rate of Change of Money Wage Rates in the United Kingdom 1861–1957', *Economica* (November 1958).

is that given by Lipsey.[1] Assume that the market for labour is out of equilibrium, and that the speed of adjustment to equilibrium is proportional to the proportional degree of excess demand for labour

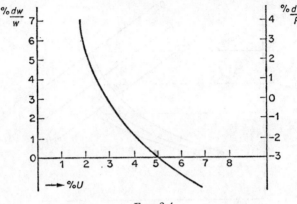

FIG. 3.4

as shown by the continuous straight line in Fig. 3.5, where D is the demand for labour and S is the supply of labour.

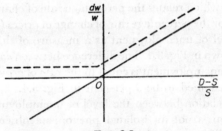

FIG. 3.5

Further assume that the percentage level of unemployment is negatively related to the proportional degree of excess demand as shown in Fig. 3.6. The relation is drawn convex to the origin on the assumption that unemployment cannot fall to zero. That is, unemployment is decreasingly sensitive to increases in the pressure of demand until it

[1] R. G. Lipsey, 'The Relation Between Unemployment and the Rate of Change of Money Wage Rates in the U.K. 1862–1957: A Further Analysis', *Economica* (February 1960).

reaches some frictional minimum below which it can fall no further. Combining Figs 3.5 and 3.6 gives a negative (and convex to the origin) relation between dw/w and $\%U$ (as shown in Fig. 3.4), the slope of which depends on the ratio of the slopes of the two curves in Figs 3.5 and 3.6, and the position of which depends on the slopes *and* positions of the two curves (which is demonstrated later).

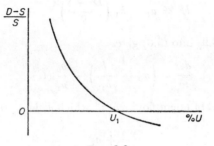

FIG. 3.6

In Fig. 3.5 the straight line relation between dw/w and $(D-S)/S$ is drawn on the assumption that free market forces prevail in the labour market, that there is no wage inflation without excess labour demand, and that wages are equally flexible in the downward direction as well as upwards. In reality, the relation is likely to have some positive intercept, which reflects the type of autonomous trade union pressure on wages that was referred to earlier in the discussion of pure cost models of the inflationary process. It is also likely to have some convexity reflecting some floor below which any reduction of the rate of change of wages is resisted. These practical realities are represented by the dotted line in Fig. 3.5.

In Fig. 3.6 the intercept on the horizontal axis, U_1, represents the percentage level of unemployment which exists when the supply and demand for labour are in balance. It is the amount of unemployment existing when the labour market is in 'equilibrium'. This level of unemployment may be called non-demand-deficient unemployment, which will consist of frictional and structural elements.

The level of unemployment at which the linear[1] Phillips relation $[dw/w = a + b(U)]$ cuts the unemployment axis is made up of both the slope and intercept terms of its two constituent relations, as can be

---

[1] Despite what has been said above, we now work with a linear relation for simplicity.

50   INFLATION, SAVING AND GROWTH

easily shown by taking linear approximations of both relations in
Figs 3.5 and 3.6. From Fig. 3.5 we have (with a positive intercept)

$$\frac{dw}{w} = a_0 + b_0 \left(\frac{D-S}{S}\right) \tag{3.8}$$

and from Fig. 3.6 we have (linearising)

$$U = a_1 - b_1 \left(\frac{D-S}{S}\right) \tag{3.9}$$

Substituting (3.9) into (3.8) gives

$$\frac{dw}{w} = \left(a_0 + \frac{a_1 b_0}{b_1}\right) - \frac{b_0}{b_1}(U) \tag{3.10}$$

so that the level of unemployment at which $dw/w = 0$ is

$$\frac{b_1 a_0}{b_0} + a_1 \tag{3.11}$$

This term can provide some measure of the degree of non-demand-
deficient unemployment in an economy (a_1) if the slope of the
Phillips relation (b_0/b_1), and the rate of upward push on wages which
is independent of the pressure of demand (a_0), are known. For
example, if the slope of the Phillips relation is unity, a_0 is 3, and the
level of unemployment at which $dw/w = 0$ is 5 per cent, then the
level of non-demand-deficient unemployment (a_1) is 2 per cent. In
developed countries the level of non-demand-deficient unemployment generally lies between 2 per cent and 4 per cent. In the urban
sector in developing countries the rate is probably much higher. In
a recent study by Koot, which establishes a trade-off between inflation and unemployment for Chile, the level of unemployment
apparently required for wage stability is approximately 20 per cent.[1]
While the information is not given to calculate a_1 precisely, it
is likely to be considerably higher than 4 per cent unless the
autonomous rate of change of wages is very high. A high value of a_1
would be quite consistent with what we know about the nature and
origins of high levels of unemployment in the urban areas of
developing countries.[2] If wage rate data are available, the use of

[1] R. S. Koot, 'Wage Changes, Unemployment and Inflation in Chile',
Industrial and Labour Relations Review (July 1969).
[2] See D. Turnham, *The Employment Problem in Less Developed Countries:
A Review of the Evidence* (Paris: O.E.C.D., 1971).

the Phillips relation can be a useful way of ascertaining the degree of structural and frictional unemployment in the absence of more direct measures.

Structural Models of Inflation

The level of structural unemployment is closely related to the structure of demand and to the sectoral distribution of unemployment across markets. If some markets are expanding while other markets are contracting, and labour cannot easily move between activities because of a lack of co-operating factors, the economy is likely to experience fairly rapid inflation with high unemployment, particularly if wages and prices in contracting markets are inflexible downwards, and wage and price increases in expanding markets transmit themselves to other sectors. These arguments form the basis of structural models of inflation which ascribe inflation to disequilibrium between markets and which point to the possibility that even though an economy may be in balance in the aggregate, inflation may still be experienced because of imbalances in sub-markets. Inflation is seen as a natural concomitant of growth and structural change.

The dependence of the aggregate rate of wage or price inflation on the sectoral distribution of demand can be illustrated with the following model. As before, write the aggregate relation between the rate of wage inflation and excess demand as

$$\frac{dw}{w} = b\left(\frac{D-S}{S}\right) = b\left(\frac{X}{S}\right) \qquad (3.12)$$

and let the relation between the rate of wage inflation and excess demand in individual sub-markets (e.g. industries i) be represented as

$$\frac{dw_i}{w_i} = \frac{b_i X_i}{S_i} \qquad \text{or} \qquad dw_i S_i = w_i b_i X_i \qquad (3.13)$$

If all $X_i = 0$, a disaggregated model of wage inflation must predict the stability of aggregate wages, the same as the aggregate model when $X = 0$. But suppose that all sub-markets are not in equilibrium, despite $X = 0$, and that the b_i's differ. A positive or negative rate of aggregate wage change with no excess demand in the aggregate is possible depending on the relation between the b_i's and the degree of excess demand in individual sub-markets (X_i). Let the aggregate

rate of change of wages equal the sum of changes in individual markets weighted by the relative supplies of labour in the base period, i.e.

$$\frac{dw}{w} = \frac{\Sigma dw_i S_i}{\Sigma w_i S_i} \tag{3.14}$$

Substituting equation (3.13) into (3.14) gives

$$\frac{dw}{w} = \frac{\Sigma b_i w_i X_i}{\Sigma w_i S_i} \tag{3.15}$$

If the b_i's differ, non-zero wage inflation in the aggregate is quite compatible with zero excess demand for labour in the aggregate. For example, suppose that there are n markets with negative excess demand and m markets with positive excess demand and that b_i is an increasing function of excess demand (implying, other things remaining the same, that the slope of the Phillips curves in individual markets is positively related to the pressure of demand), then, despite $\underset{n}{\Sigma X_i} = \underset{m}{\Sigma X_i}$ (so that $X = 0$), $dw/w > 0$ because

$$\frac{\displaystyle\sum_{i=m}^{i=m} b_i w_i (X_i)}{\displaystyle\sum_{i=m}^{i=m} w_i S_i} > \frac{\displaystyle\sum_{i=n}^{i=n} b_i w_i (X_i)}{\displaystyle\sum_{i=n}^{i=n} w_i S_i}$$

In other words, the inflationary effects of excess demand in some markets exceed the deflationary effects of an *equal* amount of excess supply in others.

There are a number of theoretical and institutional reasons why the reaction of wages to the pressure of demand, measured directly by $(D - S)/S$ or indirectly by U, may be an increasing function of the degree of excess demand. The most important considerations are that reductions in the rate of wage inflation may be decreasingly sensitive to reductions in the pressure of demand, and that reductions in unemployment are decreasingly sensitive to increases in the pressure of demand for labour. As already shown, both of these 'non-linearities' (see Figs 3.5 and 3.6) will produce a non-linear relation between the rate of wage inflation and unemployment. It is then easily shown that if the Phillips curves for individual sub-markets in the economy are non-linear, the position of the aggregate relation between dw/w and U will depend on the sectoral distribution of

demand. A simple diagram can illustrate the point. Take two markets, a and b, of equal size so that

$$U = (u_a + u_b)/2$$

and

$$dw/w = \left[\left(\frac{dw}{w}\right)_a + \left(\frac{dw}{w}\right)_b\right]\Big/2$$

and assume that the two markets have identical non-linear Phillips curves, as shown in Fig. 3.7.

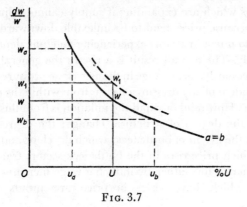

Fig. 3.7

If the level of unemployment in the two markets was equal at U (i.e. $u_a = u_b = U$), the aggregate rate of wage inflation would be w. Suppose, however, that unemployment in market a is u_a, giving a rate of wage inflation in market a of w_a, and unemployment in market b is u_b, giving a rate of wage inflation in market b of w_b. The aggregate rate of wage inflation would now be w_1 at the same rate of aggregate unemployment U (since $U = (u_a + u_b)/2$). For any given aggregate pressure of demand, the aggregate rate of inflation will be higher the greater the dispersion of demand between markets. The more 'non-linear' the market curves, the 'worse' the aggregate relation between wage inflation and unemployment will be. For example, if wage inflation in market b was the same as in market a, despite the higher level of unemployment, the aggregate rate of inflation would be the same as that in market a. The aggregate rate of

wage inflation would be dictated by the conditions in the most buoyant sector of the economy. The argument applies equally to a productivity-based theory of wage determination where the aggregate rate of wage inflation would be dictated by the rate of incease in productivity in the fastest growing sector. If prices are based on costs, both models also predict that the rate of increase in prices will be higher the greater the dispersion of demand, or productivity growth, between industries.

Even if prices are not based on costs, the same structuralist arguments can still be applied to price inflation. As demand shifts from one sector of the economy to another, according to differences in the income elasticity of demand for products, prices will tend to rise in those sectors which are expanding if supply cannot adjust immediately. But because prices tend to be inflexible downwards, prices do not fall by so much in sectors experiencing an equivalent amount of excess supply. The overall result is a rise in the general price level without, necessarily, any change in the aggregate pressure of demand, and independent of any pressure on costs from within the economy or from outside. How mild or rapid the inflation is from this source will depend on the degree of structural change; the degree of supply inelasticity; the extent of bottlenecks which develop; and also on the extent to which price rises in the bottleneck sectors transmit themselves to other sectors either by inducing wage increases or because the goods which have risen in price are inputs into other activities.

It is argued that inflation of the structural type has been acute in some countries of Latin America as a result of the lack of preparedness for industrialisation. In particular, the inadequacy of food supplies to feed a growing, and increasingly urbanised, population has pushed up the price of food and contributed to balance-of-payments problems, the inflationary effects of which spread to other sectors of the economy through the impetus given to wage demands and the effects of currency devaluation on the price of imports. The evidence for this will be discussed in Chapter 9. What is important to realise is that every economy is prone to inflation to some degree as a result of structural change and rigidities in the economic system; the more so in developing countries where the very process of development is one of structural change from a rigid to a more flexible economic and social system. Inflation may well be the price of growth in the process of structural change.

Expectations Models

It has been argued above that there is a trade-off between inflation and the full utilisation of resources, but that because of the level of non-demand-deficient unemployment the price of full employment may be a very high rate of inflation indeed. It is sometimes contended, however, that the possibility of choice between inflation and unemployment only exists in the short run. In the long run there is no choice because wage-earners come to expect inflation, and the Phillips trade-off curve becomes a vertical straight line. A sufficient condition for the trade-off curve to pivot to a vertical position is that the coefficient relating the rate of change of wages to the rate of change of prices is unity. If the coefficient is unity not only are there no redistribution effects of inflation between wages and profits[1] but there can be no gain from inflation in the form of a fuller utilisation of resources. In the models of expected inflation it is impossible to run the economy at a higher level of employment than the so-called 'natural rate' without generating ever-accelerating inflation. A simple model which captures the main arguments is as follows

Let

$$\left(\frac{dw}{w}\right)_t = f(U) + a_0 \left(\frac{dP}{P}\right)_t^e \qquad (3.16)$$

where $\left(\frac{dP}{P}\right)^e$ is the expected rate of inflation.

If the expected rate of inflation is equal to the past rate of inflation

$$\left(\frac{dP}{P}\right)_t^e = \left(\frac{dP}{P}\right)_{t-1}$$

so that

$$\left(\frac{dw}{w}\right)_t = f(U) + a_0 \left(\frac{dP}{P}\right)_{t-1} \qquad (3.17)$$

Suppose, as before, using the constant mark-up assumption, that the rate of inflation is the difference between the rate of increase in wages and the rate of increase in labour productivity, then

$$\left(\frac{dP}{P}\right)_t = \left(\frac{dw}{w}\right)_t - \left(\frac{d(O/L)}{(O/L)}\right)_t \qquad (3.18)$$

[1] Assuming that the autonomous rate of wage increase is equal to the rate of growth of labour productivity.

Substituting (3.18) into (3.17) gives

$$\left(\frac{dP}{P}\right)_t = f(U) + a_0 \left(\frac{dP}{P}\right)_{t-1} - \left(\frac{d(O/L)}{(O/L)}\right)_t \qquad (3.19)$$

Let $\dfrac{\overline{dP}}{P}$ be the equilibrium solution obtained by setting

$$\left(\frac{dP}{P}\right)_t = \left(\frac{dP}{P}\right)_{t-1}$$

so that

$$\frac{\overline{dP}}{P} = \frac{1}{1 - a_0}\left(f(U) - \frac{d(O/L)}{(O/L)}\right) \qquad (3.20)$$

Equation (3.20) gives the long run (equilibrium) relation between the rate of inflation and the level of unemployment. If $a_0 < 1$, the normal trade-off relation is traced out. If $a_0 = 1$ (i.e. if wages adjust fully to expected price increases) there is no solution to equation (3.20) and the relation between the rate of inflation and the level of unemployment is a vertical straight line, as in Fig. 3.8.

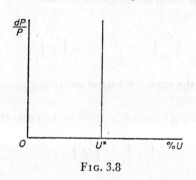

FIG. 3.8

In short, if inflation is expected, and $a_0 = 1$, then

$$(dw/w)_t = (dP/P)_t = (dP/P)_{t-1},$$

and whatever rate of inflation is initially established (including zero) will continue indefinitely. The point at which the vertical line cuts the unemployment axis is sometimes called the natural rate of unemployment, U^*. If there is no productivity growth, the natural rate of unemployment is simply the level of U at which $f(U) = 0$. Unfortunately from a policy point of view, the natural rate of unemployment cannot be known *a priori*. It is a theoretical construct

which only becomes operational *ex post*, because it is that rate of unemployment at which the actual rate of inflation equals the expected rate. The natural rate of unemployment therefore cannot be defined until the actual rate of inflation is known. If the actual rate equals the expected rate, the rate of inflation will be stable. The stable rate of inflation could be any rate of inflation, not necessarily zero. In other words, the natural rate of unemployment does not guarantee price stability, or even mild inflation.

Given the natural rate of unemployment, it is apparently only possible to reduce actual unemployment temporarily below it by

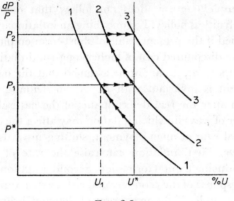

FIG. 3.9

policies of demand expansion which raise prices and reduce real wages. In the long run, it is argued, workers will bid for higher wages to match price increases, and a level of unemployment below the natural rate can only be maintained by prices rising still further. The price of reducing the level of unemployment below the natural rate is ever-accelerating inflation. This is illustrated in Fig. 3.9. Policy makers 'buy' U^*U_1 less unemployment for P^*P_1 extra inflation moving up the short-run Phillips curve 1. If workers now expect inflation rate P_1 they will bid for higher wages so that real wages rise to their former level raising unemployment back to U^*. Inflation rate P_1 is now associated with the higher unemployment rate U^*. And so the process goes on.

Apparently the choice is not between inflation and unemployment but between unemployment below the natural rate and ever-accelerating inflation, or between inflation today and inflation

tomorrow. Ever-accelerating inflation is the product of outward shifts in the short-run Phillips curve due to inflationary expectations. This is an alternative model of hyperinflation to the monetary models of hyperinflation based on a loss of confidence in money. In practice, of course, the two processes may not be mutually exclusive. Monetary expansion which contributes to expectations of price increases, and price increases which lead to a reduction in the demand for money (as well as stimulating wage rate increases), may go hand in hand.

Even if the employment gains from demand expansion are eventually lost, as expectations models predict, by the employment–inflation curve pivoting to a long-run vertical position at the natural rate of unemployment, it does not follow that demand-induced inflation is a fruitless policy. For one thing an inflationary policy may still be justified if the present value of short-term employment gains outweighs the discounted cost of higher long-run inflation.[1] Second, and more important, it cannot be assumed that the natural rate of unemployment is invariant with respect to demand expansion if inflation can alter the real determinants of the natural rate. There are a number of ways in which inflation may affect the determinants of the natural rate of unemployment, shifting inwards the vertical Phillips curve. First, inflation can raise the rate of productivity growth by inducing capital formation. Second, inflation can increase the supply response of the economy and reduce structural unemployment. For example, if the expansion of demand brings previously unemployed workers into the labour force who then get trained and become active members of the labour force, there will be less men in the pool of structurally unemployed in the future. The trade-off between inflation and unemployment will be improved, and the level of unemployment will be lower at which in subsequent periods the Phillips curve becomes vertical if the wage-price coefficient is unity. This is nothing more than the well-known proposition that a Phillips curve is specific to a given amount of frictional/structural unemployment, which is not necessarily invariant to the pressure of demand if demand pressures exert permanent effects on the composition of the (unemployed) work force. There exists a whole family of Phillips curves for different levels of frictional/structural unemployment. In developing economies, in particular, the development process may be expected to be characterised through time

---

[1] See E. S. Phelps, *Inflation Policy and Unemployment Theory* (London: Macmillan, 1972) for further discussion of this point.

by inward shifts in the trade-off curve between inflation and unemployment as the proportion of the labour force which is trained and mobile grows. The stimulus of inflation may be just what is needed to bring about the inward shifts in the curve. If the curve is shifting inwards through time there can be no unique relation between the rate of growth of wages and prices and the level of unemployment. If bursts of inflation are necessary for growth, we have here another mechanism whereby inflation may be damped. Contrary to the models which predict growing inflation as demand expands and employment increases, we have here the possibility of increased output and employment at a stable rate of inflation. It should also be remembered that many workers would probably be willing to work at a lower real wage than that prevailing, rather than not work at all, which also means that inflation could lead to a permanent reduction in the natural rate of unemployment. Even if the wage–price coefficient is unity, therefore, inflationary policies are by no means irrelevant to the question of the optimum use of resources. This argument is of particular significance in the context of developing countries where the major cause of unemployment is a lack of capital and where there is vast scope for reducing unemployment and raising the rate of growth of productivity by well-managed policies of inflationary finance.

The models of inflation based on expectations have some similarity with the more traditional explanations of accelerating inflation which stress the interaction between wages and prices.[1] In both types of model, the wage–price coefficient is a crucial parameter. In the expectations model, a coefficient of unity will give a stable rate of inflation providing prices rise in the same proportion as wage costs. In the wage–price spiral model of inflation it is the product of the wage–price coefficient and the price–wage coefficient which determines whether inflation is stable, damped or anti-damped. This is easily shown.

Let
$$\left(\frac{dw}{w}\right)_t = \gamma_0 \left(\frac{dP}{P}\right)_{t-1} \tag{3.21}$$

and
$$\left(\frac{dP}{P}\right)_t = \beta_0 \left(\frac{dw}{w}\right)_t \tag{3.22}$$

[1] In expectations models the feedback effect of wages on prices is not explicitly part of the model, although the mark-up–pricing equation is one of the equations of the model.

Substituting equation (3.21) into (3.22) gives

$$\left(\frac{dP}{P}\right)_t = \gamma_0\beta_0 \left(\frac{dP}{P}\right)_{t-1} \qquad (3.23)$$

If $\gamma_0\beta_0 = 1$, the rate of inflation is stable. If $\gamma_0\beta_0 < 1$, the rate of inflation will decelerate through time. If $\gamma_0\beta_0 > 1$, the rate of inflation will accelerate through time. If β_0 is assumed to be unity on the mark-up assumption that prices rise as fast as wage costs, it is the reaction of wages to past price increases that determines whether inflation will accelerate or not.

Expectations of inflation can clearly sustain an on-going inflation, but expectations of inflation cannot be held responsible for initiating an inflation in the first place. Nor is there much evidence that the rate of inflation based on expectations of future inflation will accelerate through time. The coefficients a_0 in equation (3.17) and γ_0 in equation (3.21) are usually found to be less than unity. As we have already shown, most countries in the world economy at least since the Second World War have experienced remarkably mild inflation with very little by way of upward trend.[1] Even in the Latin American countries with rates of inflation in excess of 10 per cent there has been a tendency for the rate of inflation to stabilise.

Conclusion

We can summarise by saying that in any economy there are two broad sources of inflationary pressure. On the one hand inflation may occur naturally in the process of structural change. On the other hand, inflation may occur when groups in the economy try to acquire more income or resources than the economy can make available at any given time. The acquisitive pressure may come from governments or from private individuals wanting to invest more than is being saved, or from the cost side with employers and/or workers bidding for a higher share of a given real income. Whatever the origins of inflation, expectations that it will continue may sustain and perhaps exacerbate it.

It is extremely difficult to classify countries according to the type of

[1] The early years of the 1970s have witnessed a doubling of inflation rates in many countries, for reasons which are not entirely clear, but there is no evidence that the rate of inflation is accelerating, and will not eventually come down.

inflation, that is, to ascribe an inflationary experience to one particular cause. All that can reasonably be done is to identify as closely as possible the initial causes of inflation in any particular case as distinct from the forces that sustain it. Diagnosis in this respect is extremely important if for some reason governments desire to reduce the rate of inflation. It would be the height of folly, for example, for a government to control a pure cost inflation, or a structural inflation for that matter, by restraining demand. Demand pressure may help to sustain the cost inflation but all that controlling demand would do in these circumstances would be to depress output which may worsen the inflation rather than ameliorate it. We shall describe in Chapter 9 the experience of some Latin American countries which have tried to cope with inflation using demand management policies but with disastrous results.

If inflation in developing countries is primarily structural in origin, inflation must be the inevitable price of growth and of development policies which seek to mobilise fully a country's resources. Even though there may be no direct causal relation leading from inflation to growth, inflation may have to be tolerated in the pursuit of growth in the face of structural change and rigidities in the price system. It is not clear that developing countries are fully aware that given the necessity and inevitability of structural change, the control of inflation may mean stifling growth. In the early nineteensixties Schonfield[1] expressed concern that developing economies in general, and Asia and India in particular, seemed to be more concerned with tackling inflation than with remedying unemployment and achieving a faster rate of growth of output. Schonfield attributed the bias in attitude and policy to the excessive inflationary experience of Latin American countries. His recommendation for India was a policy of controlled inflation which would attempt to increase employment in the rural sector of the economy, and at the same time turn the terms of trade in favour of the manufacturing sector by raising the price of manufactured goods relative to food. The price of food would be kept down by a planned expansion of food imports from the developed countries.

Little[2] was also critical of Indian development policy in the early

[1] See his three lectures delivered in New Delhi 1961, reprinted in *The Listener* (24 and 31 August, and 14 September 1961).
[2] I. M. D. Little, 'A Critical Examination of India's Third Five Year Plan', *Oxford Economic Papers* (February 1962).

sixties. He criticised the Third Indian Plan for its 'fear of inflation' and its excessive preoccupation with the dangers of monetary expansion. The Plan took the desirable rate of increase in the money supply to be slightly greater than the rate of increase of real national income to allow for some increased monetisation of the economy. According to the Plan:

It is proposed to limit deficit financing to the minimum warranted by the genuine monetary needs of the economy.

Little asks:

If the authorities are so worried by the quantity of money, why do they not take steps to reduce the multiplicative effect on the money supply of deficit finance? There are plenty of ways of imposing this on the banking system.

Little's suggested alternative to the conservative bias of the Quantity Theory approach was the Keynesian approach, advocated by Schonfield, which would be inflationary in nature. His advice was that the Indian government should spend more, and that greater risks should be taken to create more employment, especially in rural areas, and to raise agricultural output, both to cope with India's greatest problem of under-employment and to minimise the effects of demand expansion on the price of food.

The fact that inflation may be an inevitable consequence of growth for structural reasons begs the question, of course, of whether inflation itself is desirable and can be an inducement to growth. There would be nothing inconsistent in arguing that inflation must accompany growth and arguing that deliberately induced inflation is undesirable, and likely to retard growth, given that there may be certain costs involved in inducing inflation, say by monetary means. In the preceding chapter, however, it has been argued to the contrary. It is generally accepted that inflation can release some resources for investment purposes because inflation is a tax on money, and there is no reason in principle why it should be more difficult for a government to maintain a rate of demand inflation of, say, 6 per cent as opposed to 3 per cent. Growth can be accelerated if resources obtained by government are at the expense of private consumption and invested in productive capital. Even if government investment is at the expense of private investment, growth could still be accelerated if the marginal social return of the investment is greater than the

private return forgone. Temporary employment effects which act as a stimulus to development are also possible from government-induced inflation. Inflation also redistributes income within the private sector, and reduces the real interest rate, both of which may be favourable to investment. It is now time to consider in more detail models of growth which incorporate the effects of inflation and monetary expansion on the determinants of growth. We shall do this using Harrod's model of the warranted growth rate as the analytical framework.

4

Models of the Effects of Inflation on Saving and Growth

In this chapter some elementary models of growth are presented which incorporate the effects of inflation on the determinants of growth. First, however, it is necessary to clarify Harrod's model of growth as it relates to developing countries, especially the effects of divergencies between the warranted and natural rates of growth. It was suggested earlier that the typical problem of developing economies is that the natural rate of growth exceeds the warranted rate implying capital scarcity and structural unemployment. Having considered the characteristics of developing economies in terms of the basic Harrod model, we can then go on to consider classes of models in which the savings ratio adjusts to divergencies between the warranted and natural growth rates, specifically as a result of monetary expansion and inflation. The chapter is designed as a prelude to Chapter 6 in which government-initiated policies to raise the warranted growth rate by inflationary deficit finance will be discussed and assessed.

Harrod's Model of Growth

In Chapter 1 we talked loosely about the actual, warranted and natural rates of growth, and of the actual growth rate being constrained by the warranted rate in conditions where the natural rate exceeds the warranted rate, unless actual saving exceeds planned saving. We now need to be more precise. Using Harrod's notation, the actual growth rate may be written

$$G = \frac{s}{c} \qquad\qquad (4.1)$$

where $G = \Delta Y/Y$

$\qquad s = S/Y$ (the savings ratio)

and $\qquad c = \Delta K/\Delta Y = I/\Delta Y$ (the incremental capital–output ratio)

Equation (4.1) expresses the *ex-post* identity between saving and investment ($I/Y = S/Y$) which must be true in an accounting sense. Whether this rate of growth keeps existing capital fully employed, however, and whether labour is kept fully employed, depends on whether the rate of growth of demand for goods keeps pace with the growth of supply, and whether the rate of new capital formation is sufficient to provide equipment for men to work with. Here the warranted and natural rates of growth become important.

The warranted rate of growth (G_w) is that rate of growth which keeps entrepreneurs content in the sense that it keeps their capital capacity fully utilised and makes them willing to maintain the same rate of capital accumulation in the future. In Mrs Robinson's words, it is the 'growth of output which would result from the continuous operation at full capacity of the stock of capital, when the stock of capital is continuously growing at a rate dictated by the investment which just absorbs the rate of saving corresponding to full capacity income'.[1] If capital is fully employed the extra capital to provide for growth in the future must come from the increase in output itself (ΔY). Suppose that the desired, or required, incremental capital–output ratio is denoted as c_r, the extra capital in use will then be $\Delta Y c_r$. Now suppose that plans to provide extra capital in the form of saving are equal to sY. The equilibrium condition for the demand for capital to equal the supply is then

$$\Delta Y c_r = sY \qquad (4.2)$$

Hence, $\Delta Y/Y = s/c_r$ is the warranted (equilibrium) growth rate (G_w). To give a numerical example: if a country's long-run propensity to save out of income is 15 per cent, and the desired stock of capital is always three years' purchase of net income (i.e. the desired capital–output ratio is 3), the warranted growth rate would be 5 per cent. This rate could be maintained indefinitely in the absence of any change in the parameters of the model.

If the savings ratio and the required capital–output ratio are rigidly given, however, problems arise if the actual growth rate diverges from the warranted growth rate. If the actual growth rate

[1] J. Robinson, 'Mr. Harrod's Dynamics', *Economic Journal* (March 1949).

falls below the warranted growth rate there will be excess capacity, and if the actual growth rate exceeds the warranted rate there will be deficient capacity, and both divergencies will tend to produce cumulative tendencies away from equilibrium. This is easily demonstrated as follows : let $G_w c_r = s$ and $Gc = s$. Since s is common to both equations, the condition for the growth of demand to equal the growth of output is

$$G_w c_r = Gc \qquad (4.3)$$

Now if $G < G_w$, c must be greater than c_r. Actual capital accumulation per unit of output is higher than required and entrepreneurs will think they have done too much investment. Investment will be cut back reducing G still further below G_w. Conversely if $G > G_w$, c must be less than c_r. Actual capital accumulation per unit of output is less than required and entrepreneurs will think they have done too little investment. There will be pressure to accumulate more, pushing G still further above G_w. According to this analysis economies are inherently unstable in the absence of appropriate adjustment mechanisms.

The degree of instability experienced will depend partly on the workings of the multiplier which measures the ratio of the increment of output to the increment of investment. Suppose, for example, that growth at the warranted rate is disturbed by a bout of investment which due to the multiplier process raises income more than in proportion to the increase in investment. The actual growth rate now exceeds the warranted growth rate, and manufacturers will feel that they have made too little investment because the growth of demand exceeds the capital to meet it (and stocks have fallen); $c < c_r$, and there will be a tendency for entrepreneurs to want to invest more. It is a paradox of investment that if entrepreneurs as a whole do too much investment for steady growth they will think they have done too little.

How much c changes as investment takes place depends on the value of the multiplier, which depends amongst other things on the degree of capacity working of the economy. If there is excess capacity, and the consumption goods industries can respond to increases in demand, increased investment will be destabilising in the Harrod sense. If there is no excess capacity, and the consumption goods industries cannot expand output, the increase in output will be confined to the increase in investment goods and the multiplier will be

unity. In this case there will be no change in c and the 'paradox of investment' will not arise. If it is assumed that in developing economies G_w lies below the natural rate, the static multiplier must be close to unity and the problem of instability does not arise. The general tendency will be for G to exceed G_w for most of the time not because c falls as investment takes place but because of the inflationary pressure created by $G_w < G_n$ leading to 'forced' saving.

Harrod's conclusion that there is a tendency for economies to be inherently unstable was also reached by Domar, working independently.[1] In a way Domar recognised the problem more plainly than Harrod by emphasising that investment has two effects of adding to demand and adding to supply (capacity); and that to maintain equilibrium the growth of demand must obviously match the capacity-creating effects of investment. The question is, what is the rate of investment that ensures that additions to demand equal additions to supply? The question is easily answered

Let
$$\Delta Y_D = \frac{\Delta I}{s} \tag{4.4}$$

and
$$\Delta Y_s = I\sigma \tag{4.5}$$

where ΔY_D is the expansion of demand
  ΔY_s is the expansion of supply
  s is the propensity to save
  $I = \Delta K =$ net additions to the capital stock

and $\sigma = \Delta Y/\Delta K$ is the productivity of capital (the reciprocal of the capital–output ratio).

Equilibrium requires that $\Delta I/s = I\sigma$,

so that
$$\frac{\Delta I}{I} = s\sigma \tag{4.6}$$

Hence, for the balanced growth of demand and supply, investment must grow at a rate equal to the product of the savings ratio and the productivity of capital. If the marginal and average values of σ and s are the same, output must also grow at the consant rate $s\sigma$. Since the productivity of capital is the reciprocal of the capital–output ratio, $s\sigma$ is the same as Harrod's equilibrium growth rate s/c_r. A growth rate

[1] E. Domar, 'Expansion and Employment', *American Economic Review* (March 1947).

less than $s\sigma$ implies excess capacity and a growth rate in excess of $s\sigma$ implies deficient capacity. Where do the developing countries fit into this theoretical scheme?

It would be somewhat anomalous for a developing country to be growing at less than its warranted growth rate, meaning that it is operating with excess capital capacity. Developing economies, by definition, are supposed to be capital-scarce. As we shall see later there are case studies which reveal excess capacity for institutional reasons, such as import licensing systems which encourage the uneconomic use of capital, but by and large it is convenient to think of developing countries as capital-scarce, operating capital at full capacity. The tendency will be for plans to invest to exceed plans to save and for the actual growth rate to exceed the warranted rate due to inflation and forced saving. Indeed, if capital is fully employed the only way that the actual growth rate can exceed the warranted rate is through forced saving such that *ex-post* (actual) saving exceeds *ex-ante* (planned) saving. In the absence of forced saving, the actual growth rate is constrained by the warranted growth rate in a capital-scarce economy. Harrod's own policy solution in these circumstances is extremely orthodox.[1] He calls for policies to raise the warranted growth rate by non-inflationary means – by budget surpluses, with government investment to maintain adequate demand. The opposite view is expressed here that there are several expansionist policies that can be, and ought to be, pursued that can raise saving and reduce the capital–output ratio without resorting to extra taxation which a budget-surplus policy would entail. Harrod represents policies of sustained expansion, involving inflationary finance and low interest rates, as damaging to growth because they would reduce saving. This expression of opinion owes more to classical than to Keynesian theory.

The Natural Rate of Growth

In the long run, no country can grow faster than its natural rate of growth (G_n), or what Harrod calls the social optimum rate of growth. If saving is insufficient to achieve the natural rate of growth, the warranted growth rate cannot be a social optimum even though it satisfies entrepreneurs by keeping their capital stock fully employed.

[1] R. Harrod, *Economic Dynamics* (London: Macmillan, 1972).

The savings ratio required to achieve the socially optimal rate of growth is given by

$$s_n = G_n c_r \qquad (4.7)$$

If G_n is 5 per cent, and the desired capital–output ratio (c_r) is 3, then the savings ratio necessary to achieve the natural growth rate is 15 per cent. If plans to save fall short of this ratio, the warranted growth rate must lie below the natural growth rate. If the social optimum growth rate is to be attained it is presumably one of the tasks of governments to try to ensure that the necessary amount of saving is undertaken. In practice, that is what a good deal of planning in developing countries is all about.

There are two basic determinants of G_n: first, the rate of growth of the labour force, and second, the rate of improvement of available technology for the production of goods and services. Harrod assumes both rates to be exogenously determined. The rate of technical progress is important as a determinant of the rate of growth of labour productivity. The natural rate of growth can thus be defined as that rate of growth permitted by the rate of growth of the work force (l), and technical progress (t), where technical progress stands for anything which increases the productivity of labour (including a rise in the capital–labour ratio, which Harrod does not acknowledge).

Therefore

$$G_n = l + t \qquad (4.8)$$

Since the capital–output ratio is assumed to be constant (i.e. technical progress is Harrod neutral), technical progress (and capital deepening) augments the productivity of labour only. The rate of growth of the labour force plus the rate of growth of labour-augmenting technical progress can be thought of as the growth of labour measured in efficiency units, or as the growth of the effective stock of labour.

The long-period question is whether the achievement of the warranted growth rate, which ensures the full capacity working of capital, will necessarily ensure stability if it diverges from the maximum possible rate that society can achieve, determined by the growth of the work force and technical progress. Suppose, following Harrod, that the economy works with fixed production coefficients, as illustrated by the production function diagram in Fig. 4.1. Capital is measured on the vertical axis, labour in 'efficiency' units (L_e) is

measured on the horizontal axis and the fixed proportionality between capital and labour is given by the ray from the origin, *OR*. It is clear that if the labour force in efficiency units grows faster than the stock of capital (that is, if the natural rate of growth exceeds the warranted rate) there will be unemployed labour. Conversely, if the warranted rate of growth exceeds the natural rate of growth there will be unemployed capital. In Fig. 4.1, if capital expands from

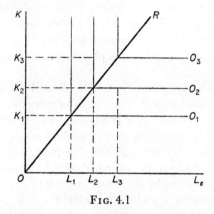

FIG. 4.1

K_1 to K_2, and 'effective' labour expands from L_1 to L_3, L_2L_3 labour will be unemployed since the technical conditions of production only permit the employment of labour L_2. To employ the quantity of labour L_3, more capital would be required than is currently available. Conversely, if capital expands from K_1 to K_3, and 'effective' labour expands from L_1 to L_2, K_2K_3 capital will be unemployed. One clear implication of the divergence between the warranted and natural growth rates, therefore, is that there will be unemployment of one factor or the other depending on the nature of the divergence. The characteristics, and experience, of developing countries suggest that in their case the natural rate exceeds the warranted rate. In the absence of sufficient saving and capital accumulation to employ the available labour force, or any change in the capital-intensity of production, the result is growing unemployment of the structural variety.

A divergence between the warranted and natural growth rates in the opposite direction is more likely to be a characteristic of developed countries where the labour force typically grows more slowly and where savings ratios are high and capital is plentiful relative to labour.

A second implication of divergence between the warranted and natural rates of growth is that there will be a divergence between the actual savings ratio and that ratio of saving to income which yields the minimum acceptable rate of profit. For example, take the developing country case in which the warranted rate of growth lies below the natural rate. Assume that the long-run propensity to save is 9 per cent of income and that the required capital–output ratio is 3, giving a warranted growth rate of 3 per cent. Suppose, however, that the natural growth rate is 5 per cent. What this means, in effect, is that given the capital–output ratio (and a fixed rate of interest), there are profitable investment opportunities for a saving ratio of 15 per cent. But the propensity to save out of income is only 9 per cent. In these circumstances there will be a tendency for plans to invest to exceed plans to save, creating inflationary pressures. If inflation raises the savings ratio this is one possible mechanism through which the divergence between the warranted and natural growth rates can be reduced. But clearly, the simultaneous existence of unemployment and inflation is no paradox in developing countries. Both phenomena arise from the same cause, namely that thrift is less than the capital accumulation required to employ the labour force fully and to satisfy entrepreneurs in search of profit. The surprise is that inflation has been so slight in the vast majority of developing countries for so long, while unemployment has been allowed to rise.

The opposite case of the warranted growth rate in excess of the natural rate is not typical of developing economies. It may, however, be a periodic feature of more economically mature countries where labour force growth rates are lower and the thrift of the community is higher. The accepted Keynesian explanation of depression and unemployment in Europe and North America in the nineteen-twenties and thirties, which spread to other countries through the breakdown of trade, is that plans to save exceeded plans to invest. But the features of mature capitalist economies need not detain us here. As Mrs Robinson once said:

A community whose only problem was that they have all the capital that there is any use for, would not really have a great deal to worry about, and we need not wring our hearts by contemplating their troubles.[1]

[1] J. Robinson, *The Rate of Interest and Other Essays* (London: Macmillan, 1952) p. 161.

Moreover, it is hardly conceivable that any of the countries now commonly classified as developing will be 'excess savers' in the foreseeable future. Population growth is still running high; there are vast reserves of under-employed labour that at some stage must be absorbed into the industrial system in the course of development, and there is a huge backlog of technology for developing countries to make up. The present developing countries will be capital-scarce for many years to come.

In summary, developing economies may be characterised as countries in which $(s/c_r) < (l + t)$. Some obvious policies suggest themselves for eliminating the discrepancy. Attempts could be made to raise s and lower c_r. The onus is on governments to formulate imaginative policies. There are also many ways in which s may rise naturally, and c_r fall. In the long term it is probably also unwise to treat the rate of growth of the work force and labour-augmenting technical progress as exogenously given constants. On the other hand, to contemplate the burden of adjustment being placed on labour force growth and technical progress would be unwise if the social optimum growth rate is not to be impaired. In Chapter 6, when policies are discussed, the emphasis will be solely on measures to raise s and to reduce c_r. Before considering these policies, however, it will be helpful to consider some simple growth models in which the savings ratio and the required capital–output ratio can adjust, and can be adjusted, to divergences between the warranted and natural growth rates. First, classical and neo-classical models will be briefly considered, followed by the neo-Keynesian models of Mrs Robinson and Kaldor which emphasise particularly the role of forced saving.

The Classical Model

The case for inflationary finance presented in Chapter 2 was essentially Keynesian in nature. Income is determined by expenditure and income determines savings. Thus expenditure can generate its own saving. In the case of a closed economy, with no foreign trade sector, saving depends on investment and the economy approaches a new equilibrium when changes in investment plans have caused income to change sufficiently for saving to match the new level of investment. Saving in the Keynesian system is something negative, which it can be misleading to think of as a resource in the absence of effective demand.

The Keynesian approach is in distinct contrast to the classical view

of saving, investment and income determination, in which saving is a prerequisite of investment and the rate of interest is the price of capital which brings savings and investment into equilibrium at full employment. Saving is a function of the rate of interest, and is always a virtue because plans to save and invest will always be equal. The development process is seen as being led by saving with investment following, rather than the other way around. It is the classical view of the development process which underlies such phrases in the development literature as the 'mobilisation of savings', and which also underlies the belief that tight money and high interest rates are desirable for development because high interest rates encourage saving. Money and the availability of credit are no substitute for prior savings. The historical origin of this viewpoint is not hard to trace. Without a well-developed credit and finance system, desired investment had to take place out of the accumulated profits of business. Historically, savers and investors were one and the same people.

The classical prior savings approach to development still dies hard in today's developing economies and in models of development which still purport to typify the development process. The reason cannot be blindness to money and monetary institutions, but the fear of inflation. Typifying the classical position are Chandler's Bombay lectures.[1] In them he argues that interest rates are too low in developing countries because they discourage saving and encourage the wasteful use of capital. It is conceded that low interest rates encourage investment, but Chandler argues that it is not the lack of willingness to invest that constrains investment but rather a lack of saving. An increase in the rate of interest becomes a precondition of increased investment. Investment to generate its own saving is dismissed on the grounds of its inflationary repercussions.

Lewis's model of development with unlimited supplies of labour, which has had a deep impact on development thinking, is also firmly in the classical tradition.[2] In Fig. 4.2, capitalists in the industrial sector employ labour at a constant real wage, OW, which is determined by the real wage in the subsistence sector. Profit is the surplus over wage payments. Given the marginal revenue product curve of labour, NR, labour is employed up to the point OM, and profits are

[1] L. Chandler, *Central Banking and Economic Development* (University of Bombay Press, 1962).
[2] A. Lewis, 'Economic Development with Unlimited Supplies of Labour', *Manchester School* (May 1954).

equal to the area *WNP*. Investment is assumed to depend on saving out of profits, which if ploughed back in the capitalist sector will shift the marginal product curve outwards to NR_1. At a constant wage rate OW, profits expand to WNP_1. The share of profits in national income rises, and thus the savings ratio rises, because the importance of the capitalist sector in relation to the national economy increases as labour is drawn in from the subsistence sector. The essential message

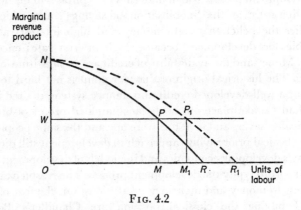

FIG. 4.2

is that capital accumulation depends on saving out of profits; that saving is necessary for investment.

Neo-Classical Growth Theory

The idea that investment can finance its own saving is equally foreign to neo-classical growth theory. The saving and investment functions are one and the same thing. Investment always equals planned saving. If the warranted growth rate falls below the natural growth rate, equilibrium is restored by a rise in the interest rate which is supposed to raise the savings ratio and reduce the capital–output ratio. If the interest rate is not free to rise (and wages do not fall) there is apparently no way that deficient capital accumulation can be remedied. The equilibrating mechanisms assumed by neo-classical theory can be nicely illustrated using a diagram suggested by Kennedy.[1] In Fig. 4.3 the vertical line S/Y represents a fixed amount

[1] C. Kennedy, 'A Static Interpretation of Some Recent Theories of Growth and Distribution', *Oxford Economic Papers* (June 1960).

of planned saving and the ray from the origin, I/Y, gives the relation between the growth rate and the investment ratio, the slope of which measures the (fixed) output–capital ratio. The warranted growth rate, G_w, is determined where the two curves intersect. The natural growth rate, G_n, is shown to be above G_w. The necessary investment to achieve the natural growth rate exceeds planned saving by the amount PQ. In the neo-classical model this divergence is remedied

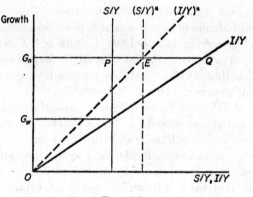

FIG. 4.3

by a rise in the interest rate which reduces the capital–output ratio (i.e. which raises the slope of I/Y, say to $(I/Y)^*$), and which increases the savings ratio to $(S/Y)^*$ so that the natural growth rate is achieved at E.

As in Harrod's model, the long-run equilibrium growth rate is exogenously determined independently of the savings ratio. In equilibrium the effects of an increase in the savings ratio are offset by a rise in the capital–output ratio. To illustrate, take the Cobb–Douglas version of the neo-classical growth model, $Y = TK^\alpha L^{1-\alpha}$, so that

$$\frac{dY}{Y} = \frac{dT}{T} + \alpha \frac{dK}{K} + (1 - \alpha) \frac{dL}{L} \qquad (4.9)$$

where Y is income or output

$\quad T$ is an index of (neutral) technical progress

$\quad K$ is a measure of capital

$\quad L$ is a measure of labour

and $\quad \alpha$ is capital's share of total income.

Since $dK = I = sY$, where I is net investment and s is the savings ratio, equation (4.9) may be written

$$\frac{dY}{Y} = \frac{dT}{T} + \alpha \frac{sY}{K} + (1 - \alpha) \frac{dL}{L} \qquad (4.10)$$

If output and capital are assumed to grow at the long-run equilibrium growth rate $(dL/L) + (dT/T)/(1 - \alpha)$, it can be seen from equation (4.10) that an increase in the savings ratio will raise dK/K. But it can also be seen from equation (4.9) that the growth of income is a non-proportional function of the growth of capital. Specifically, any rise in dK/K will exceed the increase in dY/Y, causing Y/K to fall and the capital–output ratio to rise. As Y/K falls, dK/K falls and also dY/Y, but dY/Y falls less than dK/K so that Y/K ultimately ceases to fall. The long-run equilibrium growth rate is re-established.

The crucial difference between the neo-classical growth model and that of Harrod is that whereas in the neo-classical model the warranted and natural growth rates can be brought together by variations in the capital–output ratio, in Harrod's model the capital–output ratio is fixed. In the neo-classical model unemployment caused by excess saving is eliminated by an increase in the capital intensity of production, and unemployment caused by deficient saving is eliminated by a decrease in the capital intensity of production. In contrast to the fixed coefficient production functions of Harrod's model, illustrated in Fig. 4.1, neo-classical theory assumes smooth, continuous production functions so that changes in relative factor prices, resulting from changes in the relative supply and demand for factors, can alter the relative factor intensity of production. The neo-classical position is summarised in Fig. 4.4 below.

0_1 and 0_2 represent variable coefficient production functions. K_1 and L_1 represent the 'optimum' quantities of capital and labour to be employed given the relative price of factors, $P_K P_L$. Now suppose that the quantity of capital increases to K_2 and the amount of labour to L_2. At the previous capital–labour ratio given by the ray from the origin, OZ, only L labour could be employed with K_2 capital, leaving LL_2 labour unemployed. If the production function permits substitutability between factors, however, and relative factor prices can change, the capital–labour ratio can also change. The capital–labour ratio which permits the full employment of both capital and labour is given by the ray OZ^* in Fig. 4.4. A new full-employment 'optimum' can be achieved at Y if the price of capital rises relative to

the price of labour, i.e. if the price line $P_K P_L$ pivots to $P_K^* P_L^*$. If factor prices are inflexible the economy would have to operate inside its production frontier at X.

The automatic adjustment mechanisms of neo-classical theory are appealing, but how relevant are they in the context of today's developing economies? The first point to make is that interest rates are not that flexible. Although saving may be positively related to the interest rate, interest rates in most developing economies are rarely

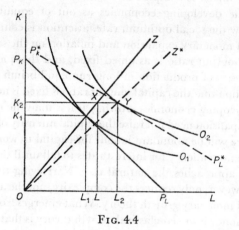

FIG. 4.4

allowed to reflect the true scarcity of capital. Interest rates tend to be heavily subsidised, at least in the organised money market. But in any case it is doubtful whether interest charges are a sufficiently important item in manufacturers' costs for techniques of production to be altered drastically in response to rising interest rates. The second point is that the neo-classical adjustment mechanism depends on the flexibility of production coefficients. In reality, production coefficients are practically rigid once capital goods have been installed and are working. Since developing countries rely to a large extent on capital inputs from abroad it should also be remembered that their choice of technology may be very limited. From a policy point of view, therefore, to rely on changes in factor prices and flexible co-efficients of production to raise the rate of capital accumulation and to reduce unemployment may be to opt for a policy of negligence. How much better from a policy point of view for the governments of developing countries to allow manufacturers credit to invest in

excess of planned savings, and for governments themselves to initiate policies and projects to reduce the capital–output ratio in conditions of capital scarcity and high unemployment. Chapter 6 explores these policies further.

Neo-Classical Monetary Growth Theory

The role of monetary factors in achieving growth equilibrium in the neo-classical model is complex and ambiguous. Since we are characterising the developing economies as out of equilibrium, with growth below the social optimum rate, attention is confined here to the effects of monetary expansion and inflation on the savings ratio. The capital–output ratio is assumed fixed, and the question of the capital intensity of production in long-run equilibrium is left aside. The assumption that the capital–output ratio is fixed is not unreasonable. In developing economies growing at less than the natural rate, monetary expansion need not raise the capital intensity of production because there will be abundant labour for capital to work with, and there will be no tendency for interest rates to fall until the warranted growth rate approaches the natural rate. Narrowing the subject in this way, however, only reduces the complexity, not the ambiguity, of neo-classical monetary growth theory. What emerges from the introduction of money into neo-classical growth theory is that money may or may not raise the speed with which an economy approaches equilibrium depending on what are considered to be the prime functions of money and whether money holdings and investment in physical capital are regarded as substitutes or complements. We shall do no more here than go over the standard models, if only to highlight the ambiguities. For simplicity, money is defined as 'outside' money consisting of notes and coins and bank money backed by government securities. These are assets to the private sector which involve no corresponding private liability. The increments to real money balances are treated as cash transfers to the public.

In the original Tobin model,[1] which first introduced money into neo-classical growth theory, and recognised money holdings as an alternative outlet for current savings, the way in which money affects the working of the economy is through its effects on real disposable income. Real disposable income is equal to real income plus increments to real money balances, and consumption is assumed to be a

---

[1] J. Tobin, 'Money and Economic Growth', *Econometrica* (October 1965).

constant fraction of real disposable income. An increase in real money balances therefore raises consumption out of *real* income and lowers the savings ratio correspondingly. A decrease in real money balances does the opposite. This is the so-called real balance effect on outside money. It arises from the existence of changes in real money balances as an argument in the consumption function

$$C = f(Y, dM_{rB}); \qquad f_1' > 0, f_2' > 0$$

where C is consumption
       Y is real income
and dM_{rB} is the change in real money balances.

Inflation and monetary contraction reduce real balances and hence reduce consumption and increase saving out of income. Deflation and monetary expansion increase real money balances and hence increase consumption and decrease saving out of income. Because of the apparent substitutability between real money holdings and the purchase of real capital, the odd result is obtained that the movement from a barter economy to a money economy reduces the savings ratio of an economy and the rate of capital accumulation. Algebraically we have

$$Y_d = Y + dM_{rB} = Y + \frac{M}{P}\left(\frac{dM}{M} - \frac{dP}{P}\right) \qquad (4.11)$$

where Y_d is real disposable income
      Y is real income

and dM_{rB} is the time derivative of the stock of real balances which is equal to the real value of the increase in the nominal quantity of money

$$\left(\frac{M}{P} \cdot \frac{dM}{M} = \frac{dM}{P}\right)$$

minus the decrease in the real value of the existing cash balances caused by inflation

$$\left(\frac{M}{P} \cdot \frac{dP}{P}\right)$$

where M/P is the real value of money balances, dM/M is the rate of monetary expansion, and dP/P is the rate of inflation.

The aggregate level of saving (S) is equal to the difference between real income (Y) and consumption (C). Given the consumption function we have

$$S = Y - c[Y + dM_{rB}] \tag{4.12}$$

where c is the propensity to consume.

The increment to the capital stock is therefore

$$dK = (1 - c)Y - c(dM_{rB}) = sY - c(dM_{rB}) \tag{4.13}$$

where s is the propensity to save.

Dividing equation (4.13) by Y gives the fraction of saving that goes into capital formation

$$\frac{dK}{Y} = s - c\left(\frac{dM_{rB}}{Y}\right) \tag{4.14}$$

The rate of growth of capital is then

$$\frac{dK}{K} = \left[s - c\left(\frac{dM_{rB}}{Y}\right)\right]\frac{Y}{K} \tag{4.15}$$

Since

$$dM_{rB} = \frac{M}{P}\left(\frac{dM}{M} - \frac{dP}{P}\right)$$

equation (4.15) may be written

$$\frac{dK}{K} = \left[s - c\frac{M}{PY}\left(\frac{dM}{M} - \frac{dP}{P}\right)\right]\frac{Y}{K} \tag{4.16}$$

Since in a growing economy $(dM/M - dP/P) > 0$, it can be seen that an increase in real money balances apparently reduces saving out of current income, and lowers the rate of capital accumulation. It follows that a positive rate of inflation $(dP/P > 0)$ and monetary contraction $(dM/M < 0)$ would raise the savings ratio and the rate of capital accumulation, while price deflation and monetary expansion would do the opposite. In short, a rise in the ratio of real money balances to real income

$$\left(\frac{dM}{P} \cdot \frac{1}{Y} > 0\right),$$

whatever the cause, reduces the amount of saving for capital accumulation, and a fall in the ratio raises the amount of saving for capital formation. Inflation would seem to be a policy variable in developing countries to raise the growth rate towards its equilibrium level. An inflationary policy could augment capital accumulation in two ways. First, the increased public revenues from the inflation tax on cash balances could be used to finance investment. Second, as the return on holding money falls there will tend to be a switch towards investment in physical capital in the private sector.

The fact that a rise in the money–income ratio should be detrimental to capital accumulation, however, is an odd result to say the least. It is not only counter-intuitive, but defies the empirical evidence. Monetisation of the economy, instead of providing resources for investment, apparently absorbs them. Yet the historical evidence indicates that over the long period the money–income ratio and the savings ratio are positively correlated. Two main explanations can be advanced for the apparent conflict between the empirical evidence and the predictions of the theory. The first is the assumption of the model that the propensity to save is given and fixed. The second is that the consumption and productive services provided by money are ignored.

The assumption that the propensity to save is fixed has the corollary that real money balances and physical capital must be substitutes for each other in the portfolios of wealth-holders. With a given level of saving, the holding of more money balances means less investment in physical capital and vice versa. This is a familiar result in neo-classical portfolio theory. Consider the standard demand for money function, $M/P = M[Y, r, (i - dP/P)]$, where r is the real rate of return on all non-monetary assets; $(i - dP/P)$ is the return on holding money (i is the nominal interest rate),[1] and $M_1' > 0$; $M_2' < 0$, and $M_3' > 0$. If r increases, the demand for money falls. If $(i - dP/P)$ increases, the demand for money rises. This is the substitution effect between money and real capital which dominates neo-classical monetary growth theory.

An alternative view, however, which is consistent with the em-

<hr>

[1] The only outside money which earns interest is bank money backed by government securities.

pirical evidence, is that in the context of a developing economy the holding of real money balances and investment in physical capital are complementary to one another. A rise in the return on physical capital, which in the neo-classical model would cause a switch from holding money balances to investment in physical capital, may itself induce the holding of a greater volume of real money balances. Conversely, a rise in the return on holding money, which in the neo-classical model would cause more money to be held and less investment in physical capital, may induce greater investment in physical capital. In either case, a rise in the propensity to save is implied, but this is not unrealistic. The factors which induce more money to be held, or more investment to take place, may themselves raise the propensity to save. The propensity to save may be strongly influenced by the very existence of real money balances made available by government during the process of gradual monetisation of the economy. If the propensity to save is not fixed there is no reason why real money balance holdings and capital accumulation should be regarded as substitutes.

The complementarity of real balance holdings and capital accumulation is also apparent if money is considered more broadly as providing a flow of consumption and productive services which will vary positively with the level of real money balances. Treating money as a 'consumer' good, its imputed services must be included as a part of disposable income. The services of money can be valued, at the margin, as the opportunity cost of holding money balances. The opportunity cost is the difference between what could have been earned from purchasing physical capital (r) instead of holding money,[1] and what is earned from the holding of real money balances which, in the absence of any nominal interest on money holdings, is

---

[1] In a more sophisticated analysis this statement would have to be qualified somewhat. The services of money cannot be measured completely by the return on physical capital because money and physical capital have attributes in common (e.g. both are stores of wealth). To value accurately the services of money really requires an asset for comparison which possesses none of the qualities of money. Strictly speaking r measures only the attributes that money has *over* physical capital. Situations can be imagined in which the utility of money balances at the margin rise without this being reflected in r; for example, where there is strong complementarity between money and real capital, as we have argued there is. In these circumstances it is possible for the services of money to rise even though real money balances and real interest rates remain unchanged.

simply the negative of the rate of inflation $(-dP/P)$. Therefore, the opportunity cost of holding money balances is $r - (-dP/P)$.[1]

Adding the consumption services of money to disposable income, the new definition of disposable income is

$$Y_d = Y + \frac{M}{P}\left(\frac{dM}{M} - \frac{dP}{P}\right) + \frac{M}{P}\left(r + \frac{dP}{P}\right) = Y + \frac{M}{P}\left(\frac{dM}{M} + r\right)$$

(4.17)

Total consumption will now be

$$c\left[Y + \frac{M}{P}\left(\frac{dM}{M} + r\right)\right].$$

Real saving, however, is equal to real income less 'physical' consumption, where 'physical' consumption is equal to total consumption minus the consumption services derived from holding money balances. Hence

$$S = dK = Y - \left[c\left(Y + \frac{M}{P}\left(\frac{dM}{M} + r\right)\right) - \frac{M}{P}\left(r + \frac{dP}{P}\right)\right] \quad (4.18)$$

Dividing both sides by K, and rearranging, the rate of growth of capital is

$$\frac{dK}{K} = \left[s - c\frac{M}{PY}\left(\frac{dM}{M} + r\right) + \frac{M}{PY}\left(r + \frac{dP}{P}\right)\right]\frac{Y}{K} \quad (4.19)$$

Alternatively, equation (4.19) may be written

$$\frac{dK}{K} = \left[s - c\frac{dM}{PY} + \frac{M}{PY}\cdot\frac{dP}{P} + r\frac{M}{PY}(1 - c)\right]\frac{Y}{K} \quad (4.20)$$

It can be seen from the above that the existence of real money balances raises the rate of capital accumulation through the consumption services provided by money. The effect of a rise in the level of real balances is now ambiguous. On the one hand it reduces saving by increasing consumption out of real income. On the other hand a higher volume of real cash balances increases consumption services and increases the savings ratio. Inflation exerts a positive influence on

[1] If interest is paid on money balances the opportunity cost of holding money would be $r - (i - dP/P)$. The only 'outside' money on which it is feasible to pay interest, however, is bank money backed by government securities.

saving through a real balance effect except to the extent that inflation may reduce the holding of real money balances (M/PY), in which case the flow of consumption services from holding money is reduced.

Given the two distinct treatments of money outlined above, the effect of monetary expansion and inflation on growth in a neo-classical framework cannot be specified precisely. On the one hand, an increase in real balances raises the savings ratio if real balances are treated as providing a flow of consumption services; on the other hand, an increase in real balances lowers the savings ratio if real balances are treated as a part of disposable income. Inflation can have a real balance effect which increases the savings ratio and raises the warranted growth rate. On the other hand, inflation can reduce the flow of consumption services by discouraging the holding of real balances, which causes real consumption to rise and the savings ratio to fall. Thus a more or less inflationary policy may raise or lower the actual growth rate depending on whether the growth-stimulating effects of the real balance effect outweigh the growth-inhibiting effects of a lower utility yield on real balances.

Up to now, the assumption has been that money balances are non-interest bearing. This is a realistic assumption as far as notes and coins are concerned but not necessarily so in the case of bank deposits backed by government securities. The possibility of interest payments on money balances further complicates the analysis of the effects of monetary expansion and inflation on capital accumulation. While a rising price level may be expected to lead to a reduction in the desired money–income ratio which will reduce the base of both the real balance effect and the utility yield effect on saving, a rise in interest rates commensurate with the rate of inflation will offset the tendency by maintaining the return on real money balance holdings. Rising interest rates may also affect favourably the propensity to save, whereas the above analysis assumes s is constant.

On balance, the view taken here is that monetary expansion and inflation are likely to be favourable to capital accumulation, particularly if accompanied by a general rise in interest rates. In countries in the process of monetising their economies it is much more realistic to think of the accumulation of money balances and capital accumulation as complements rather than substitutes in the development process. If interest rates are responsive to price changes there is no reason for real balance holdings to be cut. A strong real balance effect from inflation should outweigh the reduced consumption-yield

effect of inflation especially if nominal interest rates rise with the rate of inflation. A higher interest rate may itself encourage more real saving if there is money illusion.

There are also the productive services of money to consider. Money can be thought of as a producer good, as well as a consumer good, which saves the real resources involved in barter. One of the motives for holding money is presumably that it frees labour and capital for the production of commodities – labour and capital that, in a barter economy, would have to be devoted to achieving 'the double coincidence of wants' that the barter economy necessitates. Taking this view of money, real output and saving can be considered as an increasing function of the level of real balances (although increasing at a decreasing rate). Real balances increase real income and therefore saving and capital accumulation. In a sophisticated monetary economy, with fully developed financial institutions, there must ultimately come a point, however, when an addition to real balances does not free further resources. But up to that point real balances as producer goods belong to the production function.

Viewing money as a producer good, inflation would be detrimental to capital accumulation and the growth rate if it caused a decline in real balance holdings. In a strict neo-classical framework which recognised the productive services of money, the loss of productive services due to inflation may be the opportunity cost of financing capital accumulation by inflationary means unless the real return on holding money can be maintained in the face of inflation by, for example, the payment of interest on money holdings.

All in all, the attempt to integrate money formally into neo-classical growth theory has not been a resounding success. The results obtained depend on assumptions as to the nature and role of money, and there are no suitable criteria for choosing among the different models. Almost anything seems to be logically possible. Stein has summed up the situation well:

> The present state of monetary growth theory does not permit the economist to offer advice to the monetary authorities which represents a consensus of opinion among experts in the field. . . . Since equally 'reasonable' assumptions yield qualitatively different results monetary growth theory is an 'uncertain trumpet'; it cannot be used as a guide to policy.[1]

[1] J. L. Stein, 'Neo-classical and Keynes–Wicksell Monetary Growth Models', *Journal of Money, Credit and Banking* (May 1969).

Not only are monetary growth models of limited help in elucidating the relation between money, inflation, saving and growth, but it can also be argued that they miss one of the most important ways in which money affects growth, namely by providing an economic system with a means of credit creation. A credit system confers a number of advantages on an economy. People can borrow the savings of others and 'hire' idle resources. Depressions can be avoided and greater efficiency achieved in the use of a nation's resources. Time is saved if willing savers and anxious investors do not have to be matched. The existence of money in its credit creation function allows a monetary policy, which can play an important role in maintaining full capacity growth. Monetary authorities have a source of purchasing power which they can add to at will, enabling recipients to bid up the prices of resources and to generate forced saving. In the neo-classical model forced saving is not admitted. Consumers always win the battle over claims for resources; investors (including the government) never do. Investment always equals planned saving, with all markets in simultaneous equilibrium. But the ability to force saving is an important credit creation function of money. While the production benefits of money, which are now stressed by neo-classical theory, diminish, the credit creation function of money retains its importance through time.

In the last resort the effect of monetary expansion on an economy must depend on how governments utilise the liabilities they create. The assumption in standard neo-classical theory is that money is handed out as transfers. In practice, however, a great deal of monetary expansion (in developing economies) goes to finance capital formation. By a change in the composition of new money issued there seems no reason in principle why the government should not have any desired effect on the rate of capital accumulation that it wishes. How money is treated by the public is irrelevant. What is important is whether a government can redistribute income to itself.

Forced Saving

The distinguishing feature of neo-classical growth models is that investment always equals planned saving. There is no such thing as forced saving. All markets are continuously in equilibrium, and the savings and investment functions are one and the same thing.

Monetary factors affect the growth rate, if at all, depending on how the planned savings ratio is affected by monetary expansion.

In practice, of course, there is no guarantee that saving will be used for investment. There may be no demand for investment funds at any price. Alternatively, the demand for investment funds may be strong but there may be difficulty in channelling saving into the activities where it is most needed.

In the real world, investment is not constrained by prior saving. If entrepreneurs wish to invest more than the level of real saving currently available, they raise finance from the capital market. This is the starting point of Keynesian monetary growth theory. Keynesians argue for monetary expansion and low interest rates on the hypothesis that credit-financed investment can generate its own saving through a number of mechanisms, e.g. a marginal propensity to save above the average; a change in the factor intensity of production which increases the volume of output; a change in the output-mix, and forced saving. As Mrs Robinson has said in discussing the nature of the savings–investment relationship under full-employment conditions:

> We cannot return to the pre-Keynesian view that savings governs investment. The essential point of Keynes' teaching remains. It is decisions about how much investment is to be made that govern the rate at which wealth will accumulate, not decisions about savings.[1]

In conditions of full capacity working, inflation is the inevitable result of the Keynesian approach to development. Investment is not constrained by saving but by the inflation rate willing to be tolerated, and by organisational and foreign exchange bottlenecks. But while investment is inflationary in the short term, it need not be in the longer term. A distinction needs to be made between the static income multiplier of Keynes and the dynamic multiplier process of Domar in which investment is a double-edged sword, generating demand on the one hand and real supply capacity on the other. The task of planning in developing countries must be to tide over the time interval between the increase in demand generated by increased investment and the investment bearing fruit in the form of a higher volume of real output. A portion of extra investment needs to be directed to high and quick yielding wage goods industries. What is required is a pattern of investment demand which will match the supply of wage goods with

[1] J. Robinson, 'Notes on the Theory of Economic Development', in *Collected Economic Papers*, vol. II (Oxford: Basil Blackwell, 1960).

the expansion of demand, and which at the same time augments the country's capital stock to raise the productivity of existing investment.

There is little doubt that the traditional development literature, and the governments of developing economies, have veered towards the classical view of development in formulating and implementing policy. But there must be room for a middle view. It is not necessary to be a classicist to recognise that it is desirable to encourage saving in capital-scarce economies. In conditions of full capacity working, the more voluntary saving can be encouraged the less inflation required to finance investment-led growth. The Keynesian can welcome 'prior' saving. What he disputes is that saving is necessary before investment can take place; that investment is constrained by saving.

In contrast to neo-classical monetary growth models, Keynesian models specify independent saving and investment functions, and allow price changes in response to excess demand in the goods market which may force saving independently of any real balance effect in the consumption function.

Let the warranted growth rate lie below the natural rate so that aggregate demand exceeds aggregate supply, or plans to invest exceed plans to save. Savers and investors cannot both be satisfied simultaneously. It is reasonable to suppose that the actual rate of capital formation is less than firms desire but greater than consumers plan to save. Specifically, assume that the actual growth of capital is a linear combination of planned saving and planned investment

$$\frac{dK}{K} = \alpha \frac{I}{K} + (1 - \alpha) \frac{S}{K} \qquad (4.21)$$

where $\qquad\qquad \alpha < 1$

Now make the assumption that the rate of inflation is proportional to the degree of excess demand as measured by the difference between plans to invest and plans to save

$$\frac{dP}{P} = \lambda \left(\frac{I}{K} - \frac{S}{K}\right), \qquad \lambda > 0 \qquad (4.22)$$

Substituting the expression for I/K into (4.21) above gives

$$\frac{dK}{K} = \frac{\alpha(dP/P)}{\lambda} + \frac{S}{K} \qquad (4.23)$$

S/K is planned saving, and $\alpha(dP/P)/\lambda$ is forced saving, per unit of capital. The forced saving occurs because there is excess aggregate demand. Forced saving can clearly exist even with foresight among competitive units. Both investors and consumers can anticipate inflation, so there is no reason why there should not be a perpetual state of excess demand. Since one of the causes of inflation may be monetary expansion in excess of the rate of growth of output, monetary expansion must raise the growth rate towards its equilibrium level. The essential nature of forced saving is that it arises through the inability of consumers to fulfil plans in the face of excess aggregate demand.

The possibility of investment-led growth and forced saving forms the basis of the neo-Keynesian growth models of Mrs Robinson and Kaldor in which divergences between the warranted and natural growth rates may be narrowed, or planned investment realised, by shifts in the distribution of income from wages to profits as inflation takes place, thereby generating the extra saving to match the new investment (assuming that the propensity to save out of profits exceeds the propensity to save out of wages).

Mrs Robinson's Model

In Mrs Robinson's model growth depends on investment to which saving adapts. When a steady rate of growth is going on, the share of saving adapts to it. In effect, the actual growth rate pulls up the warranted growth rate by forcing saving. In Mrs Robinson's own words:

> Whatever the rate of investment may be, the level and the distribution of income must be such as to induce the firms and households, between them, to wish to carry out saving at an equal rate . . . the level of prices relative to money wages is such, in equilibrium conditions, as to provide sufficient profits to call forth a rate of saving equal to the rate of net investment.[1]

In contrast to neo-classical models, however, there is nothing in Mrs Robinson's model to guarantee growth at the natural rate. 'There is no law of nature that the natural rate of growth should

[1] J. Robinson, 'A Model of Accumulation', in *Essays in the Theory of Economic Growth* (London: Macmillan, 1962).

prevail. The natural rate will only be realised if firms possess the energy and inclination to carry it out.'

Saving adapts to investment through the dependence of saving on the share of profits in income which rises with the level of investment in relation to income. Profits, in turn, are uniquely related to the level of real wages. If entrepreneurs want to invest to realise the natural rate of growth, equilibrium between the rate of growth of capital (the warranted growth rate) and the rate of growth of 'effective' labour (the natural growth rate) depends on what happens to real wages when the system is out of equilibrium. The basic equation of the model is the distribution equation

$$pY = wL + \pi pK \qquad (4.24)$$

where Y　is national income
p　is the price of output and capital equipment
L　is the amount of labour employed
w　is the money wage rate
π　is the gross profit rate
and　K　is the amount of capital employed.

Dividing equation (4.24) by p, and rearranging to obtain an expression for the profit rate, gives

$$\pi = \frac{Y}{K} - \left(\frac{w}{p}\right)\frac{L}{K} = \frac{Y - \left(\frac{w}{p}\right)L}{K} \qquad (4.25)$$

which, by dividing through by L, gives

$$\pi = \frac{(Y/L) - (w/p)}{(K/L)} \qquad (4.26)$$

Given the capital–labour ratio, the rate of profit depends on the relationship between income (output) per head (Y/L) and the real wage (w/p).

On the assumption that all wages are consumed and that all profits are invested, the rate of capital accumulation is equal to the rate of profit. Since

$$S = I = \pi K$$
$$\Delta K = \pi K$$
$$\therefore \quad \frac{\Delta K}{K} = \pi \qquad (4.27)$$

The rate of profit also gives the growth rate. Rearranging equation (4.25) we have

$$\pi = \frac{Y}{K}\left(\frac{Y - \left(\frac{w}{p}\right)L}{Y}\right) \tag{4.28}$$

where Y/K is the reciprocal of the capital–output ratio and the expression in brackets is the savings ratio.

Therefore

$$\pi = \frac{Y}{K}\left(\frac{I}{Y}\right)$$

so that

$$\pi = \Delta K/K = \Delta Y/Y = \sigma s \text{ (Domar)} = s/c_r \text{ (Harrod)}.$$

We know that for the full employment of labour and capital, $G = G_w = G_n$. If the capital–labour ratio is fixed, equilibrium depends on the relation between wages and profits. The essence of Mrs Robinson's model is that if entrepreneurs want to invest more it is variation in the rate of profit and the corresponding variation in the real wage that provides the equilibrating mechanism. Investment can exceed planned saving through a change in the income distribution. But the crucial variable in the system is investment, determined by animal spirits! If the rate of investment is high enough the natural growth rate can be achieved, but economies will only grow if entrepreneurs want to invest. 'This is the nature of economic growth according to "capitalist rules of the game".'

But entrepreneurs do not necessarily have it all their own way. There is an upper limit to real investment set by what Mrs Robinson has called the inflation barrier, meaning a real wage so low that wage earners react to price increases to prevent the real wage from falling further.

There is a limit to the possible maximum proportion of quasi rent to wages, which is set by what we may call the inflation barrier. Higher prices of consumption goods relatively to money wage rates involve a lower real consumption by workers. There is a limit to the level to which real-wage rates can fall without setting up a pressure to raise money-wage rates. But a rise in money wage rates increases money expenditure, so that the vicious spiral of money wages chasing prices sets in. There is then a head-on conflict between the

desire of entrepreneurs to invest and the refusal of the system to accept the level of real wages which the investment entails; something must give way. Either the system explodes in a hyperinflation, or some check operates to curtail investment.[1]

In equation (4.26) it can be seen that if the real wage remains unchanged as investment takes place, the rate of profit stays the same and a greater volume of real investment cannot be financed. In a static context it seems that according to the capitalist rules of the game, growth can only be accelerated at the expense of a reduction in the real wage – a conclusion which comes close to the pessimistic development theories of Ricardo and Marx.

In reality we know that pessimism is unfounded because of the possibility of a continual rise in the productivity of labour (Y/L) through technical progress and capital deepening. This enables the real wage to rise over time, and also for the share of profits to rise as long as the growth of labour productivity exceeds the growth in the real wage.[2] In other words a rise in the share of profits is quite consistent with an increase in the real wage as long as the excess of money wage increases over price increases does not exceed the increase in labour productivity.

In the presence of an inflation barrier, an equilibrium may be possible if the assumptions that saving out of wage income is zero and that the capital–labour ratio is fixed are relaxed. It is easily seen from equation (4.26) that the profit rate could be raised by a decline in the capital–labour ratio – provided that the fall in the capital–labour ratio does not reduce the productivity of labour (Y/L) in the same proportion.

Kaldor's Model[3]

Kaldor also makes saving adjust to the desired level of investment through a rise in the share of profits in national income. The profit

---

[1] J. Robinson, *The Accumulation of Capital* (London: Macmillan, 1956) p. 48.

[2] See the discussion in Chapter 2. What happens to the rate of profit depends on the relation between capital deepening (K/L) and labour productivity (Y/L). Provided the capital–output ratio is fixed, the rate of profit will also rise.

[3] N. Kaldor, 'Alternative Theories of Distribution', *Review of Economic Studies*, no. 2 (1955–6).

rate rises explicitly through inflation. Kaldor's model is therefore also in the Keynesian spirit showing how a higher rate of investment and growth can be financed by the redistributional effects of inflation. The model consists of three basic equations

$$\left. \begin{array}{c} Y = W + P \\[2mm] I = S \\[2mm] S = S_w + S_p \end{array} \right\} \quad (4.29)$$

where Y is total income
       W is total wage payments
       P is profits
       I is investment
       S is saving
       S_w is saving out of wage income
and S_p is saving out of profit income.

Also, $S_w = s_w W$, and $S_p = s_p P$, where s_w is the propensity to save out of wages and s_p is the propensity to save out of profits. Thus,

$$\left. \begin{array}{l} S = I = s_p P + s_w W \\[2mm] = s_p P + s_w (Y - P) \\[2mm] = (s_p - s_w)P + s_w Y \end{array} \right\} \quad (4.30)$$

Dividing through by Y gives

$$\frac{I}{Y} = \frac{S}{Y} = (s_p - s_w)\frac{P}{Y} + s_w \quad (4.31)$$

Assuming that the propensity to save out of profits is greater than the propensity to save out of wages, the investment ratio and the profits ratio are positively related. If it is further assumed that $s_p = 1$ and $s_w = 0$, then $I/Y = P/Y$ and, multiplying both sides of the equation by Y/K, we have Mrs Robinson's result that the rate of capital accumulation, the rate of profit and the growth rate are all equal:

$$P/K = \pi = \Delta K/K = \Delta Y/Y$$

If $s_p < 1$ we have the result:

$$\pi = (\Delta Y/Y)/s_p$$

Now make investment the explicit independent variable in the system. Rearranging equation (4.31) we have

$$\frac{P}{Y} = \frac{1}{(s_p - s_w)} \cdot \frac{I}{Y} - \frac{s_w}{(s_p - s_w)} \qquad (4.32)$$

A rise in the investment ratio will raise P/Y provided $s_p > s_w$, which is guaranteed by the assumptions of the model. But what is the mechanism through which a rise in investment raises the profits and savings ratios? It must, of course, be through a redistribution of income from wages to profits. Otherwise more real investment could not be financed. One possible cause is rising prices. In conditions of static real output, plans to invest more at full capacity working lead initially to rising prices. If wages lag behind price changes, profits can increase relative to wages as a proportion of national income. Prices will stop rising when the savings ratio has risen to match the desired investment ratio. There are, however, constraints on the share of profits. One important one is that the share of wages cannot be so low that the real wage is below the subsistence level. Indeed, workers may react to a declining wage share long before the real wage has reached this point. This is nothing more than Mrs Robinson's inflation barrier. The investment ratio is constrained by the ability of workers to protect their real incomes against erosion by rising prices. The inflation barrier is as much a feature of Kaldor's model as it is of Mrs Robinson's. If real wages rise as fast as productivity, there can be no increase in the share of profits in income and no increase in the volume of real investment in relation to income. In Chapter 6 an explicit model is developed along the lines of Kaldor, giving the likely rates of inflation necessary to raise the savings ratio by given amounts on alternative assumptions about the values of s_w, s_p, the wage–price coefficient, and the initial share of wages in income.

Kalecki's Model

Perhaps the clearest statement of the dependence of the level of profits, and saving, on decisions to invest is that of Kalecki[1] who, along with Keynes, has also influenced the models of Mrs Robinson and Kaldor. Consider a closed economy with no government expenditure or taxation. By the income approach to national income accounting,

[1] M. Kalecki, *The Theory of Economic Dynamics* (London: Allen & Unwin, 1954).

gross national product equals gross profits (P) plus wages and salaries (W). From the expenditure side, gross national product equals gross investment (I) plus capitalists' consumption (C_c) and workers' consumption (C_w). Therefore

$$Y = P + W \qquad (4.33)$$

and $$Y = I + C_c + C_w \qquad (4.34)$$

Hence $$P + W = I + C_c + C_w \qquad (4.35)$$

Defining workers' saving as $S_w = W - C_w$, and rearranging, gives

$$P = I + C_c - S_w \qquad (4.36)$$

Equation (4.36) is essentially an identity which says nothing about causation. Kalecki thought of it, however, as a behavioural relation with capitalists' spending as the independent variable, and profits as the dependent variable. Clearly, capitalists can decide to consume and invest more, but they cannot decide how much they are going to earn. Thus it is the decisions of capitalists to invest and consume that determine profits. The saving of workers actually reduces profits. Kalecki's explanation of the process by which an increase in investment brings about an increase in saving is different from that of Keynes, but easily explicable. Suppose that there is no capitalist spending and all wages are spent on consumption. In such a situation, the only form of revenue to capitalists would be revenue from workers, which will exactly equal wage costs if all wages are spent on consumption. Hence, business in the aggregate cannot earn profits by selling to workers. There can only be profits if income is spent on goods which did not constitute a direct cost of production. Hence, the famous saying attributed to Kalecki, 'the workers spend what they get and the capitalists get what they spend'. If workers do not spend what they get, and capitalists do not spend either, there will be losses because revenue will fall short of wage costs.

Keynes was aware of the result that Kalecki pointed to. In the *Treatise on Money* he says:

If entrepreneurs choose to spend a portion of their profits on consumption (and there is, of course, nothing to prevent them from doing this) the effect is to *increase* the profit on the sale of liquid consumption goods by an amount exactly equal to the amount of profits which have been thus expended. . . . Thus, however much

96   INFLATION, SAVING AND GROWTH

of their profits entrepreneurs spend on consumption, the increment
of wealth belonging to entrepreneurs remains the same as before.
Thus, profits, as a source of capital increment for entrepreneurs, are
a widow's cruse which remains undepleted however much of them
may be devoted to riotous living.[1]

Inflation and the Real Interest Rate

Another feature of the Keynesian approach to development is that
inflation can reduce the real interest rate, acting as a stimulus to
investment. This contrasts with the neo-classical view that nominal
interest rates will adjust to inflation leaving the real interest rate
unchanged. Most of the empirical evidence suggests, however, that
nominal interest rates are extremely slow to adjust to inflation. If it is
believed that monetary phenomena cannot have real effects, the
explanation of what is observed must be either that money lenders
lack foresight or that there are strong institutional pressures depressing interest rates permanently. Alternatively, the theory that
monetary phenomena cannot have real effects may be faulty. It is
certainly faulty if real output can expand as inflation occurs because
there is unemployment or because inflation expands the capacity to
produce.

Keynes himself based his belief that inflation would reduce the
real interest rate on the assumption that inflationary policies will
expand output. Consider Fig. 4.5 below.

The *IS* curve represents the locus of points at which saving equals
investment at different levels of output, given the rate of interest.
The interest rates corresponding to the full-employment levels of
output are given by the intersection of the *IS* curves and the vertical
lines *FF* and F_1F_1 representing different levels of full-employment
output. Now suppose that with a level of output *OF*, and an interest
rate of 6 per cent, prices are expected to rise by 4 per cent. The
demand curve for investment will rise 4 per cent shifting the *IS* curve
up 4 per cent to IS_1. This will lead to a new equilibrium interest rate
of 10 per cent if the full-employment output remains unchanged at
OF. If full-employment output expands, say, to OF_1, however, the
new equilibrium interest rate will be less than 10 per cent, say 9 per
cent. The nominal interest rate rises by less than the rate of inflation

[1] J. M. Keynes, *Treatise on Money*, vol. i (London: Macmillan, 1930)
p. 139.

and the real interest rate falls. If output expanded at the same rate as the rate of inflation, nominal interest rates would remain unchanged. Keynes is not explicit about the mechanism by which inflation at full employment may bring about an output expansion but it could be through the capacity-creating effects of investment or through the Phillips curve mechanism discussed in Chapter 3.

An alternative model in which the money rate of interest rises less than the rate of inflation, even holding output constant and allowing

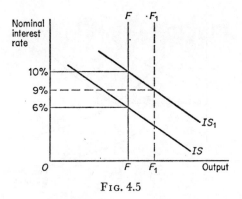

Fig. 4.5

inflation to be fully anticipated, has been developed by Mundell.[1] The basis of the model is that inflation reduces real money balances and that the resulting decline in wealth stimulates increased saving. This gives an impetus to investment and growth. Consider Fig. 4.6 below.

The *IS* curve is the locus of points at which real saving equals real investment for different combinations of the real interest rate (r) and real money balances. It is positively sloped because an increase in the real interest rate lowers investment and an increase in real money balances lowers saving. The *LM* curve is the locus of points at which the supply of money balances equals the demand for money balances for different values of the money rate of interest (i) and real money balances. It is negatively sloped because at low rates of interest the demand for real money balances is higher. Where *LM* = *IS*, the real rate of interest equals the money rate (i.e. $i_0 = r_0$ if Fig. 4.6).

The effect of inflation is to open up a gap between the money rate of interest and the real rate of interest equal to the rate of inflation.

[1] R. Mundell, 'Inflation and Real Interest', *Journal of Political Economy* (June 1963).

Inflation increases the opportunity cost of holding money balances. Since the LM schedule is derived on the basis of the money rate of interest, the LM curve must shift downwards, in relation to the real interest rate, by the amount of inflation RT. That is, the community is now willing to hold only M_1 money balances at the real interest rate, r_1, and at the money rate of i_1.

Inflation also creates a discrepancy between the productivity of investment and the return on saving, equal to the rate of inflation. To

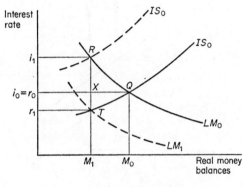

Fig. 4.6

maintain equality between saving and investment at any given rate of inflation, the money rate of interest must rise by the rate of inflation, RT. Only at i_1 will saving equal investment at the level of real balances, M_1. Since the IS schedule is derived on the basis of the real interest rate, the IS curve must shift upwards, in relation to the money interest rate, by the amount of inflation, RT.

Hence the net result of inflation is to reduce the real rate of interest from r_0 to r_1 and to raise the money rate from i_0 to i_1. Inflation alters the intertemporal distribution of income and the equilibrium capital stock, independently of whether inflation is anticipated or not. The result comes about because of a decline in the value of real money balances. Inflation reduces real money balances, and real investment and saving are both higher than in the absence of inflation.

Reconciling the Prior Saving versus Forced Saving Approaches to Development

There must be a middle view between the classical prior saving approach to development finance and the Keynesian forced saving

approach. A start would be for the prior saving school to admit the possibility of forced saving and to reduce their aversion to demand inflation. Equally, the Keynesians could admit that saving depends on factors other than the functional income distribution and that for any given desired investment ratio and growth rate inflation will be less the more voluntary saving can be encouraged.

At the practical level, the flow of funds approach offers the most constructive approach at integration.[1] The flow of funds approach recognises that some sectors of the economy have surplus saving while others have deficient saving, so that the policy issue becomes the best way of rectifying a deficiency or excess of aggregate saving and inducing the flow of excess saving in the surplus sectors to the deficit sectors to maximise efficiency in the use of investible resources.

The household sector of an economy normally invests less than it saves. Household savings are absorbed into idle money balances, precious metals and second hand claims to wealth of all types. Real resources remain idle unless the sellers of assets to the household sector invest, or idle resources are employed by other sectors of the community including the government. If the responsibility falls on the government to employ the surplus saving of the household sector, or the government wishes to invest more than the community wishes to save, monetary expansion may be required.

For the transfer of resources from surplus to deficit sectors of the economy, surplus sectors require financial assets in which to hold their transferable savings. If saving goes directly into investment in the sector in which it is generated, outside the confines of the monetary system, it will not necessarily be invested in the most socially useful enterprises. Deficit spending units can either issue their own liabilities which the surplus sectors take up, or financial intermediaries can channel surplus household saving into deficit sectors by issuing debt which the surplus spending units take up, and then by allocating the loanable funds among the deficit sectors. The more developed is the practice of financial intermediation, the more likely it is that saving will be allocated to the most efficient deficit sectors. To achieve efficiency in the use of investible resources the ratio of financial assets to total savings of the household sector must be allowed to grow as fast as possible.

[1] This point has been forcefully argued by D. R. Khatkhate, 'Analytic Basis of the Working of Monetary Policy in Less Developed Countries', *I.M.F. Staff Papers* (November 1972).

To encourage the household sector to hold financial assets as substitutes for 'idle' money and artifacts, a high interest rate policy may be needed. This need not necessarily raise the cost of investment, however, if funds are drawn to the organised money market away from the unorganised money market where very high rates of interest prevail. If this happens there is no necessary conflict between the classical view that high interest rates are necessary to encourage saving and the Keynesian view that low interest rates are necessary to encourage investment. The development of financial intermediaries and an organised money market can raise the rate of saving and reduce the *overall* interest rate at one and the same time, by diminishing the importance of the unorganised money market. Let us now consider money and banking in a developing economy in more detail.

5

Money in a Developing Economy

Whether or not monetary expansion leads to inflation, and is conducive to output growth in this way, the growth of the money economy
and the development of a country's financial system must be considered an integral part of the development process. As Hicks has
said:

> The beginning of a process of expansion . . . might occur because
> of real factors (inventions and the like) raising the real (prospective)
> rate of profit. But it might also occur because of financial improve-
> ments . . . , thereby permitting access to funds, for improvements
> which could have been made earlier, if the necessary funds had
> been forthcoming. It is not savings only that are required, but a
> channel of communication between potential savings and potential
> real investment.[1]

The importance of financial intermediation between the real sectors
of the economy is that financial intermediaries can offer liquidity to
lenders while at the same time providing borrowers with long-term
capital. Savers are more willing to lend and investors to borrow than
if savers could only lend directly to investors.

The growth of a developing economy's financial system is important
both for the classical model of development which stresses the role of
voluntary saving and for the Keynesian model of development which
emphasises decisions to invest and investment-led growth. On the one
hand, financial institutions can encourage the production of surpluses
for reinvestment and encourage firms to use resources which might
otherwise be used for consumption or lie idle. On the other hand, the
possibility of credit creation enables investors to bid resources away

[1] J. Hicks, *Capital and Growth* (Oxford University Press, 1965) p. 290.

from consumers for the purpose of capital formation. This is the primary importance of the banking system in Keynesian models of development: to enable entrepreneurs to do the investment they wish to do in the absence of prior saving. Profits are clearly not a substitute for credit where plans to invest exceed plans to save. In short, the development of the financial system can permit the accumulation of capital and the expansion of income in excess of the level which would prevail in its absence.

A well-developed financial system is also important for the efficient allocation of capital between competing uses. In particular, the capital market needs to be integrated and the interest rate structure unified. The consequence of a fragmented capital market in which interest rates vary from sector to sector is that some sectors of the economy may be able to borrow at rates of interest far below the rate of interest in other sectors of the economy where the productivity of capital is higher. The allocation of capital is distorted, leading to inefficiency in its use and a higher capital–output ratio than if the capital market was unified. The solution must be to encourage funds into the organised money market and to extend the provision of financial institutions into sectors of the economy which lack them. Attempts to overcome fragmentation of the capital market by the subsidisation of already privileged sectors of the economy, as so often happens, not only distorts investment further but tends to conceal capital's true scarcity.

In summary, greater financial sophistication in an economy may be expected to lead to a higher level of income, more saving and a more efficient allocation of investible resources. The task is to build up the financial infrastructure.

A financial infrastructure comprises four elements each of which contributes to the process of financial deepening,[1] and to the encouragement of saving, by offering higher real returns to savers and by diversifying savers' portfolios. These four elements comprise the introduction of money and the replacement of barter as a means of exchange; the establishment of a central bank; the development of a commercial banking system; and the development of a well-coordinated capital market. A financial infrastructure is not something that the developing countries can just afford to let grow as happened

---

[1] Financial deepening is defined as an increase in the ratio of financial assets to income.

in most of the present developed countries.[1] The financial infrastructure must be actively fostered in the interests of development,
drawing on the experience and lessons of countries with sophisticated
financial systems.

The basic objectives of a financial policy for development must be
to encourage savers to hold their saving in the form of financial assets
to permit saving to flow freely between sectors of the economy; to
ensure that new saving is allocated efficiently to the most socially
productive uses, and to provide incentives to saving and production in
order to minimise the inflationary repercussions of investment-led
growth through monetary expansion.

In the early stages of development most of the saving is done by the
household sector of the economy; and the household sector invariably
invests less than it saves. In the absence of financial assets, household
saving typically takes the form of the acquisition of tangible assets
such as jewellery, precious metals and land. While the acquisition of
such assets, provided they are 'second hand', frees resources for
investment, there is no guarantee that the seller of the assets will use
the sale proceeds for investment. The proceeds may be consumed or
hoarded. Alternatively, investment may take place in relatively
unprofitable activities. If the sale proceeds are hoarded, the freed
resources are still available for use, but if they are consumed the
resources are lost forever. Moreover, the assets acquired may themselves be resources with positive opportunity costs if they are left idle.
Land and certain precious metals come into this category. The
existence of monetary assets and financial intermediaries provide a
stronger guarantee that the act of saving will lead to investment, and
to investment in the most productive activities. If saving goes
directly into investment outside the confines of the monetary system,
it will not necessarily be invested in the most profitable enterprises.
Financial intermediaries exist to channel surplus saving in one sector
to more profitable sectors elsewhere in the economy.

Thus there are two main ways in which the financial system can
aid the growth of the capital stock. First, financial institutions
can distribute new saving more productively, and second, they can
provide incentives to saving and investment. Financial intermediaries
can distribute new capital more efficiently than otherwise because
there is no obvious reason why the distribution of saving in an

[1] U. Hicks, *Development Finance, Planning and Control* (Oxford University
Press) 1965.

economy should correspond with the most efficient distribution of investment. Financial institutions can also achieve economies of scale in the costs of transferring saving to investors by spreading risks and by saving time that would be involved if each individual saver had to find the most productive investor. On the second point, a financial system can stimulate saving by offering a wide range of financial assets; and the very existence of assets makes the return on saving higher than it would otherwise be. There is a limit to the utility yield and psychic return to hoarded money. But the return to the growth of financial assets cannot go on rising for ever. Ultimately the stimulus to saving from the growth of financial assets must come to an end. In most developing economies, however, this point is a long way off. Some of the gain in savings that comes with financial deepening may be illusory. Saving may be drawn to uses which get counted in national income statistics away from uses that do not and were not previously measurable. On the other hand reasons have been given as to why the savings ratio may be expected to rise. In particular, savers' horizons are extended and investment opportunities are widened.

The first prerequisite in the development of a financial infrastructure is money as a medium of exchange. Secondly, banking institutions are needed to act as deposits for savings, and which can also provide credit so that the money supply can be readily expanded to meet the needs of the economic system. Some form of central bank is indispensable for the co-ordination of the growth of the financial system and for the control of credit. To assist the development of the capital market a range of financial assets is needed, especially available in small units to attract the small saver. The organised money market needs to encroach as much as possible on the unorganised money market, to unify the interest rate structure and to restrict lending for consumption purposes which the unorganised market tends to indulge in heavily.

Money and Development

It has been argued that there are several ways in which the financial development of an economy can contribute to development. At the same time governments can lay claim on a country's real resources by monetary expansion. In the early stages of development perhaps the greatest potential contribution comes from the release of re-

sources, and from the saving of resources by the avoidance of resource waste as money replaces barter as a medium of exchange. As monetary transactions replace barter, the public's demand for money for transactions purposes increases relative to income. To hold more money in relation to income, the public must give up real resources of an equivalent value. In substituting currency for barter there is an act of real saving involved corresponding to the increase in the real stock of money held. With the government exchanging notes and coins for resources, the resources released can be used by the government to increase the level of investment over and above that permitted by taxation and borrowing from the public. One of the primary benefits stemming from the monetisation of an economy is that it possesses the potential for generating a real investible surplus.

The use of money not only releases resources, but also saves and generates resources. Barter is extremely wasteful of resources. The objects used for barter, which may be costly to produce, could be used as inputs in production and may depreciate. Barter also requires a double coincidence of wants which absorbs time, which itself is a resource if the marginal product of labour time is positive. Money, by contrast, is virtually costless to produce; it does not depreciate readily, and its use saves time by avoiding the necessity of matching the wants of sellers and buyers. Money also facilitates exchange and therefore acts as an encouragement to specialisation and the division of labour. In this way the development of the money economy can contribute to the growth of an economy's productive potential – raising the productivity of labour. Historically, the major impetus to the monetisation of most of the present developing economies was the desire of agriculturalists to specialise in the production of native crops for export and to have a convenient means of purchasing goods, often imported, which were available in the towns. When peasant producers started to specialise in the production of goods for export, and came to rely on other producers for goods which they previously produced themselves, it was natural for the money economy to spread from the foreign trade sector to the rest of the domestic economy.

In a growing economy, monetary expansion is required to facilitate the needs of trade and to allow growth to take place. Monetary expansion for this purpose can also be appropriated by governments for development purposes.

Neither the growth of the money supply to meet the increased demand for money, nor the monetary expansion to facilitate the

growth of output, necessarily involves inflation. This should be clear from the fundamental equation of exchange

$$MV = PY \tag{5.1}$$

or
$$M = K_d PY \tag{5.2}$$

where M is the nominal money supply
V is the income velocity of circulation of money
$K_d(= 1/V)$ is the demand to hold money per unit of income
P is the average price of final goods and services
and Y is real income.

Taking rates of growth of the variables in equation (5.2) (denoted by lower case letters), i.e. $m = k_d + p + y$, it can be seen that if the demand for money per unit of income is increasing $(k_d > 0)$, m can be positive without the price level rising. Similarly if real income is expanding $(y > 0)$, m can also be positive without the price level rising. Without monetary expansion, $k_d > 0$ and $y > 0$ releases resources, which monetary expansion by government can then appropriate. The government's proceeds from monetary expansion will equal $(m - p)$.

One of the problems confronting the government of a developing country committed to faster economic development is to determine the optimum rate of expansion of the money supply. Clearly if k_d and y are greater than zero, the optimum rate of expansion cannot be zero, otherwise real income growth would be impaired.[1] Besides the fact that the demand for money is likely to be expanding, and real growth is positive, some monetary expansion which is inflationary may also be beneficial to growth as we have tried to argue in previous chapters. Further, an economy may possibly hold surplus foreign exchange reserves which it wishes to repatriate. Not all developing countries suffer from a shortage of foreign exchange. All these considerations will influence the desired rate of expansion of the money supply.

[1] Unless, of course, the objective is to initiate a deflationary spiral. Such a policy has been seriously suggested by Professor Friedman to equate the return on money holdings with the rate of return on alternative assets in order to encourage the holding of money which is costless to produce. Since there are easier ways to encourage the holding of money (such as offering interest rates on current account bank deposits), and many prices are probably inflexible downwards anyway, Friedman's monetary rules are not considered in detail here. Interested readers are referred to M. Friedman, *The Optimum Quantity of Money and other Essays* (London: Macmillan, 1969).

There seems to be some consensus in the literature that a ratio of about 5:3 between the percentage increase in the money supply and the rate of real growth can be considered non-inflationary.[1] For example, if real growth is 6 per cent per annum, then something like a 10 per cent per annum expansion of the money supply would be non-inflationary. Making no allowance for the influence of inflation on real output growth, the above example would imply that the demand for money, k_d, was growing by about 4 per cent per annum. This sort of rate is not uncommon in developing countries. In Chapter 6 reference is made to the work of Bhambri[2] on Nigeria which uses a figure of 5 per cent expansion in the demand for money per unit of income in estimating the proportion of investment that can be financed by non-inflationary monetary expansion given the growth of demand for money and the growth of output of the economy.

The empirical estimates of the demand for money in relation to income (income velocity) invariably find that the income elasticity of demand for money is higher in developing countries than in the developed countries. Typically what tends to happen is that initially velocity falls as income grows and then rises in the later stages of development. This is generally true whatever definition of money is taken to compute income velocity (although sometimes when a narrow definition of money is taken the income velocity shows no significant change). As we should expect, the income elasticity of demand is higher, and velocity lower, the broader the definition of money taken.

Ezekeil and Adekunle[3] found in a cross-section study of thirty-seven countries that the money–income ratio rises systematically with the level of development as measured by per capita income as long as money is defined to include at least demand deposits. Measuring income velocity in three ways using currency (V_1); narrow money (V_2), and broad money (V_3), and relating each measure of velocity to per capita income (Y/N), gave the following regression results

[1] A. C. Harberger, 'Some Notes on Inflation in Latin America' in *Inflation and Growth in Latin America*, ed. W. Baer and I. Kerstenetsky (London: Irwin, 1964).

[2] R. S. Bhambri, 'Demand for Money and the Investible Surplus', *Nigerian Journal of Economic and Social Studies* (March 1968).

[3] H. Ezekeil and J. O. Adekunle, 'The Secular Behaviour of Income Velocity: An International Cross Section Study', *I.M.F. Staff Papers* (July 1969).

$$\log V_1 = 1 \cdot 16 - 0 \cdot 03 \log Y/N$$
$$(t=0 \cdot 39)$$
$$\log V_2 = 1 \cdot 30 - 0 \cdot 22 \log Y/N$$
$$(t=2 \cdot 75)$$
$$\log V_3 = 1 \cdot 55 - 0 \cdot 40 \log Y/N$$
$$(t=4 \cdot 44)$$

The signs of the regression coefficients show clearly velocity falling and falling significantly, except in the case of the currency–income ratio where the regression coefficient is not significantly different from zero ($t = 0 \cdot 39$).

Estimates of the income elasticities of demand for money for individual countries show a wide variety of results depending on the definition of money taken, on the other variables included in the estimating equations, and on the stage of development reached. Taking a fairly narrow definition of money, and considering inflation and the rate of interest as additional explanatory variables, Adekunle[1] gives estimates of the income elasticity of demand for money of $0 \cdot 77$ for Ceylon; $0 \cdot 81$ for the Republic of China; $0 \cdot 94$ for Costa Rica; $1 \cdot 35$ for India, and $0 \cdot 60$ for Mexico. Fry has made estimates of $1 \cdot 1$ for Iran; $1 \cdot 1$ for Pakistan taking narrow money and $2 \cdot 12$ taking broad money (including time deposits); and $1 \cdot 38$ for Turkey taking narrow money and $1 \cdot 75$ taking broad money.[2] The much higher elasticity of demand for broad money probably reflects, in the main, a switch out of more traditional forms of saving into time deposits and other financial assets as the financial system becomes more sophisticated and as the return to be earned on monetary assets becomes more apparent. As such, a high income elasticity of demand for money, taking a broad definition of money, cannot be taken as indicative of an extensive release of resources for investment. The resources would probably have been freed to some extent by the act of saving in a different form. In particular, an increase in the ratio of time deposits to income can only be construed as a release of resources for investment to the extent that time deposits represent genuine new saving, or if the deposits were previously being used for exchange payments and now replace barter in the same way as the holding of narrow money.

[1] J. O. Adekunle, 'The Demand for Money: Evidence from Developed and Less Developed Countries', *I.M.F. Staff Papers* (July 1968).

[2] M. F. Fry, 'Manipulating Demand for Money' in *Essays in Modern Economics*–Proceedings of the A.U.T.E. Conference 1972, ed. M. Parkin (Harlow: Longman, 1973).

Whilst the ratio of real money balances to income may rise with development, releasing resources for investment, what happens to the ratio also depends on the rate of inflation. On the one hand inflation has a real balance effect which raises the savings–income ratio; on the other hand inflation may reduce the desired ratio of money balances to income thus reducing the savings ratio if a portion of the excess money balances is consumed and not saved by the purchase of alternative monetary assets. Whether aggregate saving is impaired depends on whether the favourable real balance effect is outweighed by a reduction in saving brought about by a fall in the desired money–income ratio.

The empirical evidence on the demand for money in relation to inflation is mixed but on balance most studies of individual countries seem to conclude that inflation does not have a significant impact on the velocity of circulation of money except when inflation is severe.[1] A cross-section study by Melitz and Correa on international differences in income velocity reaches the same conclusion.[2] Melitz and Correa rationalise their findings in terms of the mildness of the inflationary experience and the costs involved of switching out of money into asset substitutes which are inflation-proof. Even where a statistically significant negative relation between inflation and the money–income ratio is found the elasticity of the ratio with respect to inflation appears to be quite low. Taking different measures of income velocity for sixteen Latin American countries over the period 1950–69 Hanson and Vogel estimate elasticities of income velocity with respect to inflation of between 0·07 and 0·12.[3] The elasticities are certainly very low and suggest that inflation can operate effectively as a tax on money even in countries which have been experiencing high rates of inflation for many years. It seems unlikely that the decline in saving from a reduction in the money–income ratio would more than offset the receipts from the inflation tax. In fact, it is possible that the negative relation between the money–income ratio and inflation may simply reflect a switch from money to other forms

[1] See P. Cagan, 'The Monetary Dynamics of Hyper-Inflation' in *Studies in the Quantity Theory of Money*, ed. M. Friedman (University of Chicago Press, 1956).

[2] J. Melitz and H. Correa, 'International Differences in Income Velocity', *Review of Economics and Statistics* (February 1970).

[3] J. S. Hanson and R. C. Vogel, 'Inflation and Monetary Policy in Latin America', *Review of Economics and Statistics* (August 1973).

of asset holding – from money to interest-bearing securities, for example – in which case saving would not be impaired at all.

A further advantage of the growth of the money economy is that it gives rise to banking and credit mechanisms which themselves can act as a stimulus to saving and investment. When the range of financial assets is small in a developing country, physical assets tend to form the major part of saving; for example, the acquisition of jewellery, precious ornaments, gold, land and so forth. In principle, this should not mean that saving is any less available for productive investment than it would be if the saving was in the form of the acquisition of monetary assets. The crucial question is how the sellers of the assets purchased by the savers dispose of the return from the sale. If the seller does not consume, the act of saving by purchasing jewellery, gold, land, etc. releases resources for investment just as real as if financial assets had been purchased. In practice, however, some of the sale proceeds are likely to be consumed, which means that the saving of one person is partly offset by the dissaving of another and less resources are released for investment than if financial assets had been acquired of the same value. This is undoubtedly one of the reasons why saving and capital accumulation appear low in developing countries, whereas the capacity to save for capital formation is much greater and could be taken advantage of with a range of financial assets as substitutes for physical assets as a means of saving. Saving by the purchase of such assets as gold and land, which can be used as inputs in the productive system, also represents a loss to the community if the assets lie idle.

Therefore, while it is fallacious to think that the particular form that saving tends to take in developing countries necessarily precludes the release of resources for investment, in practice there are grounds for believing that alternative financial assets would lead to a higher volume of real saving and the greater availability of resources for development. There is a greater guarantee that the proceeds to the seller of newly issued financial assets will be used for investment purposes and that the holding of the assets will absorb less of society's real resources. The importance of money is that it leads to the provision of banking, deposit facilities and debt instruments of governments which become alternative assets in which to hold wealth.

Fractional reserve banking further allows credit creation. The ability of the economic system to create credit is important for two main reasons. First, it can compensate for the failure of the economic

system to transmit current saving into domestic investment. If hoarding takes place, for example, resources are released but saving is not directly available for investment. The creation of credit through the banking system can compensate. The second need for credit creation is for the continuous expansion of credit to facilitate growth. This point has been forcefully argued by Kaldor who maintains that this is the real significance of the invention of paper money and of credit creation through the banking system.[1] Because development is a cumulative phenomenon sustained by increasing returns, a monetary and banking system is vital to enable the expansion of investment so as to generate the savings required to finance additional investment out of the *additions* to production, which production itself makes possible through increasing returns. In other words, credit creation is necessary to finance increasing returns. In a barter system, or with a purely metallic currency, the ability of the system to expand in response to opportunities would be severely restricted.

The Role of Banks

In most developing countries of the world – in Latin America, Asia and Africa – banks, at least as we know them today, had their origins in the banks of developed countries which established offices in the developing countries to conduct the finance of external trade. The job of the banks was to provide credit for financing the collection and export of primary commodities and to finance the distribution of consumer goods imports. Then as the economies developed the banks took on the role of deposit banking as well. They collected deposits, which in many cases exceeded loans made, and the surpluses were transferred to the developed countries. For many years, several colonial banks in different parts of the world were involved in exporting capital from the less developed to the developed countries. In many countries, in the course of time, the branches of foreign banks were transformed into separate affiliates from the parent bank abroad with varying degrees of participation and autonomy. In other countries the overseas banks were transformed into national institutions. In both cases they contributed to the formation of a national banking system.

[1] N. Kaldor, 'The Irrelevance of Equilibrium Economics', *Economic Journal* (December 1972).

The development of a national banking system, comprising a central bank, branch banks and special national development banks and credit agencies, has become an integral part of the development programme of most developing countries. Besides sound economic reasons for establishing a central bank, the desire has often been a matter of fashion as well, to demonstrate monetary and financial independence and also to demonstrate political independence in the case of ex-colonial countries. A reaction against the archaic and detrimental monetary and financial systems operated by colonial powers in many of the present developing countries was to be expected. For example, it could be argued that the Currency Board system which was operated by Great Britain in a large part of British colonial Africa impeded rather than fostered development. The workings of the Currency Board system in eight major African territories have been vividly elucidated by Newlyn and Rowan.[1] The system operated by requiring that a country's currency could only be issued against the exchange of British sterling. The currency in circulation always had to be backed 100 per cent by British sterling assets. The volume of a country's currency thus became a function of its balance-of-payments position as under a gold-standard system. If the balance of payments was in surplus, British sterling assets could be acquired and the money supply expanded; if in deficit, the money supply contracted. In effect, the country's medium of exchange had to be imported and paid for, as for ordinary goods, in the form of exports. Money therefore involved a substantial real resource cost, and human costs in terms of impediments to development. Under the Currency Board system there was no monetary authority capable of influencing the money supply in accordance with the wishes of the government, and no authority concerned with the operations and development of monetary and financial institutions. It was extremely difficult for the monetary system to respond to the needs of development. Economic expansion was forced to rely on bank money and on increases in the velocity of circulation of money which absorbed real resources. In fact, the system suffered from all the deficiencies of the old gold standard system, with growth continually constrained by the balance of payments. Yet most developing countries need balance of payments deficits to grow!

The motivation to establish a central monetary authority with the

[1] W. Newlyn and D. C. Rowan, *Money and Banking in British Colonial Africa* (Oxford University Press, 1954).

power to issue money has therefore had a strong economic rationale in many developing countries. It is clear, looking at central bank charters for developing countries, that economic development has been one of the goals in mind, if not the major goal. To give some illustrative examples: Kenya's Act reads, 'The principal objects of the Bank shall be to regulate the issue of notes and coins, to assist in the development and maintenance of a sound monetary, credit and banking system in Kenya conducive to the orderly and balanced economic development of the country.' Tanzania's Act reads, 'The activities of the Bank shall be directed to the promotion of credit and exchange conditions conducive to the rapid growth of the national economy in Tanzania.' Similarly, the Central Bank of Ceylon is charged with, amongst other things, 'promoting and maintaining a high level of production, employment, and real income, and encouraging and promoting the full development of the productive resources of Ceylon.'

The major functions expected of a central bank consist of the issuing of currency, which transfers real resources to government in the manner described earlier; the development of a fractional reserve banking system through which it can provide liquidity and control credit; acting as a banker to the government by financing deficits and advising on economic policy; developing other financial institutions, especially institutions to finance development and to provide a market for government securities; maintaining an interest rate structure conducive to development; encouraging saving by monetary and other means; maintaining a high level of demand to achieve capacity growth, and applying selective credit controls in the interests of developing particular sectors of the economy. As the experience of many countries indicates, it is very much easier with a strong central bank to give priority to the needs of the government and the public sector. A central bank can require member banks to hold reserves in government bonds, and the rapid growth in the market for bonds can permit development without excessive monetary expansion.

The stabilisation role of the central bank in developing countries is essentially secondary to its development role, in contrast to developed countries where the financial system is already well equipped to meet the requirements of economic growth. In any case, stabilisation is particularly difficult in a developing economy where credit control, the main lever of stabilisation policy, is ill-developed; and where major economic fluctuations occur because of fluctuations in export

earnings or because of the volatility of overseas investment, and where only a small proportion of domestic investment is dependent on bank finance.

The importance of building up an indigenous banking system, and the establishment of widely dispersed branch banks, should be clear from what has already been said. Above all, banks can encourage thriftiness in the community and can ultimately lead to a more efficient allocation of savings than if investment takes place in the sector in which the saving originates, outside the confines of the monetary system. A system of banks can help to break down sectoral bottlenecks through the mobilisation of financial resources and by unifying interest rates. In a study of financial intermediaries and national savings in developing countries, U Tun Wai has compared the extent of financial saving in countries (that is, the acquisition of financial assets by the non-financial sector) with the extent of economic saving, and finds a strong correlation.[1] He concludes that financial intermediation exerts a positive influence on saving, especially in developing countries.

Branch banks need to be numerous and dispersed if they are to act as collecting points for savings of small average amounts from a large number of sources. Expatriate banks in colonial Africa were notorious for their small number of branches and their unwillingness to open small accounts. Today, in the developing countries as a whole, the average number of banks per million of population is 10 compared with 180 in developed countries.[2] The encouragement of branch banking has met with considerable success in many parts of the developing world. One of the purposes of the extensive bank nationalisation in India in 1969 was to expand branch banking and to ensure that banks would play an increasingly important role in promoting productive activities and the growth of employment opportunities by a wider dispersal of credit in previously neglected regions and sectors of the economy; in particular, to rural agriculture and small businesses. To June 1972 the fourteen newly nationalised banks had set up 3,056 new branch offices. The opening of four branch banks in villages near New Delhi attracted two million rupees in one day, including a 200,000 pile from a local temple! Lewis has remarked that experience shows that the amount of savings depends partly on

[1] U Tun Wai, *Financial Intermediaries and National Savings in Developing Countries* (New York: Praeger, 1972).
[2] Ibid. p. 46.

how widespread savings institutions are.[1] 'If they are pushed right under the individual's nose . . . people save more than if the nearest savings institution is some distance away.' In addition, as we have remarked already, the existence of banks and monetary assets frees saving from the problem of finding investment opportunities if that is the only alternative form of saving; bank deposits represent a new form of saving with less risk and greater liquidity than many other types of asset; interest rates offered by banks may attract a greater volume of net saving, and, perhaps most important of all, an organised banking system can avoid dissaving by replacing moneylending institutions which typically lend for consumption purposes, which the banks do not do to such an extent.

The fact remains, however, that banking is still rudimentary in most developing countries. The ratio of bank deposits to national income in some countries is as low as 10 per cent, and the proportion of demand deposits to the total money supply averages between 25 and 30 per cent. These figures contrast with developed countries where the ratio of bank deposits to national income typically exceeds 30 per cent and where demand deposits constitute the major part of the total money supply.

Development Banks[2]

Special development banks figure prominently in the financial structure and development effort of most developing countries. Their establishment normally reflects difficulties in raising finance for development through existing financial channels, in particular where capital markets are not well developed. Almost every developing country possesses a development bank of one description or another, established with government and/or international backing. Their role is to provide finance for industry; to develop a capital market; and to provide guidance and stimulus to the leading sectors of the economy to accelerate development. Development banks are given different emphasis in different countries. In some countries they act as direct investors in productive enterprises; in others, they act primarily as guarantors of loans floated by private industry. In all cases the emphasis tends to be on long-term finance, and on help to

[1] A. Lewis, *Theory of Economic Growth* (London: Allen & Unwin, 1955).
[2] This section draws heavily on W. Diamond, *Development Banks* (Baltimore: Johns Hopkins Press, 1957).

specific sectors of the economy, such as agriculture or small business. The case for development banks for these specific purposes is that ordinary commercial banking institutions are frequently reluctant to support projects of a long-term nature which involve risk.

Development banks also have a role to play in stimulating the capital market. This they can do by selling their own stocks and bonds, by helping enterprises float or place their securities, and by selling from their own portfolio of investments. The banks are typically financed from a mixture of public, private and international sources. Attracting private capital can be difficult, but government inducements can be provided; for example, in the form of tax exemption on interest receipts and dividends. In this way, governments can provide a subsidy to development banks in their early stages of growth.

Development banks are to be found throughout the developing countries. The following are some examples: in India there is the Industrial Finance Corporation of India, established in 1948, which is designed to make medium- and long-term credits more readily available to industrial concerns in India, particularly in circumstances where normal banking arrangements are inappropriate or recourse to capital issues is impracticable. In Greece the Greek National Investment Bank was set up in 1963 to assist efforts to raise productivity in the industrial sector, to develop a capital market and to encourage joint ventures by Greek and foreign investors. In addition, the Hellenic Industrial Development Bank was formed in 1964 from the merger of three smaller existing development financing institutions, which is now the major source of medium- and long-term financing for industry in Greece. In Turkey the Turkish Industrial Development Bank, established in 1950, was charged with three tasks: first, to support and stimulate the establishment of new private enterprises and the expansion and modernisation of existing private enterprises; second, to encourage and assist the participation of private capital, both domestic and foreign, in industry established in Turkey; and third, to encourage and promote the private ownership of securities pertaining to Turkish industry and to assist in the development of a securities market in Turkey. The Turkish Industrial Development Bank is probably the most important single development agency in Turkey, and the most prominent institutional source of private industry finance. In Mexico there is one of the oldest development banks, the Nacional Financiera of Mexico, set up in

1934, which finances a large part of the investment in the public sector and which also lends to the private sector. In Pakistan there is the Pakistan Industrial Credit and Investment Corporation, which is internationally supported by the World Bank.

The Unorganised Money Market

One of the objects of the extension of the money economy and the development of the financial system must be to reduce the size of the unorganised money market which operates largely in the agricultural sector. There are two reasons for concern. The first is the very high rates of interest charged which discourage investment in productive assets. The second is that a large fraction of borrowing in the unorganised money market is for consumption purposes. A diminution of the importance of the unorganised money market in the total financial structure could, paradoxically, reduce the overall level of interest rates and increase saving at the same time.

The high price of funds in the unorganised market is a reflection of the strength of demand for loanable funds relative to supply. There is a limited supply of funds in the market reflecting a general shortage of capital in developing economies. In addition, there are high risks involved including the risk of default. The main sources of supply are village shopkeepers, merchants, moneylenders and landlords. The supply of institutional credit from the organised money market to the sectors of the economy where the unorganised market prevails is very limited. There has always existed a reluctance on the part of institutional investors to lend to the agricultural sector.

There is a heavy demand for loanable funds in the unorganised market not only for investment purposes but also for consumption. Consumption demand figures prominently to finance marriages, religious festivals, funerals, etc., which social customs dictate should be of a standard far in excess of that which could be provided for out of current income alone.

Rates of interest in the unorganised market vary from one type of lender to another and from country to country. According to data collected by U Tun Wai, the weighted average interest rate in the unorganised money market in a representative cross-section of developing countries in the 1950s was 36 per cent, compared with an average effective rate of 12 per cent charged by credit institutions in

the organised money market.[1] In Thailand the rate varied from 25 per cent charged by merchants to 45 per cent charged by landlords. Effective rates in excess of 100 per cent, however, are not uncommon in many countries, in particular in South America.

The policy objective must be for the organised money market to reach out into the agricultural areas. Laws and decrees setting maximum rates of interest that money-lenders can charge are not workable and do not get to the heart of the problem anyway. What is required is a greater supply of loanable funds from the organised market to the agricultural sector. This flow can be fostered in a number of ways including loans to the agricultural sector through the national development banks and the encouragement of private agricultural credit institutions such as co-operatives, land mortgage banks and village banks. At the same time the demands for consumption purposes must somehow be curbed, preferably by economic and social change itself. Social change is important in this context because of the fungibility of funds. It is conceivable, for example, that finance provided for productive purposes may ultimately be used for consumption, by farmers borrowing from the organised money market for purposes which were formerly self-financed and using internally generated funds thus released for consumption.

The importance of unifying the interest rate structure of developing countries and reducing the fragmentation of the capital market cannot be overstressed, both from the point of view of encouraging saving and from the point of view of the use of saving productively. A fragmented capital market with low interest rates in the industrial sector and very high interest rates in rural areas means that projects are inevitably biased towards the industrial sector where the returns to society may be lower. And within the rural areas themselves, limited outlets for saving, due to the fragmented capital market, can lead to the wasteful use of resources. If peasant farmers have cash surpluses, they need to be encouraged to hold them until they can invest in worthwhile projects, as opposed to being forced into hasty decision-making because of the low return on holding money and the lack of alternative investment outlets. Fragmented capital markets can lead to over-investment and wasteful investment in some sectors, and under-investment in others. Financial policy must gear itself much more to decreasing the fragmentation of the money market. In doing

[1] U Tun Wai, 'Interest Rates Outside the Organised Money Markets of Underdeveloped Countries', *I.M.F. Staff Papers* (November 1957).

so, the complementarity between the accumulation of money balances and physical capital, which was argued in Chapter 4, becomes even more plausible.

Empirical Evidence on the Relation Between Money and Growth

On the basis of what has been argued so far we should expect to find a positive relation between the rate of monetary expansion and the rate of growth of output, at least up to the point at which excessive inflation becomes damaging to growth for the reasons already discussed. To find a positive relation, however, presents serious difficulties of identification. Monetary expansion can induce growth; on the other hand monetary expansion may merely be responding to growth in a passive way. A single equation regression between the rate of monetary expansion as the independent variable and the growth of output as the dependent variable may indicate that monetary expansion induces growth, when it is simply responding to the needs of the system. It can be argued, however, and has been by Fan,[1] that the money supply in developing countries is much less subject to control by the authorities than in the developed countries, where the endogeneity argument would apply with some force, which makes it legitimate to treat money as exogenous and as the independent variable in the system. Using this argument Fan examines the relation between monetary growth and the growth of output in eight Asian and eighteen Latin American countries over the period 1959–66. In Asia he finds that monetary expansion of up to 17 per cent per annum has more effect on real income than on inflation. The rank correlation across countries between the rate of monetary expansion and the rate of growth of income is 0·68. The equation relating real growth to monetary expansion is

$$y = 4{\cdot}249 + 0{\cdot}279\ m\ (r^2 = 0{\cdot}59).$$
$$\text{(S.E.} = 0{\cdot}110)$$

In Latin America a simple linear relation between monetary expansion and growth gave an insignificant negative relation. This is largely accounted for by a handful of countries with massive rates of expansion of the money supply. A quadratic function approximates

[1] L. S. Fan, 'Monetary Performance in Developing Economies: A Quantity Theory Approach', *Quarterly Review of Economics and Business* (Summer 1970).

the data much better, showing the beneficial aspects of monetary expansion up to a point, after which monetary expansion detracts from growth, probably due to the excessive inflation generated. The quadratic estimated by Fan for the eighteen Latin American countries is (standard errors in brackets)

$$y = 4\cdot79 + 0\cdot132(m) - 0\cdot004(m^2); \qquad (r^2 = 0\cdot26)$$
$$ (0\cdot116) \qquad (0\cdot002)$$

which gives an 'optimum' rate of increase in the money supply of 16·5 per cent. It is interesting to note (see Chapter 9) that the relation between the savings ratio and inflation in Latin America is also quadratic.

In a cross-section study of forty-three countries, taking average values of the variables 1956–65, Wallich also finds that the relationship between monetary expansion and the growth of output is peaked.[1] In Wallich's sample of countries, however, the coefficients of the quadratic imply that growth would be maximised with a 28 per cent expansion of the money supply, which even expansionists would regard as excessive. Wallich also finds in his study that growth is positively related to the degree of financial intermediation of the monetary system. This conclusion concurs with that of U Tun Wai, already mentioned, who found a positive relation between the degree of financial intermediation and the savings ratio.

Another approach to an examination of the relationship between financial deepening and economic development is to include a measure of real balances in the production function. This has been attempted for the American economy for the period 1929–67 with the conclusion that real balances contribute significantly to growth.[2] The inclusion of real balances in the production function reduces the characteristic residual term and improves the statistical fit of the equations. The significance of the real balance term is not impaired when considered against time as a variable as well.

In conclusion, there is a lot of evidence which suggests that monetary expansion and growth are associated. Even if monetary growth is not a growth-inducing force, it is certainly a necessary condition for growth to take place. But a number of reasons have been

---

[1] H. C. Wallich, 'Money and Growth: A Country Cross-Section Analysis', *Journal of Money, Credit and Banking* (May, 1969).

[2] A. Sinai and H. H. Stokes, 'Real Money Balances: An Omitted Variable in the Production Function?', *Review of Economics and Statistics* (August 1972).

given for thinking that the monetary development of an economy plays an important role in its overall development in the early stages of growth. The rates of monetary expansion which would apparently maximise the growth rate, however, seem to be somewhat in excess of what was considered earlier to be the likely non-inflationary rate of expansion (i.e. not more than double the real growth rate). What this suggests is that inflation itself must also be a growth-inducing force. We have already argued why this might be so; the evidence here supports that view. The evidence is admittedly crude but it points in that direction.

6

Raising the Warranted Rate
of Growth

The Redistribution Effects of Inflation on Saving

It was seen in Chapter 2 that there are two broad approaches to the
question of the way inflation may promote growth. One is the
Keynesian approach which stresses income redistribution between
wages and profits. The other is the Quantity Theory approach in
which inflation redistributes income from the holders of money
balances to the monetary authorities. In the first case what is involved
is redistribution within the private sector, and in the second case
redistribution between the private and the public sector. The two
processes are not mutually exclusive, of course. Demand inflation is
likely to involve both forms of redistribution. Rising prices which
originate from the desire of government to transfer real resources to
itself will also tend to redistribute income within the private sector
between wage-earners and profit-earners, creditors and debtors.
Similarly, a profit inflation emanating from excess demand in the
private sector will involve a tax on money which may or may not
redistribute resources to the government sector depending on how the
holders of money balances react to the tax.

The way in which a tax on money releases resources for investment
is a complex process. On the one hand real purchasing is reduced.
Other things remaining the same, saving must increase. This is one
interpretation of the term forced saving. The inability to consume as
much as before is reinforced by the fact that inflation reduces the real
value of money balances. If the public wishes to restore the real value
of its money holdings to its previous level, its holding of money must
rise. Hence consumption out of real income must fall and saving
increase. If the public seeks to avoid the tax on money, however, it
will reduce its holdings of real balances which may or may not reduce

saving out of real income depending on which assets are purchased as substitutes for money. If consumption goods are purchased, real saving will fall. At the same time, because the real value of saving is decreasing, the public may decide voluntarily to save less out of current income which could partially or fully offset the positive redistribution effects of inflation on saving.

In the private sector, whether there is redistribution between wages and profits depends exclusively on whether the rate of growth of real wages matches the rate of growth of productivity. If it does not there will be a redistribution of real income in favour of profits because some of the gains of labour productivity will be appropriated by the profit-earners. Given the rate of productivity growth, how much the saving ratio will rise for any given rate of inflation will depend on the precise relationship between the rate of change of wages and prices; by how much the propensity to save out of profits exceeds that out of wages, and on labour's initial share of income. As we have seen in Chapter 2, the relationship between the rate of change of wages and prices depends on two factors: the rate of autonomous wage increases and the wage–price coefficient. It is often asserted that redistribution within the private sector can only generate extra saving in the short run because inflation will ultimately become anticipated by workers who will bargain for wage increases in advance of price increases to ensure a growth of real wages at least equal to the rise in labour productivity. The value of the wage–price coefficient is ultimately an empirical question. Some evidence will be given later. It does seem from case studies in developed countries, however, that people's price expectations cannot be inferred from data on past price movements.[1] People disagree on their perceptions of past price changes. And what is more relevant, people do not necessarily project the recent past into the future. These findings of survey research on consumer reactions to inflation are consistent with the results of econometric research which show that the wage–price coefficient is typically less than unity in both the short and the long run. But as we have seen in Chapter 2, even a wage–price coefficient in excess of unity is not sufficient to guarantee that labour's share will not fall as a result of inflation.

How much aggregate saving increases as a result of inflation will depend on the combined extent of the redistribution effects in the two

[1] E. Mueller, 'Consumer Reactions to Inflation', *Quarterly Journal of Economics* (May 1959).

sectors if the effects are in the same direction, and on the balance of the two effects if the effects in the two sectors are in the opposite directions. In examining the empirical evidence of the relation between inflation and saving, as we shall do in the concluding chapter, it is impossible to distinguish between the effects in the two sectors unless the aggregate saving ratio of countries is disaggregated into government saving, corporate saving and personal saving. The two sectors can be modelled separately, however, and the general conditions stated under which forced saving is likely to be most successful. The impact of inflation will be more favourable: the more monetised the economy and the higher the money–income ratio, the higher is the government's propensity to save, the higher is the propensity to save out of profits, the lower is the rate of increase in money wage rates, and the less is voluntary saving discouraged.

Now let us consider in more detail the relation between inflation and saving, looking especially at the inflation rate implied to induce extra saving and growth of a specified amount. Then let us consider government revenue from an inflationary tax on money, and the inflation necessary to induce extra growth in a model of income redistribution to government.

A Two-Sector Model of the Effect on Saving of Income Redistribution between Wages and Profits

To isolate the effect of inflation on saving through income redistribution between wages and profits, the model to be developed assumes no money illusion in the goods market, no real balance effect in the consumption function, and that resources are fixed and fully employed so that the inflation rate is equal to the growth of money income and there can be no increase in the savings ratio as a result of the utilisation of under-utilised resources. The model is therefore worked out on the most unfavourable assumptions. Estimates of the extra inflation required to raise the savings ratio by a specified amount, based on the parameters of the model alone, will be overestimates.

It should be clear that in conditions of static real income, with no real balance effect, and ignoring the effects of a tax on money, the only way that inflation can raise the savings ratio is through redistribution of income between those with low propensities to save and

those with high propensities to save. This proposition can be illustrated as follows

Let $$dY = dS + dC \tag{6.1}$$

where dY is the change in money income (or prices)

dS is the change in saving

and dC is the change in consumption.

Assume that it is desired to raise the savings–investment ratio from its initial level a to a higher level x, and let c be the average propensity to consume and c' be the marginal propensity to consume (hence $a = 1 - c$). The change in income may therefore be written as

$$dY = Y(x - a) + dYx + dYc' \tag{6.2}[1]$$

$$\therefore dY = \frac{Y(x - a)}{1 - c' - x}$$

dY (or the change in the price level) only has a finite value if $c' + x < 1$. In conditions of full employment this condition is unlikely to hold unless changes in the distribution of income produce a fall in the average propensity to consume. This follows from the fact that since $a + c = 1$, and $x > a$, c' must be less than c if $c' + x$ is to be less than unity. In short, the marginal propensity to consume must be lower than the average propensity which, on the assumptions outlined at the outset, can only come about through a redistribution of income from low savers to high savers. That is, inflation cannot be successful in forcing saving in the absence of income redistribution. Below, a model is developed which allows for the redistribution of income between wage-earners and profit-earners.[2] The model is formulated

[1] The term dYx is the consequential change in spending to keep investment a constant proportion of income following the initial increase in investment $Y(x-a)$.

[2] The model was first presented in my paper 'Inflation and the Savings Ratio Across Countries', *Journal of Development Studies* (January 1974). In my book *Growth and Development* (Macmillan, 1972) I used Maynard's model of the efficiency of inflation to analyse the inflation–saving relation in a two sector model of wage-earners and profit-earners–see G. Maynard, *Economic Development and the Price Level* (London: Macmillan, 1962). On closer inspection of his model, however, it appears that a rise in the savings ratio can be financed by a finite amount of inflation even if the wage–price coefficient is unity and the propensities to consume of the two income recipients are the same. This cannot be right. I therefore prefer the model presented here.

in continuous time so that the time path of the savings ratio in relation to inflation can also be simulated if desired.

Assume two classes, workers and capitalists, and two factor returns, wages and profits. Saving is a function of income with no autonomous element, so that saving at time t may be written

$$S_t = W_o e^{wt} \cdot s_w + (Y_o e^{pt} - W_o e^{wt}) s_p \qquad (6.3)$$

where W_o is the initial wage bill

w is the rate of growth of the wage bill (= rate of growth of the wage rate)

s_w is the propensity to save out of wages

Y_o is the initial level of income

p is the rate of growth of money income (= rate of growth of the price level)

and s_p is the propensity to save out of profits.

Dividing equation (6.3) by $Y_o e^{pt}$, to obtain an expression for the savings ratio at time t, and rearranging, gives

$$\left(\frac{S}{Y}\right)_t = \frac{W_o}{Y_o} \cdot e^{wt-pt} \left(s_w - s_p\right) + s_p \qquad (6.4)$$

Let $w = a + \alpha p$, where a is the rate of autonomous wage growth and α is the wage–price coefficient. Equation (6.4) may then be written

$$\left(\frac{S}{Y}\right)_t = \frac{W_o}{Y_o} \cdot e^{p(\alpha-1)t+at} \left(s_w - s_p\right) + s_p \qquad (6.5)[1]$$

---

[1] In a growing economy, it is easily shown that the savings ratio is equal to

$$\left(\frac{S}{Y}\right)_t = \frac{W_o}{Y_o} \cdot e^{p(\alpha-1)t-rt+at} (s_w - s_p) + s_p$$

where r is the rate of growth of labour productivity. For any given rate of inflation, the higher the rate of productivity growth, the higher the savings ratio: $\partial(S/Y)_t/\partial r > 0$. This proposition was demonstrated indirectly earlier in Chapter 2 where it was shown that for any given growth of real wages, the higher the rate of productivity growth the higher the share of profits in income and the higher the savings ratio if $s_p > s_w$. On the other hand, it can be seen from the above equation that the higher the rate of productivity growth, the higher the rate of inflation necessary to achieve a given increase

Differentiating (6.5) with respect to p gives

$$\frac{\partial \left(\frac{S}{Y}\right)_t}{\partial p} = (\alpha - 1)t \frac{W_o}{Y_o} \cdot e^{p(\alpha-1)t+at} (s_w - s_p) \qquad (6.6)$$

The change in the savings ratio with respect to the rate of inflation depends on four factors: (1) the difference in the propensity to save out of wages and profits $(s_w - s_p)$; (2) the wage–price coefficient (α); (3) labour's initial share of income (W_o/Y_o); and (4) the rates of inflation and autonomous wage increase already prevailing (p and a). It is clear from equation (6.6) that if $\alpha = 1$, and/or $s_w = s_p$, there can be no redistribution effects on saving from generating extra inflation: $\partial(S/Y)_t/\partial p = 0$. If, however, $\alpha < 1$ and $s_p > s_w$, which is the normal case to consider, $\partial(S/Y)_t/\partial p > 0$. We also have $\partial^2(S/Y)_t/\partial p^2 < 0$, which means that the savings ratio rises with extra inflation but at a decreasing rate. The savings ratio cannot exceed 100 per cent! The relation is also time dependent in a rather complex way, depending on the values of the parameters of the model. To obtain a prediction of the coefficient relating the saving ratio to the inflation rate using time series or cross-section data, however, the time subscript is irrelevant; t assumes the value of unity. Given the values of the parameters for any sample we have from equation (6.6) a prediction about the coefficient linking changes in the savings ratio to changes in the inflation rate that comes about as a result of income redistribution. The reciprocal of the coefficient gives the increase in the rate of inflation required to raise the savings ratio by one percentage point. Some calculations are presented in Table 6.1 of the extra inflation required to raise the savings ratio by one percentage point using different values of the parameters W_o/Y_o, $(s_w - s_p)$, and α in equation (6.6). The dependence of $\partial(S/Y)/\partial p$ on p and a is ignored because for

---

in the savings ratio, i.e. the higher r, the lower $\partial(S/Y)_t/\partial p$. The rationalisation of this result is that the higher the rate of productivity growth the more labour's share is being reduced for any given growth of money wages; and the lower labour's share, the greater is the inflation that is necessary to re-distribute income to achieve a given increase in the savings ratio. Clearly, more extra saving can be obtained from a given increase in r than the same increase in p, but it is limits to raising r which constitute the development problem!

reasonable initial values of p and a the term $e^{p(\alpha - 1)t + at}$ is approximately unity.[1]

It can be seen from Table 6.1 that the calculations of the inflation rate required to raise the savings ratio solely through redistribution

TABLE 6.1

*Extra Inflation Necessary to Raise the Savings Ratio
by One Percentage Point*

Case 1 $W_0/Y_0 = 0.7$

α	-1.0	$(s_w - s_p)$ -0.5	-0.1
0·1	1·58	3·16	15·80
0·5	2·85	5·70	28·50
0·9	14·28	28·56	142·80
1·0	∞	∞	∞

Case 2 $W_0/Y_0 = 0.6$

α	-1.0	$(s_w - s_p)$ -0.5	-0.1
0·1	1·85	3·70	18·91
0·5	3·33	6·66	33·30
0·9	16·66	33·33	166·60
1·0	∞	∞	∞

Case 3 $W_0/Y_0 = 0.5$

α	-1.0	$(s_w - s_p)$ -0.5	-0.1
0·1	2·22	4·44	22·20
0·5	4·00	4·00	40·00
0·9	20·00	40·00	200·00
1·0	∞	∞	∞

between wages and profits within the private sector of the economy are extremely sensitive to the parameter values assumed in the model. On classical assumptions that $s_w = 0$ and $s_p = 1$ all the inflation

[1] The higher p, and the lower a, the more extra inflation necessary to increase the savings ratio by a given amount. If p is initially zero we can talk simply of the inflation rate to generate additional saving, as opposed to the *extra* inflation necessary.

rates, regardless of α and W_o/Y_o, are relatively mild, but the classical assumptions are a little unrealistic. Houthakker's long-run estimates of $s_w = 0.02$ and $s_p = 0.24$ (reported in Chapter 2), combined with $W_o/Y_o = 0.7$ and $\alpha = 0.5$, give an inflation rate of 13 per cent (starting from zero) to raise the savings ratio by one percentage point. A wage–price coefficient of 0.9 raises the required rate of inflation to 66 per cent. In Chapter 9 an attempt is made to estimate the co-efficient of the savings ratio on the inflation rate to see what inflation rate to raise the savings ratio is implied by the international cross-section evidence. On the surface, ignoring other mechanisms, the inflation required to have any noticeable impact on the warranted rate of growth looks fairly forbidding.

The Redistribution of Real Income to Government: Inflation as a Tax on Money

If a government wishes to devote more of a country's real resources to investment one of the ways it can do so is to invest itself on society's behalf, financing the investment by expanding the money supply. In conditions where capital is already fully employed, and where production techniques cannot be altered to absorb unemployed labour, monetary expansion will be inflationary. Inflation is the means by which the real resources are effectively transferred to government. Inflation imposes a tax on money holdings which consists of the reduction in the real purchasing power of money and the real resources that the holders of money must forgo to restore the real value of their money holdings. The base of the tax is the level of real cash balances (M/P), and the tax rate is the rate at which the real value of money is deteriorating, which is equal to the rate of inflation (dP/P). The real yield from the tax is the product of the tax base and the tax rate, i.e.

$$\frac{M}{P}\left(\frac{dP}{P}\right).$$

If the rate of inflation is equal to the rate of monetary expansion, the real tax yield R will equal the real value of the new money issued, i.e.

$$R = \frac{M}{P}\left(\frac{dM}{M}\right) = \frac{dM}{P}.$$

If the rate of inflation exceeds the rate of monetary expansion some of the potential yield will be lost due to a reduction in the base of the tax. If the base falls more than in proportion to the tax rate, the yield from the inflationary tax will decline.[1] As in standard tax theory, the yield from the inflation tax will be maximised when the elasticity of demand for real balances with respect to the rate of inflation is -1. The proof is as follows

$$\text{Let } \frac{M}{P} = f\left(\frac{dP}{P}\right) \tag{6.7}$$

where (M/P) is the demand for real money balances,
and (dP/P) is the rate of inflation

and
$$R = \left(\frac{dP}{P}\right) \cdot f\left(\frac{dP}{P}\right) \tag{6.8}$$

where R is the real tax yield.

Differentiating R with respect to the inflation rate and setting equal to zero gives

$$\frac{\partial R}{\partial(dP/P)} = \left(\frac{dP}{P}\right) \cdot f'\left(\frac{dP}{P}\right) + f\left(\frac{dP}{P}\right) = 0 \tag{6.9}$$

$$\therefore \left(\frac{dP}{P}\right) \cdot f'\left(\frac{dP}{P}\right) = -f\left(\frac{dP}{P}\right) \tag{6.10}$$

or
$$f'\left(\frac{dP}{P}\right) = \frac{-f(dP/P)}{(dP/P)} \tag{6.11}$$

The elasticity of demand for real balances with respect to inflation is

$$\varepsilon = \frac{d(M/P)}{d(dP/P)} \frac{(dP/P)}{(M/P)} \tag{6.12}$$

Now
$$f'\left(\frac{dP}{P}\right) = \frac{d(M/P)}{d(dP/P)} = \frac{-f(dP/P)}{(dP/P)} \tag{6.13}$$

Substituting (6.13) into (6.12) gives

$$\varepsilon = \frac{-f(dP/P)}{(dP/P)} \cdot \frac{(dP/P)}{(M/P)} = -1$$

[1] The evidence presented in Chapter 5 suggests that this is extremely unlikely.

The inflation rate which maximises the yield from the inflation tax can be calculated from equation (6·9).

Strictly speaking, the 'optimal' inflation rate obtained above only holds for a stationary economy. In a growing economy there is the additional yield to consider from the provision of the additional real balances that are demanded as income rises. The yield from the provision of additional cash balances for transactions purposes declines monotonically with the rate of inflation. It can be shown that when this consideration is taken into account, the rate of inflation that maximises the yield from the inflation tax will be lower than the unit elasticity rate in equation (6.9).[1]

The real yield from the inflationary tax available for investment as a percentage of national income, R_I/Y, will be the product of the money–income ratio $(M/P)/Y$, the rate of inflation (equal to the rate of increase in the money supply dM/M), and the proportion of the increase in the real money supply captured for financing development, $R_I/(dM/P)$, i.e.

$$\frac{R_I}{Y} = \frac{M}{PY} \cdot \frac{dM}{M} \cdot \frac{R_I}{dM/P} \qquad (6.14)$$

If the money–income ratio is, say, 0·4, and 50 per cent of the expansion of the money supply is captured for development purposes, then a 10 per cent expansion of the money supply would yield 2 per cent of the national income for the development programme. As we saw earlier the base for the inflationary tax is the money–income ratio. In practice, the base on which the inflationary tax can be levied in developing countries is quite small. The money–income ratio is typically less than 0·4. Clearly, the lower the ratio the more the inflation necessary to command a given percentage of the national income for development purposes. For simplicity we have also assumed that in the course of monetary expansion the money–income ratio remains stable. For reasons given earlier, however, inflation may lower it; thus, the tax would be partially avoided and the tax yield lowered. On the other hand, while inflation may reduce the desired money–income ratio, the monetisation and development of the economy will contribute to raising the ratio, so that on balance there

[1] See M. Friedman, 'Government Revenue from Inflation', *Journal of Political Economy* (July/August 1971). It can be seen from equation (6.9) that if the base of the inflation tax is lowered the rate of inflation which maximises the tax yield will also be lowered.

132 INFLATION, SAVING AND GROWTH

may be no change in the ratio as monetary expansion takes place. What happens to the ratio in conditions of a sustained policy of monetary expansion is ultimately an empirical question.

The proportion of national income that is captured for investment purposes by monetary expansion also depends on the proportion of the increase in the money supply that is used for investment purposes. Assuming that 100 per cent of the new money issued is used for investment, it can be seen from equation (6.14) that the real yield from the tax for investment purposes is simply equal to the real value of the new money issued, i.e.

$$R_I = (M/P).\ (dM/M) = dM/P$$

Non-Inflationary Finance of Investment

If the economy is growing, and the demand to hold money is rising, a portion of the expansion of the money supply will be non-inflationary so that a fraction of government investment may be financed without causing any increase in the general price level. This point was discussed briefly in Chapter 5. Now let us consider it in more detail. The extent of the non-inflationary finance of investment is easiest to calculate if it is assumed that the banks operate a 100 per cent reserve system. This simplification is permissible to illustrate the principle involved. The basis of the model is the familiar equation of exchange $M = K_d PY$, where M is the money supply ($=$ demand); K_d is the inverse of the income velocity of circulation, P is the average price level and Y is real income. Using lower-case letters to denote rates of growth of the variables we have

$$m = k_d + p + y \tag{6.15}$$

It is clear that the rate of non-inflationary monetary expansion is $k_d + y$. The question is what proportion of investment requirements to sustain a given rate of growth can be financed by non-inflationary monetary expansion?

The approximate increase in the amount of money demanded is equal to the product of the money stock and the rate of growth of the money stock which, assuming $p = 0$, gives

$$dM = M \cdot m = M(k_d + y) \tag{6.16}$$

$$\therefore \qquad \frac{dM}{Y} = \frac{M}{Y}(k_d + y) = K_d(k_d + y) \tag{6.17}$$

If y is the required growth rate and c_r is the required capital–output ratio, the investment ratio to achieve the growth rate is

$$\frac{I}{Y} = c_r y \tag{6.18}$$

Dividing (6.17) by (6.18) gives

$$\frac{dM}{I} = \frac{K_d(k_d + y)}{c_r y} \tag{6.19}$$

Equation (6.19) gives the proportion of total investment that can be financed by newly created money without leading to a rise in the price level. To give an example, let $K_d = 0 \cdot 3$; $k_d = 0 \cdot 04$; $y = 0 \cdot 03$ and $c_r = 3$. Therefore

$$\frac{dM}{I} = \frac{(0 \cdot 3)(0 \cdot 04 + 0 \cdot 03)}{3(0 \cdot 03)} = 0 \cdot 23$$

That is, 23 per cent of total investment can be financed without inflation. For any desired growth rate, the proportion of total investment that can be financed without inflation will be higher the faster the demand for money in relation to income is rising. The estimated figure of 23 per cent is high because of the unrealistic assumptions of the model, but the model illustrates well the potential for non-inflationary finance of development that results from the demand for money balances as the economy grows, and from the rise in the money–income ratio in the process of development.

The main reason for the apparently high capacity to finance investment by non-inflationary means is the assumption of a 100 per cent reserve system. With the more realistic assumption of a fractional reserve system, the public surrenders real resources to the government only to the extent of the increase in the demand for bank money, not that part of the additional money supply created by domestic banks. If a transactor receives a loan from a bank to make purchases, offering goods as collateral, real resources are not surrendered to anyone. Bhambri has developed and applied a model similar to the above which relaxes the assumption of a 100 per cent reserve system.[1] He

[1] R. S. Bhambri, 'Demand for Money and the Investible Surplus', *Nigerian Journal of Economic and Social Studies* (March 1968).

shows that with a fractional reserve system the amount of investment
that can be financed by non-inflationary means is

$$\frac{dM_G}{I} = \frac{K_d(k_d + y - a)}{A \cdot c_r \cdot y} \tag{6.20}$$

where M_G is the stock of 'government' money
A is the credit multiplier
and a is the rate of change of the credit multiplier.

Using the values $c_r = 3$; $y = 0.05$; $K_d = 0.1$; $k_d = 0.04$; $A = 1.6$,
and $a = 0.03$, Bhambri estimates for Nigeria that newly created
money should enable the government to finance approximately 2·5
per cent of total investment without inflation. If government investment is approximately 20 per cent of total investment, this means that
about 12 per cent of government investment can be financed by
monetary expansion without leading to a rise in the price level
(assuming the economy grows at 5 per cent per annum).

The analysis suggests, therefore, that the public's increased
demand for money in the development process can provide an
important flow of investment finance. The amount of total resources
released, however, is relatively small. If the increased demand for
money enables the government to finance approximately 2·5 per cent
of total investment without inflation, and total investment is 20 per
cent of income, the increased demand for money releases resources
for investment of $(0.2)(0.025) = 0.0050$, or one-half of one per cent
of national income. It should also be stressed that as developing
economies become fully monetised the extent of the surplus available
through an increase in the demand for money will decline over time.

Mundell's Model of Credit-Financed Growth[1]

An attempt has been made by Mundell to calculate the tax on money
(i.e. the inflation rate) implied by a government's attempt to raise the
growth rate by borrowing from the central bank for the finance of
new investment projects, assuming monetary expansion to be the
only source of growth. It is interesting to compare the results of
Mundell's model with the calculations made earlier of the rate of
inflation required to raise the savings ratio (and hence the growth

[1] R. Mundell, 'Growth, Stability and Inflationary Finance', *Journal of
Political Economy* (April 1965).

rate) through redistribution of income within the private sector, assuming this to be the only source of growth.

The basis of Mundell's model is the fundamental equation of exchange $MV = PY$, as before. Taking logarithms of the variables and differentiating with respect to time to give the growth rate of the variables we have

$$y = m + v - p \qquad (6.21)$$

where y is the growth rate of output
    m is the growth rate of the money supply
    v is the rate of change of income velocity
and p is the rate of change of the price level.

The equation for output may be written as

$$Y = \sigma K \qquad (6.22)$$

where σ is the productivity of capital

and K is capital.

Assuming σ is constant, and differentiating with respect to time, equation (6.22) may be written as

$$\frac{dY}{dt} = \sigma \frac{dK}{dt} \qquad (6.23)$$

Now suppose that all government investment is financed by borrowing from the central bank and that all other investment is ignored. The real value of government investment may be written as

$$\frac{G}{P} = \frac{1}{P} \cdot \frac{dR}{dt} = \frac{dK}{dt} \qquad (6.24)$$

where R is bank reserves

and G is government investment.

The relation between bank reserves and the money supply (M) is

$$R = rM \qquad (6.25)$$

where r is the fractional reserve ratio.

Differentiating (6.25) with respect to time gives

$$\frac{dR}{dt} = r \frac{dM}{dt} \qquad (6.26)$$

Substituting (6.26) into (6.24) gives

$$\frac{dK}{dt} = r\frac{1}{P}\left(\frac{dM}{dt}\right) \qquad (6.27)$$

and substituting (6.27) into (6.23) gives

$$\frac{dY}{dt} = r\sigma\frac{1}{P}\frac{dM}{dt} \qquad (6.28)$$

Dividing (6.28) by Y gives

$$\frac{1}{Y}\cdot\frac{dY}{dt} = r\sigma\frac{1}{PY}\cdot\frac{dM}{dt}$$

or

$$y = r\sigma(m)\frac{M}{PY} \qquad (6.29)$$

Equation (6.29) gives the relation between the rate of growth of output and the rate of growth of the money supply. If the income velocity of circulation of money is assumed to be constant then from (6.21) the rate of change of prices is equal to the rate of monetary expansion minus the growth of real output. Substituting equation (6.29) for y in equation (6.21) gives an expression for the rate of inflation of

$$p = m - r\sigma(m)\frac{M}{PY} = \left(1 - \frac{r\sigma}{V}\right)m$$

or

$$p = \left(\frac{V}{r\sigma} - 1\right)y \qquad (6.30)$$

Given values for r and σ, and assuming that V does not vary positively with inflation (which is probably not too unrealistic in the case of mild inflations but which puts inflationary finance in a more favourable light in the event of rapid inflation), the relation can be established between the inflation rate and the credit-financed growth rate. For example, suppose $V = 3$, $\sigma = 0.5$ (implying a capital–output ratio of 2) and $r = 0.3$, then from equation (6.30) we have $p = 19y$. That is, the inflation rate is 19 times the credit-financed growth rate. Therefore, to raise the growth rate by one percentage point would require a 19 per cent tax on money. If the productivity of capital is 0.5, extra saving of 2 per cent of national income would be required to raise the growth rate by one percentage point. Hence the inflation–

saving coefficient implied by the model is of the order of 9·5; that is, 9·5 per cent inflation is apparently required to raise the savings–investment ratio by one percentage point.

It is easy to see how inflation is generated in Mundell's model. The supply of money always exceeds the demand for money, with excess supply in the money market leading to excess demand in the goods market. The increase in the demand for money is $r\sigma/V$, where $r\sigma$ is the increase in output and $1/V$ is the desired ratio of money to income. The expenditure of r units of bank reserves on capital goods increases the supply of money by one unit. The supply of money always exceeds the demand (i.e. $r\sigma/V < 1$) because $V > 1$ and r and $\sigma < 1$.

Taking reasonable parameter values for our earlier model of income redistribution within the private sector, the rates of inflation implied to raise the savings ratio by one percentage point are not dissimilar in the two models despite the fact that the models are representations of two distinct processes.

There are a number of features of the present model that need further elaboration, however. Some features of the model exaggerate the inflationary repercussions of credit-financed growth while others underrate the likely inflationary impact. Let us consider the latter features first. First, the model ignores the effect of government investment on private investment. If extra government investment is not wholly at the expense of consumption, but partly at the expense of private investment, a given inflation rate will be accompanied by less growth; or, to put it another way, more inflation will be necessary to achieve a given increase in the growth rate. (As an offset to this, however, inflation may be expected to redistribute income from low savers to high savers in the manner described earlier in the chapter, thereby providing more resources for investment in the private sector. Moreover, the greater availability of credit through the banking system that credit expansion provides could stimulate borrowing from the banking system for investment purposes.)

A second factor which may lead to an underestimation of the inflationary repercussions of credit-financed growth is the assumption that the income velocity of circulation of money is constant and does not vary positively with the inflation rate; or, in other words, that the demand for money does not vary inversely with the rate of inflation. If this assumption is relaxed it can be seen from equation (6.30) that higher values of V as inflation accelerates will, in turn, involve higher inflation rates for any given growth rate. A positive

relation between the velocity of circulation of money and the rate of inflation is one of the dominant characteristics of hyperinflation. Real growth associated with hyperinflation is extremely unlikely. New government investment is likely to be at the expense of private investment as confidence in money wanes and the future becomes uncertain.

The effect of inflation on velocity is easily incorporated into the model. Assume that velocity is a linear function of the inflation rate

$$V = V_o + \beta_o(p) \tag{6.31}$$

Substituting (6.31) into (6.30) gives

$$p = \left(\frac{V_o + \beta_o(p)}{r\sigma} - 1\right) y$$

$$\therefore p = \left[\frac{(V_o/r\sigma) - 1}{1 - (\beta_o/r\sigma)y}\right] y \tag{6.32}$$

Inflation is no longer a linear function of the growth rate, y, as in equation (6.30). The inflation–growth coefficient increases with the growth rate. In short, there is a limit to which growth can be financed by borrowing from the central bank. The maximum growth rate is $y = r\sigma/\beta_o$. This is the value of y when the denominator of equation (6.32) is zero. If β_o is zero (i.e. velocity does not increase with inflation), the old result in equation (6.30) holds. But suppose $\beta_o = 10$, so that velocity will have doubled at around 30 per cent inflation. This gives an inflation rate of $(57y)/(3–200y)$. For a growth rate of one per cent ($y = 0\cdot01$), this gives an inflation rate of 57 per cent ($p = 0\cdot57$). The maximum growth rate possible (i.e. the point at which inflation becomes 'infinite') is $1\cdot5$ per cent.

Now let us discuss the features of Mundell's model which put credit-financed growth in an unfavourable light as measured by the inflation rate required to raise the growth rate by a given amount. These features relate first to the empirical questions of whether the values chosen for the parameters, r and σ, are not too low, and secondly to the economic context to which the model refers, particularly whether the economy is fully employed or under-employed and whether it is relatively open to trade or relatively closed.

The fractional reserve ratio, r, is used as the relation between bank reserves and the money supply, and was given a value of $0\cdot3$. Strictly

speaking, however, the ratio that should be employed is the percentage of money holdings that are backed by government securities which will be higher than the fractional reserve ratio – probably in the region of 0·5.[1] The reason why this is the more appropriate ratio to employ is that a proportion of the expansion of bank deposits will reflect the purchase of government securities, and to this extent the need for borrowing from the central bank for any given expenditure requirement is reduced. The ratio of total bank deposits held by the public which are backed by government securities is likely to be close to 50 per cent in developing countries, compared with a fractional reserve ratio of 30 per cent. From equation (6·30) it can be seen that the inflation–growth coefficient is quite sensitive to the value of r assumed in the model. Taking a value for r of 0·5 instead of 0·3 reduces the coefficient from 19 to 11, other things remaining the same (where r is the 'new' ratio referred to).

A second point concerns the productivity of capital, σ, which is the inverse of the capital–output ratio. The capital–output ratio is assumed constant, irrespective of the government investment undertaken and the change in factor combinations that government investment may bring about. The fact that investment goods may be imported is also ignored. In a developing economy with unemployed labour, especially in agriculture, and which trades with the outside world, there must be some scope for government investment, financed by credit expansion, to raise the overall productivity of capital. In countries where agriculture is primitive, where there are bottlenecks in supply, and where the basic infrastructure of the country is rudimentary, government investment of the 'right' type can raise directly the productivity of the total capital stock, and also indirectly by substituting more productive social investment for private investment, if private investment is forgone. If this were not the case one of the primary purposes of government investing on society's behalf would be defeated. In the agricultural sector, in particular, small doses of capital can reap substantial returns to output. Directly productive investment in seeds and fertilisers, and investment in agricultural inputs such as research stations, are some obvious examples of projects to which investment can be applied. Also road building, and the improvement of communications in general, expands the market for goods and the capacity to produce. If output was previously limited by demand, or if production is subject to increasing returns as

[1] I am indebted to my colleague, Charles Kennedy, for this point.

new land is brought under cultivation and overheads are spread wider, the productivity of both capital and labour will increase. These are externalities that can only be captured by government investment in the absence of subsidies to private producers (which themselves would have to be financed).

Capital goods purchased from abroad may be more productive than domestically produced capital goods. If the actual growth rate of an economy is constrained by the warranted rate, any increase in planned investment is likely to be financed partly domestically (by forced saving) and partly by resources from abroad (running a balance of payments deficit). Resources from abroad may not only raise the overall productivity of capital but may also raise the level of saving utilised if the savings ratio increases with income and if the use of domestic saving was previously hindered by deficiencies of domestically produced capital goods. A government-sponsored and financed investment programme can act as a catalyst for foreign resources and the productivity of capital raised as a result.

But these are more long-term considerations. In the short term the major impact of inflationary finance on the capital–output ratio must come from quick yielding projects, or if under-utilised resources in certain sectors of the economy can be brought into play. The short-term increases in supply that are generated will act as an offset to the excess supply of money in the money market. Thereafter, however, the major impact of inflationary finance must be on the structure of investment through a change in the composition of real assets and through a change in factor combinations (induced, perhaps, by a change in relative factor prices if production coefficients are flexible). A rise in the price of capital relative to labour should induce the substitution of labour for capital, reducing the capital–output ratio, other things remaining the same. Short of any natural tendency for the price of capital to rise relative to the price of labour, the government can deliberately induce substitution by policies of taxation and subsidies. Reducing the required capital–output ratio is another method, in addition to raising the savings ratio, of raising the warranted rate of growth. Let us now consider in more detail methods of reducing the capital–output ratio.

Reducing the Capital–Output Ratio

The rate of growth of the capital stock depends on both the investment ratio and the capital–output ratio

$$\frac{dK}{K} = \frac{I/Y}{K/Y} \qquad\qquad (6.33)$$

where the variables are defined as before.

For any given ratio of investment to income the rate of capital accumulation will be higher the lower the required capital–output ratio. If the rate of growth of effective labour in an economy exceeds the rate of growth of capital an alternative strategy to raising the savings (investment) ratio is to adopt policies to lower the required capital–output ratio. There are four broad policy choices: first, relatively short-run policies of investment in bottleneck sectors where capacity-creating effects are substantial; secondly, long-run policies to alter the structure of investment in favour of projects with high spillovers and external economies; thirdly, policies to raise the utilisation of existing capacity; lastly, policies to alter techniques of production in favour of more labour-intensive activities. Some of these policies to reduce capital requirements per unit of output may also raise the savings ratio at the same time, in particular if under-utilised resources are brought into use and the marginal propensity to consume is less than the average. Moreover, not all the policies necessarily entail inflation.

Investment, the Capital–Output Ratio and the Multiplier

Government investment financed by monetary expansion is normally regarded as inflationary because in the short run the investment adds more to the demand for goods than it does to the supply. This view, in turn, is based on the assumption that existing capital is working at full capacity and that it takes time for the new capacity to generate output. Those who dislike inflation, and who prefer price stability to employment creation, have argued in consequence that Keynesian-type policies of deficit finance are inappropriate in developing countries where unemployment if primarily structural and not the result of deficient demand. An early paper by Rao, typifying the anti-Keynesian school, argued:

> the secondary, tertiary and other increases in income, output and
> employment visualised by the multiplier principle do not follow,
> even though the marginal propensity to consume is very high. . . .
> This is because the consumption goods industries to which the

increased demand is directed are not in a position to expand output and offer effective additional employment.[1]

Proponents of this view have always been particularly worried about the inelasticity of food supply for the obvious reason that a large fraction of increases in money income is likely to be spent on food. Reddaway[2] has also questioned whether putting unlimited supplies of labour to work will have significant real income multiplier repercussions as Keynesian theory would suggest (although he does admit the possibility of output expansion from existing capital as a result of the under-utilisation of capital). Referring to road building with bare hands he says:

the secondary consequences of this, in the shape of additional demand for consumer goods, mainly serves to increase the demand for food; and the output of food is not limited by the lack of demand, even though there is plenty of unemployed labour attached to agriculture. The extra demand consequently falls on the balance of payments (and/or) it serves to drive up prices. There is growth in the national income corresponding with the work done on road building, but there is little or no multiplier effect.[3]

The question is whether the Keynesian multiplier is the relevant concept to consider, or, at least, whether it is the only factor that should be considered in discussing employment creation by inflationary finance. There would seem to be far too much emphasis on the demand-generating effects of investment and far too little attention paid to the capacity-creating effects. The Keynesian multiplier is static and ignores both the direct and indirect capacity-creating effects of the investment undertaken. The question of real income multiplier repercussions depends on what kind of investment is made and on how long its gestation period is likely to be, which the Keynesian multiplier is not concerned with. A carefully chosen and designed pattern of investment in bottleneck sectors of the economy containing unemployed labour can have real multiplier effects in a very short space of time. To analyse the relation between investment,

[1] V. K. R. V. Rao, 'Deficit Financing, Capital Formation and Price Behaviour in an Underdeveloped Economy', *Indian Economic Review* (February 1953).

[2] W. B. Reddaway, 'The Economics of Underdeveloped Countries', *Economic Journal* (March 1963).

[3] Ibid. pp. 8–9.

RAISING THE WARRANTED RATE OF GROWTH   143

inflation and the capital–output ratio in both the short- and the long-term, Domar-type theory,[1] which stresses the capacity-generating effects of investment, needs to be considered in conjunction with the stress on demand in Keynesian static multiplier theory.

In the agricultural sector of developing countries, and in the production of consumer goods in the industrial sector, there are abundant opportunities for investment which can yield outputs several times the money value of capital involved in a very short space of time. In agriculture the use of fertilisers and the provision of transport facilities, which open up previously uncultivatable areas or which extend markets, are prime examples. Credit expansion for these activities can soon generate output sufficient to absorb the demand-creating effects of the new money in circulation. Unemployed labour in rural areas needs very little money capital to work with. For example, in Ecuador it has been estimated that with between $10 and $15 of money capital per hectare, settlers can clear and cultivate land which yields output of between $88 and $145 for internal consumption and export, respectively.[2] This is a very high output–capital ratio and the gestation period is short. There are several examples throughout the world of successful employment-generating schemes, using very little capital per unit of labour and yielding high returns. Morocco has a programme (Promotion Nationale) to employ rural under-employed labour and to economise on scarce capital and skilled labour.[3] Under the scheme employment is provided on various types of projects in half-monthly units of twelve-day work periods. Workers are paid in cash and wheat. Since 1961 when the programme was started about 60,000 man-years of employment have been created per year, involving more than half a million men. Nearly one-half of the jobs have related to agricultural development, the rest to infrastructure improvements and to the provision of social overhead capital. Some of the investments, irrigation schemes in particular, have yielded quick and high returns, especially evaluating costs and returns at social prices as

[1] See Chapter 4.
[2] A. Bottomley, 'Keynesian Monetary Theory and the Developing Countries', *Indian Economic Journal* (April–June 1965).
[3] A brief description is provided in D. Jackson and H. A. Turner, 'How to Provide More Employment in a Labour Surplus Economy', *International Labour Review* (April 1973).

opposed to market prices. The projects not only have low capital–output ratios; they also redistribute income to rural areas and, through their employment-generating effects, discourage rural–urban migration. It is often forgotten that while employment-generating schemes may involve some inflation in developing economies, which redistributes income against wage-earners and the poor, it also tends to redistribute income back to these groups in the form of employment gains. The sum total of inflationary consequences from programmes of inflationary finance cannot be said unequivocally to worsen the income distribution.

Given the expansion of output possible, the inflationary consequences of expanding demand may, in practice, be minimal. The key variable is the output–capital ratio. Policies to raise the growth rate without inflation require a substantial rise in the output–capital ratio. The policies that have been described above are limited in the sense that the number of quick-yielding projects with high capacity generating effects is likely to be limited. But there is also the possibility of longer-term infrastructure projects to raise the output–capital ratio. What is required as part of a development programme is a judicious mix of long-term infrastructure projects and shorter-term high yielding projects. With such a programme it is possible for deficit financing to have dynamic real multiplier effects, with minimal inflation, which reduce the capital–output ratio and raise the rate of capital accumulation for a considerable period of time.

Changing the Structure of Investment

There are many projects in developing countries that would not be undertaken if decision-making was left entirely to private entrepreneurs. These are projects which have a high social return but which are perceived to have a low private return because not all the benefits of the investment can be captured by the private entrepreneur himself. Many projects with a high social return may also be risky for a private entrepreneur because of the long gestation period of the project and uncertainties concerning supplies of inputs and the demand for output. Governments can spread risks and hence insure against them more easily. One of the main arguments for government intervention in a market economy is to undertake investments which yield high social returns but which would not be profitable if operated by private individuals and which therefore

would not be undertaken. Government projects of this sort, financed by monetary expansion, may not only raise the investment ratio; they also possess the potential to reduce the overall capital–output ratio by altering the structure of investment in favour of higher yielding projects. Projects with high social returns replace projects with lower social returns. We are not talking here about 'prestige' projects which absorb large quantities of capital for very little output, but about basic infrastructure projects such as investments in the health and educational facilities of a developing nation, and research and development expenditure which improves the stock of knowledge, all of which possess the potential to yield returns to large sections of the community. One of the purposes of a government investment programme, financed by monetary expansion, must be to seek out projects where the returns to society are higher than the forgone private return on resources, assuming the resources would have been put to alternative investment uses. (Of course, if government investment is all at the expense of consumption the net output gain to society is bound to be positive as long as the social return is positive. It is probably more realistic, however, to think of government investment taking place partly at the expense of private investment as well.) There are many projects of the infrastructure type which offer scope for reducing the overall capital–output ratio in the early stages of development, and which can exert a permanent influence on the maximum sustainable rate of growth.

Under-utilisation of Capital

Although developing countries are characterised as working at full capacity – it would be perverse if they were not – full capacity working may be a false assumption in practice. Whether the sheer expansion of monetary demand could raise capacity utilisation and lower the capital–output ratio must depend on why capacity is under-utilised. The possibility of deficient effective demand in certain sectors of the economy cannot be dismissed entirely. In the short term, at least, Keynesian-type unemployment is a possibility for the obvious reasons that demand can shift from one commodity to another and that most developing economies are private enterprise economies where profits can vary and where there is minimal insulation from changes in exogenous demand especially in the demand for

exports. Shifts and variations in demand primarily require policies of demand management to counteract them.

It is unlikely, however, that a lack of effective demand is the primary reason for the under-utilisation of capital that has been observed in many developing countries. Pakistan may be taken as a case study where the facts have been well documented. In a study by Islam[1] it was found that only 17·3 per cent of firms manufacturing consumer goods were operating at more than 80 per cent capacity, and 62·1 per cent of the firms operated at less than 40 per cent capacity. In intermediate goods production only 4·3 per cent of firms operated at more than 80 per cent capacity, and 78·3 per cent at less than 40 per cent capacity. In the capital goods industries, 5·6 per cent were operating at more than 80 per cent capacity, and over one-half the firms at less than 40 per cent capacity. Winston reports similar findings.[2] In 1965–6 the average industrial firm operated its equipment only 33 per cent of the time, defining maximum capacity as a 20-hour working day. The interesting question is why should developing countries invest scarce resources in capital that remains idle for more than half the time? The reasons would seem to be a combination of social and economic factors.

One important consideration is exchange-rate policy, in particular the tendency for the currencies of developing countries to be over-valued, and for developing economies to operate import licensing systems which favour the purchase of new capital equipment irrespective of need. Over-valuation of the exchange rate means that there is an excess demand for foreign exchange with which to buy imports in relation to the supply of foreign exchange available from the sale of exports. In the absence of devaluation, foreign exchange has to be rationed by some licensing system. A licensing system which favours the purchase of capital equipment not only encourages the use of capital equipment without much regard to its productivity, but can also encourage inefficiency through the bribery and corruption it makes possible. For example, such a system can lead to over-invoicing by manufacturers who then use the excess foreign exchange they receive to make profits at black market rates. Schemes where foreign suppliers over-invoice domestic importers and bank

[1] N. Islam, 'Comparative Costs, Factor Proportions and Industrial Efficiency in Pakistan', *Pakistan Development Review* (Summer 1967).

[2] G. C. Winston, 'Capital Utilisation in Economic Development', *Economic Journal* (March 1971).

the excess foreign exchange, which is later sold to other importers at a substantial profit, are well entrenched in countries which operate import licensing systems. With this sort of possibility manufacturers attempt to expand capacity with as much foreign capital as possible. New capital equipment is preferred to the maintenance of existing equipment, and the purchase of investment goods is encouraged in excess of requirements by giving capital equipment foreign exchange priority. In short, currency over-valuation and import licensing systems can lead to manifold inefficiencies in the use of capital which lower its rate of utilisation. This is the predominant cause of under-utilised capacity in Pakistan.

If capital is purchased from abroad the reliance on spare parts from foreign suppliers can also be an important factor in determining utilisation if there are production bottlenecks in the supplying country, or if foreign exchange shortages in the home country prevent the purchase of the necessary parts.

Apart from the under-valuation of capital, capital utilisation seems to vary according to fairly well defined economic characteristics of industries, such as the volume of competing imports as a percentage of total supply, the volume of export sales as a proportion of total domestic production and the size of the market relative to the 'optimum' size of plant which has been adopted (which in many cases is the minimum size available).

There are also social factors to consider. In spite of considerable unemployment there is a general reluctance on the part of workers in developing countries to operate a shift system. If capital was worked more intensively in this way, a small dent could be made in the unemployment problem. Assuming that it was profitable for manufacturers to operate a shift system, there is little that can be done about this factor short of strict measures of industrial discipline. Attitudes of the work force can be expected to change with time if the experience of the developed countries can be taken as a guide. The development of shift working has been one of the forces making for the long-run downward trend in the incremental capital–output ratio in industrialised countries.

Poor operative efficiency may be another factor determining the low rate of utilisation.

Overall, the prevalent opinion seems to be that in many industries, improvements in operative efficiency, shift systems, and the productive technology (in the form of smaller sized plants using more

indigenous technology and less capital from abroad) offer considerable scope for the expansion of output from a given investment in capital.

The question of the appropriate technology is an important one. It is important not only as a determinant of capacity utilisation but for the bearing it has on the twin problems in developing countries of raising the growth rate on the one hand and the level of employment on the other; goals which may conflict. The factor proportions prevailing in the industrial sector of developing countries must bear a heavy responsibility for the high levels of unemployment and underemployment currently prevailing in the urban areas. At the same time it must be conceded that more labour-intensive technology may reduce the growth rate by reducing the productivity of labour. The escape from the dilemma involves seeking out projects and technologies which lower the capital intensity of production but which are high yielding so that the capital–output ratio does not rise. Developing economies must raise their expenditure on research and development to build up their own science and technology. Developed countries could help by devoting a higher percentage of development assistance to support science and technology in developing economies and by devoting a proportion of their own research and development expenditure to problems directly relevant to developing countries. The international community could also help by the establishment of an international technology transfer bank giving developing countries better access to appropriate technology than is currently available.

Altering the Capital Intensity of Techniques

More labour-intensive techniques will reduce the capital–output ratio if the productivity of labour is not impaired. What has been said so far, and the analysis to follow, assumes that there are projects in which governments can invest, which not only have high labour–capital ratios but also high output–labour ratios so that the output–capital ratio also rises, and the capital–output ratio falls.

The inverse relation between the labour–capital ratio and the capital–output ratio is easily demonstrated. We have

$$\frac{K}{Y} = \frac{K/L}{Y/L} \qquad (6.34)$$

A fall in K/L will lower K/Y, provided a lower K/L does not lower Y/L (the productivity of labour). A similar demonstration is possible using the Cobb–Douglas production function

$$Y = TL^\alpha K^{1-\alpha} \qquad (6.35)$$

Dividing both sides by K gives

$$\frac{Y}{K} = \frac{TL^\alpha}{K^\alpha} = T\left(\frac{L}{K}\right)^\alpha \qquad (6.36)$$

Assuming T and α are constant, a higher L/K raises Y/K and reduces K/Y.

For a profit-maximising enterprise the combination of factor inputs which maximises output for a given cost (or minimises cost for a given output) is given by the equality of the ratio of the marginal products of factors to the ratio of their prices. We can derive this result in the normal way by maximising the production function in equation (6.35) subject to the cost constraint $C = wL + rK$, where w is the wage rate and r is the rental on capital. The cost constraint is nothing more than the price line on an isoquant diagram which we have already come across in Chapter 4 (see Fig. 4.4). To maximise $Y = TL^\alpha K^{1-\alpha}$ subject to $C = wL + rK$, and to obtain the optimum factor combinations, we form the Langrangean function

$$Y = TL^\alpha K^{1-\alpha} + \lambda(C - wL - rK) \qquad (6.37)$$

where λ is the undetermined Langrangean multiplier, and partially differentiate Y with respect to L and K.

$$\frac{\partial Y}{\partial L} = T\alpha L^{\alpha-1} K^{1-\alpha} - \lambda w$$

and

$$\frac{\partial Y}{\partial K} = TL^\alpha(1 - \alpha)K^{-\alpha} - \lambda r$$

Setting the partial derivatives equal to zero, and taking their ratio, gives

$$\frac{K}{L} = \frac{w}{r}\left(\frac{1 - \alpha}{\alpha}\right) \qquad (6.38)$$

Given that $1 > \alpha > 0$, to cheapen the cost of labour (w) relative to capital (r) will result in a greater labour intensity of production. An

increase in the cost of capital relative to labour will produce the same result.

In an economy which is capital-scarce and labour-abundant it would seem sensible on the surface to use labour-intensive techniques of production. This would not only raise the growth of output for any given ratio of investment to income, but would also reduce unemployment. Yet we witness in the urban sectors of developing economies high unemployment and production technologies which are not dissimilar to those in highly developed industrial countries. The origin of the situation is no mystery. The technology has been imported voluntarily by the countries themselves in the desire to industrialise, and by foreign investors who have brought their technology with them. A characteristic of sophisticated modern technology is that it is not only capital-intensive but also has fairly rigid technological coefficients of production. In the case where technological coefficients are completely fixed it means that not only is the rate of growth of employment constrained by the rate of growth of the capital stock, and the rate of growth of output constrained by the slowest growing factor, but also that any change in relative factor prices is incapable of altering the combinations in which factors of production are employed. Once the technology is installed there is only one combination of factor inputs that it is profitable to employ. These propositions are illustrated in Fig. 6.1 below.

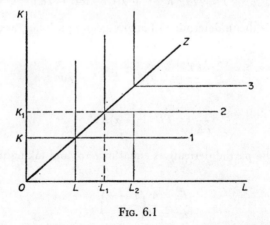

Fig. 6.1

Production functions 1, 2 and 3 represent fixed technological coefficients of production (sometimes called Leontief production

functions). Capital OK requires OL units of labour. Capital OK_1 requires OL_1 units of labour. If capital expands from OK to OK_1 and labour expands from OL to OL_2, L_1L_2 labour will be unemployed. To cheapen labour relative to capital cannot absorb the unemployed labour because the expansion path OZ represents the only profitable combination of factor inputs. Contrast this with the smooth neo-classical production functions shown in Fig. 6.2.

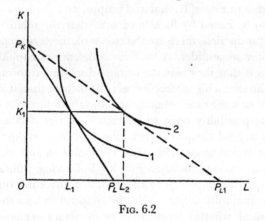

FIG. 6.2

Now, unemployed labour L_1L_2 can be absorbed by a fall in the relative price of labour from P_KP_L to P_KP_{L1}. At the same time the economy moves to a higher production function with the same stock of capital OK_1. The capital–labour ratio falls and the output–capital ratio rises. It will be remembered from Chapter 4 that it is through variations in the factor intensity of production that equilibrium growth is achieved in neo-classical growth theory.

Even if production relations were reasonably flexible in the urban industries of developing countries, it is by no means certain that the cost of labour would fall, and/or the cost of capital rise, sufficiently for the unemployed to be absorbed. Indeed, one of the continuing causes of unemployment may be that wages in the urban sector have been allowed to rise despite unemployment, and that the cost of capital is subsidised. Neither of these factors has been conducive, to say the least, to the employment of more labour with existing techniques or to research and investment in more labour-intensive technology in the first place. If anything, there has been a continuing bias towards labour-saving technology as in the developed countries. How much of the growth of unemployment in recent years has been due to rising

wages, how much to labour saving technical progress and how much to fixed technical coefficients of production is impossible to say. All three factors probably bear some responsibility for the situation that now exists. All that can be said with some confidence is that an attack on all three fronts should prove to be beneficial, if at the same time rural–urban migration can be curbed by policies of employment promotion in the agricultural sector.

If the growth rate of capital and output, and the level of employment, is to be raised by fiscal means to alter the relative prices of factors of production, there are the effects on the savings potential of the economy to consider. A traditional defence of capital-intensive techniques is that they bias the income distribution towards profit-earners who save a higher fraction of their income than workers. The use of shadow wage rates to encourage the labour intensity of production is one possibility open to governments, but if labour is then employed beyond the point where the marginal product of labour equals the actual wage paid, extra consumption will exceed extra production, reducing the aggregate level of saving. Subsidies could be paid to private employers to maintain their investible surplus. The effect on community saving would then depend on how the subsidies were financed, whether by taxation or monetary expansion.

The clash between lowering the capital–output ratio and maintaining the savings ratio, which arises because of the implications for saving of different technological choices, is illustrated in Fig. 6.3, which depicts the relation between technology and production in the industrial sector.

Assume that the wage is given in the industrial sector so that the wage bill, OW, rises linearly with the amount of labour employed. Further assume that all wages are consumed so that the line OW also gives the level of consumption for any level of employment. With a fixed amount of capital, OK, the employment of labour, OR, maximises the level of saving where a tangent to the output curve is parallel to the wage bill (consumption) curve at S. A more labour-intensive technology than that given by the capital–labour ratio, OK/OR, would increase employment (and also output up to the employment level OT), but would reduce the level of saving. To prevent the savings ratio from falling would require a shift in the production function to Y_I giving a level of output TX at the level of employment OT. The flatter the wage bill (consumption) curve the less the conflict between a more labour-intensive technology and the level of saving. If the

market wage was zero, savings and the output–capital ratio could apparently be maximised simultaneously.

One way to increase the employment of labour beyond OR is to reduce the wage below the market wage by granting wage subsidies to employers. With a 100 per cent subsidy employers could afford to employ labour up to the point OT. Community saving at employment

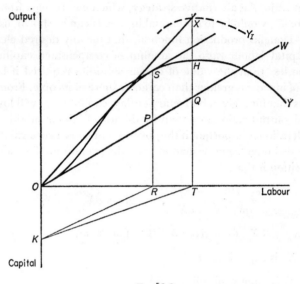

FIG. 6.3

level OT would still be lower, however, than with the more capital-intensive technology. The investible surplus in the industrial sector is now HT but workers still receive the same market wage which they consume, leaving a level of saving equal to HQ. What ultimately happens to saving with the new factor proportions depends on how the subsidy is financed. If the subsidy is financed by taxation, and taxes are met by reducing consumption, saving would increase to HT. If taxes are partly met out of saving, aggregate saving will increase but not to the level HT. Presumably a tax system could be designed which maintained the old level of saving, SP, if this was thought 'optimal' in some sense, having regard to the balance between consumption and investment (or consumption today and consumption tomorrow).

An alternative to financing the subsidies by taxation would be to finance them by monetary expansion. Swingeing taxation is avoided, real saving is induced by the inflation it brings, but inflation will be moderate because increases in output will accompany increases in monetary demand.

So far attention has been concentrated on reducing the price of labour to reduce the capital intensity of production and the capital–output ratio. An alternative strategy, which can be seen from equation (6.38), would be to tax capital inputs. It can be shown, using the Cobb–Douglas production function, that for any desired change in the capital–labour ratio the amount of compensated capital taxes will be less than the value of labour subsidies required if labour's share of income is greater than capital's share of income. From this it follows that for a given budgetary outlay, capital taxes will lower the capital–output ratio more than by the use of labour subsidies. This consideration is important if the government faces a constraint on the size of its budget. Let us demonstrate the proposition formally. The proposition is that

$$\frac{\partial(K/L)}{\partial X_K} > \frac{\partial(K/L)}{\partial X_L}, \qquad \text{given } \partial X_K = \partial X_L$$

and $\partial X_K < \partial X_L$, for a given $\partial(K/L)$, if $w_L > w_K$,

where X_K is capital taxes

X_L is labour subsidies

w_L is labour's share of income $= wL/Y$

and w_K is capital's share of income $= rK/Y$

The proof is as follows:[1]

$$\frac{\partial(K/L)}{\partial X_K} = \frac{\partial(K/L)}{\partial r} \cdot \frac{\partial r}{\partial X_K} \qquad (6.39)$$

and
$$\frac{\partial(K/L)}{\partial X_L} = \frac{\partial(K/L)}{\partial w} \cdot \frac{\partial w}{\partial X_L} \qquad (6.40)$$

---

[1] I am grateful to my colleague Mr R. Dixon for assistance. For an alternative proof see A. T. Peacock and G. K. Shaw, 'Fiscal Measures to Improve Employment in Developing Countries: A Technical Note', *Public Finance*, vol. 26, no. 3 (1971).

Now $\dfrac{K}{L} = \dfrac{w \cdot w_K}{r \cdot w_L}$, therefore

$$\frac{\partial(K/L)}{\partial r} = \frac{w \cdot w_K}{r^2 w_L} \qquad (6.41)$$

and

$$\frac{\partial(K/L)}{\partial w} = \frac{w_K}{r w_L}. \qquad (6.42)$$

Let $dX_K = dR$ be the change in profits

$dX_L = dW$ be the change in the wage bill

$$r = \frac{R}{K}$$

and $\quad w = \dfrac{W}{L}.$

Therefore

$$\frac{\partial r}{\partial R} = \frac{\partial r}{\partial X_K} = \frac{1}{K} \qquad (6.43)$$

and

$$\frac{\partial w}{\partial W} = \frac{\partial w}{\partial X_L} = \frac{1}{L} \qquad (6.44)$$

Substituting (6.43) and (6.41) into (6.39), and (6.44) and (6.42) into (6.40) gives

$$\frac{\partial(K/L)}{\partial X_K} = \frac{w \cdot w_K}{r^2 w_L} \cdot \frac{1}{K} \qquad (6.45)$$

and

$$\frac{\partial(K/L)}{\partial X_L} = \frac{w_K}{r \cdot w_L} \cdot \frac{1}{L} \qquad (6.46)$$

Dividing (6.45) by (6.46) gives

$$\frac{\dfrac{\partial(K/L)}{\partial X_K}}{\dfrac{\partial(K/L)}{\partial X_L}} = \frac{\dfrac{w \cdot w_K}{r^2 \cdot w_L \cdot K}}{\dfrac{w_K}{r \cdot w_L \cdot L}} = \frac{wL}{rK} = \frac{w_L}{w_K} \qquad (6.47)$$

Hence, the proposition is proved. If $w_L > w_K$, then for an equal change in capital taxes and labour subsidies, capital taxes save more capital. Secondly, for a given change in K/L, the change in labour subsidies must be greater than the change in capital taxes. The intuitive explanation for the result can be seen if we consider the ratio of

factor shares wL/rK. If $wL > rK$ the same subsidy to labour as a tax on capital means a smaller proportional change in wages than in profits. If relative shares are to remain the same, which is the Cobb–Douglas assumption, a given proportional change in w/r due to labour subsidies must mean a lesser rise in the L/K ratio than a change in w/r due to capital taxes. From which it follows that for a given change in the L/K ratio the value of the subsidy to labour must be greater than taxes on capital.

Capital taxes would seem to have not only theoretical advantages but also practical advantages as well. Compared with labour subsidies, they may be administratively easier to operate, especially in developing countries where a large proportion of capital inputs are imports. This advantage of capital taxes has been especially stressed by Peacock and Shaw.[1] All that would be required would be the extension of the system of import levies which is used to tax consumer imports. The effects of a capital tax would also be much more pervasive than labour subsidies in that whereas the effects of selective labour subsidies would be confined to particular sectors of the economy in which they applied, a tax on (say) capital imports would influence the prices of existing capital assets including capital goods domestically produced. Thus, substitution of labour for capital would be encouraged across a wide range of activities where production techniques were flexible.

Care would have to be taken with labour subsidies in the urban areas for fear of encouraging excessive in-migration. It seems more desirable to tax capital, the effect of which is all-pervasive, and to promote labour-using activities in the rural areas of the type already discussed earlier in the chapter.

There is also the point that labour subsidies should ideally be applied only to marginal workers. Subsidies to employ workers who would be employed anyway are wasteful. In practice, however, the administrative difficulties of confining subsidies to the employment of marginal workers would be insurmountable. This consideration gives added weight to the case for capital taxes.

Empirical Evidence on the Capital–Output Ratio

Despite the relative abundance of labour in developing economies there is not much evidence that in the industrial sector of developing

[1] Ibid.

economies the capital–output ratio is any lower than in the same industries in developed countries. In an early study, Bhatt made comparisons in twenty-three industries between the United States, Australia, Canada, New Zealand, South Africa, Mexico, Peru and India.[1] The results were very mixed but there was no consistent tendency for the capital–output ratio in a given industry in developing countries to be lower than in the same industry in developed countries. On the contrary, in over one-half of the twenty-three industries at least one developing country had a higher capital–output ratio than one of the developed countries. Bhatt suggested as an explanation that the ratio may be biased downwards in the developed countries due to higher depreciation rates, and biased upwards in the developing countries because of the under-utilisation of capacity, but he found no firm evidence for either of these hypotheses.

An alternative hypothesis is that wage costs per unit of output in an industry do not differ significantly between countries because high wages are associated with high productivity and low wages with low productivity. Wage costs per unit of output (W/O) can be expressed as the ratio of wage costs per unit of labour (W/L) and output per unit of labour (O/L), i.e.

$$\frac{W}{O} = \frac{W/L}{O/L}$$

Wages per man divided by the productivity of labour is sometimes called the efficiency wage. Even if the wage rate $(W/L = w)$ is lower in developing countries because of labour abundance (which it undoubtedly is), wage costs per unit of output may nonetheless be high if the productivity of labour (O/L) is low. The consideration of the efficiency wage is often advanced as an explanation of why developing countries apparently do not export goods which are relatively labour intensive as factor endowment theories of trade predict. A high efficiency wage is an equally plausible explanation of why the capital–output ratio is as high in developing countries as it is in developed countries.

If low operative efficiency is the primary cause of the relative capital intensity of techniques in developing countries the remedy is

---

[1] V. V. Bhatt, 'Capital–Output Ratios of Certain Industries: A Comparative Study of Certain Countries', *Review of Economics and Statistics* (August 1954).

plain. There must be more investment resources devoted to improving the skills, education and health of the work force. If wage increases match productivity increases there will be little incentive for the capital–labour ratio to change, but a rise in the productivity of labour at a given capital–labour ratio is a sufficient condition for the capital–output ratio to fall (see equation 6.34).

A final question concerns the relation between inflation and the capital–output ratio. It is well documented that the actual capital–output ratio and the growth rate are inversely related in the short term for cyclical reasons associated with variations in the pressure of demand and the degree of capacity utilisation. What would be useful and interesting would be evidence of a long-run inverse relation brought about by a sustained increase in the pressure of demand. It was argued earlier that there are a number of ways in which the governments of developing countries can increase the long-run sustainable rate of growth of the economy by inflationary means, raising the savings ratio and reducing the required capital–output ratio. On the other hand, it is sometimes contended that inflation diverts investment resources into assets which have low yields in terms of real output; that it diverts resources into speculative assets such as inventories, foreign currency and precious metals. Clearly, a lot depends on the degree of inflation under consideration. If the rate of inflation is high it may well be that the productivity gains secured by government investment are offset by production losses from a switch of assets within the private sector. This is a matter of empirical enquiry. One of the few studies attempted is by Shaalan who examines the relationship between incremental output–capital ratios and inflation to see whether the productivity of capital tends to be greater or less in periods of inflation, which could reflect the type of investment undertaken in periods of inflation.[1] In Argentina and Chile, the two countries examined, the evidence suggests that periods of sharply rising prices were associated with relatively low average ratios of marginal output to capital, whereas the opposite was true in periods when inflation was more moderate. Not too much should be read into this limited evidence however. The inflation rates of Argentina and Chile have hardly been typical of the developing countries in general. Furthermore, the relation between inflation and the capital–output ratio is an extremely complex one, and cannot be assumed to

[1] A. S. Shaalan, 'The Impact of Inflation on the Composition of Private Domestic Investment', *I.M.F. Staff Papers* (July 1962).

reflect only the pattern of investment being undertaken in the economy at the time. The marginal output–capital ratio may be low because of production bottlenecks in certain sectors, which accounts for the associated inflation. Also, in inflationary periods there may be a tendency for techniques to become more capital intensive, especially if wages are rising rapidly. Shaalan's study picks up primarily short-term influences, from which it is impossible to infer the long-run relation between the overall productivity of investment and government investment financed by inflationary means.

7

Per Capita Income, the Growth of Income and the Savings Ratio

If the growth rate, and the level of per capita income, can be raised by government policies which induce capital formation and lower the capital–output ratio, the domestic savings ratio may rise independently of the inflation rate because of the dependence of the savings ratio on the level of per capita income and the growth of income itself. The time series and cross-section evidence is overwhelming that the savings ratio is positively related both to the level of per capita income as a measure of living standards and also to the growth of income.[1] Economic theory predicts a positive relationship. The interdependence between savings, growth and per capita income presents statistical identification difficulties in the estimation of the precise relationships, but the fact that there is mutual dependence suggests that development via capital formation is a cumulative process which, if given a push, can gather its own momentum.

[1] Saving in most countries is defined as the difference between investment and foreign capital inflows. It should be pointed out from the outset that part of the reason for the strong positive relation between the savings ratio and the level of per capita income may be the result of the fact that as development proceeds investment expenditure is more faithfully and accurately recorded. In the traditional agricultural sector of developing countries it is often difficult to separate consumption and investment decisions and a large part of investment may go unrecorded. Moreover, the large discrepancies in recorded savings ratios between rich and poor countries should not be taken as indicative of such large discrepancies in levels of investment. A lot of consumption in developing economies represents forms of investment.

Per Capita Income and the Savings Ratio

Let us call the relation between the savings ratio and per capita income the Keynesian income hypothesis. Keynes revolutionised macro-economic theory by relating aggregate saving (S) to aggregate income (Y). Specifically, Keynes seemed to be hypothesising a savings function of the form $S = f(Y)$, where $f' > 0$, and $f'' > 0$, such that the savings ratio would rise with the level of income. The hypothesis of the consumption–income ratio falling and the savings ratio rising with the level of income can also be represented by a linear savings function with a negative intercept (shown in Fig. 7.1), which is frequently found when cross-section studies of saving in relation to income are undertaken.[1]

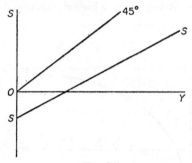

Fig. 7.1

The saving function, SS, drawn in relation to the 45° line shows saving growing as a proportion of income. In equation form

$$S = -\alpha_0 + \beta_0(Y) \tag{7.1}$$

Dividing through by the population level (N) gives

$$\frac{S}{N} = -\alpha_1 + \beta_1 \left(\frac{Y}{N}\right) \tag{7.2}$$

where S/N is per capita saving
and Y/N is per capita income

---

[1] It is nonsense to suppose that the 'long-run' savings function is linear, emanating from the origin, as some textbooks would have us believe. Britain was not saving 20 per cent of its gross national product in the Stone Age, and Japan was not saving 40 per cent of its national income forty years ago. The savings ratio rises with the level of development and per capita income through time, levelling off in maturity, as the empirical evidence to follow shows.

From equation (7.2) an expression can be obtained relating the savings *ratio* to per capita income by multiplying equation (7.2) by N and dividing by Y giving

$$\frac{S}{Y} = -\alpha_1 \frac{N}{Y} + \beta_1$$

$$\therefore \frac{S}{Y} = \beta_1 - \alpha_1 \left(\frac{Y}{N}\right)^{-1} \tag{7.3}$$

The Keynesian absolute income hypothesis predicts, therefore, that the savings ratio will rise with the level of development as measured by per capita income, but at a decreasing rate. As $Y/N \to \infty$, $S/Y \to \beta_1$. β_1 is the asymptote to which the savings ratio will tend, as illustrated in Fig. 7.2 below.

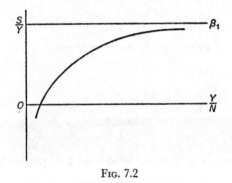

FIG. 7.2

A number of studies have fitted equation (7.2) to cross-section data for different samples of countries and found a significant non-proportional relation. For example, Leff has fitted the function to data in logarithmic form for samples of developed and developing economies and finds that the elasticity of savings per capita with respect to income per capita exceeds unity in both cases.[1] Houthakker has regressed the log of domestic consumption per capita on the log of income per capita for thirty-four countries, and finds an elasticity of less than unity, indicating the consumption ratio to fall (and the

[1] N. Leff, 'Dependency Rates and Savings Rates', *American Economic Review* (December 1969).

savings ratio to rise) with the level of per capita income.[1] Williamson,[2] using pooled time series data for a sample of Asian countries, estimates the equation (standard errors in brackets)

$$\frac{S}{N} = \underset{(1\cdot31)}{-9\cdot45} + \underset{(0\cdot010)}{0\cdot203} \left(\frac{Y}{N}\right) \qquad (r^2 = 0\cdot829)$$

The significant negative intercept term implies that the average propensity to save rises with the level of per capita income.

When equation (7.3) is fitted directly to cross-section data the positive dependence of the savings ratio on per capita income is also very apparent. Taking cross-section data for sixty-three countries over the period 1958–68 (see Appendix 1)[3] gave the following estimated relation (standard errors in brackets)

$$\frac{S}{Y} = 20\cdot848 - \underset{(155\cdot156)}{993\cdot393} \left(\frac{Y}{N}\right)^{-1} \qquad (r^2 = 0\cdot402)$$

The correlation coefficient is high for cross-section analysis, and is statistically significant at the 0·95 confidence level. The same function fitted to separate samples of developing and developed countries approximated the data less well, for the good reason that the two groups of countries relate essentially to two fairly distinct portions of the total function in Fig. 7.2. Within the group of developing countries the scatter relation looks virtually linear; and a linear function gives the best approximation to the data. In the group of developed countries the relation does not differ significantly from zero. Apparently, the savings ratio does level off when countries reach a certain stage of development, which would justify the notion of a linear savings function emanating from the origin in Fig. 7.1. In the developing economies, however, there is a strong tendency for the savings ratio to rise in response to a rise in the level of per capita income.

[1] The estimated equation is

$$\log C/N = \underset{(0\cdot017)}{-0\cdot03 + 0\cdot948} (\log Y/N).$$

See H. S. Houthakker, 'On Some Determinants of Saving in the Developed and Underdeveloped Countries' in *Problems of Economic Development*, ed. E. A. G. Robinson (London: Macmillan, 1965).

[2] J. G. Williamson, 'Personal Saving in Developing Nations, An Intertemporal Cross Section from Asia', *Economic Record* (June 1968).

[3] Puerto Rico, Vietnam, Zambia, Israel and Japan were excluded from the sample.

In addition to fitting a hyperbola (equation 7.3) to the international cross-section data, other functional forms were also tried, including an exponential and a parabola. In our sample of sixty-three developing and developed economies, the parabola gave the best statistical approximation, measured by the proportion of the variance in S/Y explained; in fact, the parabola explains a higher proportion of the variance than the hyperbola already reported. The fitted parabola was estimated as (standard errors in brackets)

$$\frac{S}{Y} = 10{\cdot}675 + \underset{(0{\cdot}0017)}{0{\cdot}0149} \left(\frac{Y}{N}\right) - \underset{(0{\cdot}0000006)}{0{\cdot}0000038} \left(\frac{Y}{N}\right)^2 \qquad (r^2 = 0{\cdot}622)$$

The savings ratio reaches a maximum of 25 per cent at approximately $2000 per capita income.

A similar result has been obtained by Sommers and Suits using the investment ratio as the dependent variable.[1] Taking a sample of 100 countries, they found the relation between the investment ratio and per capita income parabolic with a negative quadratic term

$$\frac{I}{Y} = 14{\cdot}93 + \underset{(0{\cdot}0018)}{0{\cdot}0105} \left(\frac{Y}{N}\right) - \underset{(0{\cdot}000000058)}{0{\cdot}00000242} \left(\frac{Y}{N}\right)^2 \qquad (r^2 = 0{\cdot}40)$$

In this model the investment ratio reaches a maximum of 26·4 per cent at a per capita income level of $2200 (at 1966 prices).

If this functional form is accepted as an approximation to reality, and the results of cross-section analysis are taken as a reliable guide to individual country behaviour, it implies, of course, that the savings–investment ratio will level off and eventually fall at high levels of per capita income, lending support to the view sometimes expressed that growth in mature developed economies will ultimately decelerate as a result of declining rates of capital accumulation. In fact, the Sommers' and Suits' equation is part of a three equation model of economic growth which, not surprisingly, on simulation, predicts a steady state. The prediction hinges crucially on the negative quadratic term in the investment ratio function. If the investment ratio does eventually fall to zero then, of course, growth will be impossible. The possibility of eventual stagnation for mature developed economies need not detain us here, however. For one thing there are only

[1] P. M. Sommers and D. B. Suits, 'A Cross Section Model of Economic Growth', *Review of Economics and Statistics* (May 1971). The investment ratio differs from the domestic savings ratio to the extent of the deficit on the balance of payments (see Chapter 8).

two countries in our sample that have experienced per capita incomes in excess of $2000 per annum, and only eight countries in the Sommers' and Suits' sample that have experienced per capita incomes in excess of $2200 per annum. To draw conclusions about the behaviour of saving and investment in highly developed countries more countries are needed in the high per capita income range, and the cross-section results need to be supported by time series evidence. But in any case, we are more concerned here with the broad mass of countries in the lower and middle part of the income range where the evidence is that the savings ratio will rise as per capita income increases which, in turn, will raise the growth rate in the growth framework we have outlined.

The reasons why the savings ratio should rise as per capita income increases are not clear cut. It is as if saving is a luxury good in the early stages of development, which then loses its appeal. It is too glib to say that the marginal propensity to save exceeds the average propensity to save; although clearly it must do for the savings ratio to rise. A number of factors no doubt play a contributory role. One factor, already mentioned in discussing the ability to expand the money supply without inflation, is the growth of the money economy. As money replaces barter for transactions, the public wish to hold a higher proportion of their income in the form of money which they can only do by giving up command over real resources. This hypothesis is supported by what we know about the income elasticity of demand for money in developing economies. It tends to be greater than unity (see Chapter 5). As an economy becomes fully monetised, however, the demand for money will tend to grow in proportion to income leaving the savings ratio unchanged.

A second possible factor is that population growth decreases with increases in the level of per capita income so that population growth absorbs household saving to a lesser and lesser extent. In the early stages of development the effect of population growth is to cause the marginal product of labour to fall below the level of average consumption cutting per capita saving in relation to income. The deceleration of population growth in the later stages of development eases the problem so that the savings ratio and the level of per capita income appear positively correlated. Faith in this explanation must depend partly on the existence of a negative relation between the level of per capita income and the rate of population growth.

Another plausible hypothesis is that as development proceeds, the

income distribution, both personal and functional, grows more unequal but at a decreasing rate, and ultimately becomes more egalitarian. If higher income groups have higher propensities to save than lower income groups, and profit-earners have a higher propensity to save than wage-earners, the savings ratio will be positively related to the degree of inequality in the income distribution (the personal income distribution) and to the share of profits in total income (the functional income distribution). The transformation of economies from a primitive subsistence state into highly industrialised societies is bound to be accompanied in the early stages by widening disparities in the personal distribution of income and a rise in the share of profits in total income. Some men are more industrious than others, and more adept at accumulating wealth than others. Without confiscatory taxation, income inequality is bound to grow with industrialisation because of the inequality of wealth holding that industrialisation produces. Profits, too, are a feature of capitalist industrialisation, which will increase in the development process as a proportion of income if the capitalistic sector grows in relative importance in the total economy, and if profits as a proportion of industrial output rise because labour is available to industry at a constant real wage.

The hypothesis that inequality in the size distribution of income increases in the early stages of development and then declines is borne out by the international time series and cross-section evidence. The work of Kuznets[1] shows clearly that in many developed countries the extent of inequality has decreased in the later stages of industrialisation, and that the degree of inequality in developing countries is greater than in the present developed countries – largely due to a heavy concentration of income among the top 5 to 10 per cent of income recipients. The work of Kravis[2] also shows that the degree of inequality tends to be negatively related to the level of per capita income but not in a simple (linear) way. Inequality first increases and then declines. Now we have the wealth of data assembled by Adelman

[1] S. Kuznets, 'Economic Growth and Income Inequality', *American Economic Review* (March 1955); and 'Quantitative Aspects of the Economic Growth of Nations: Distribution of Income by Size', *Economic Development and Cultural Change*, Part II (January 1963). See also his *Economic Growth and Structure* (Heinemann, 1966) and *Modern Economic Growth* (Yale University Press, 1966).

[2] I. B. Kravis, 'International Differences in the Distribution of Income', *Review of Economics and Statistics* (November 1960).

and Morris to draw on.[1] Table 7.1, which is based on the Adelman and Morris data, shows the size distribution of income for fifty-six countries. The table also shows two measures of income concentration calculated from these figures: the Gini ratio[2] and the maximum equalisation percentage which indicates what percentage of total income would have to be shifted between the quintiles of income recipients in order to achieve an equal distribution of income. The data shows fairly conclusively that inequality increases up to a certain stage of development and then declines. In the sample of countries in Table 7.1, income inequality appears to reach a maximum in countries with per capita incomes of around $300. The average Gini coefficient for forty-three developing countries is 0·467, compared with 0·392 for thirteen developed countries. The maximum equalisation percentage is 35·8 for the developing countries compared with 28·4 for the developed countries. The greater degree of income inequality in the developing countries appears largely due to the

[1] I. Adelman and C. T. Morris, 'An Anatomy of Income Distribution Patterns in Developing Countries', *I.M.F. Development Digest* (October 1971).

[2] The Gini coefficient of concentration varies from 0 to 1 and measures the area between the curve relating the percentage share of total income to the percentage share of total population (the Lorenz curve) and a 45° line showing complete equality in the income distribution. If, for example, we were to draw a Lorenz curve for the group average of countries with per capita incomes below $100 in Table 7.1, it would look something like this:

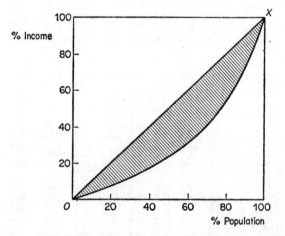

The ratio of the shaded area to the area enclosed by the 45° line, *OX*, is 0·419 (the Gini coefficient).

TABLE 7.1

Size Distribution of Personal Income before Tax in Fifty-six Countries: Income Shares received by Quintiles of Recipients in the Neighbourhood of 1965

Country and level of G.D.P. per head	Percentiles of recipients						Gini ratio	Maximum equalisation percentage	G.D.P. per head in 1965 (U.S. $)
	Below 20%	21–40 %	41–60 %	61–80 %	81–95 %	96–100 %			
Under $100									
Chad (1958)	8·0	11·6	15·4	22·0	20·0	23·0	0·35	25·0	68
Dahomey (1959)	8·0	10·0	12·0	20·0	18·0	32·0	0·42	30·0	73
Niger (1960)	7·8	11·6	15·6	23·0	19·0	23·0	0·34	25·0	81
Nigeria (1959)	7·0	7·0	9·0	16·1	22·5	38·4	0·51	40·9	74
Sudan (1969)	5·6	9·4	14·3	22·6	31·0	17·1	0·40	30·7	97
Tanzania (1964)	4·8	7·8	11·0	15·4	18·1	42·9	0·54	41·0	61
Burma (1958)	10·0	13·0	13·0	15·5	20·3	28·3	0·35	28·5	64
India (1956–57)	8·0	12·0	16·0	22·0	22·0	20·0	0·33	24·0	95
Madagascar (1960)	3·9	7·8	11·3	18·0	22·0	37·0	0·53	39·0	92
Group average	*7·0*	*10·0*	*13·1*	*19·4*	*21·4*	*29·1*	*0·419*	*31·6*	*78·3*
$101–200									
Morocco (1965)	7·1	7·4	7·7	12·4	44·5	20·6	0·50	45·4	180
Senegal (1960)	3·0	7·0	10·0	16·0	28·0	36·0	0·56	44·0	192
Sierra Leone (1968)	3·8	6·3	9·1	16·7	30·3	33·8	0·56	44·1	142
Tunisia (1971)	5·0	5·7	10·0	14·4	42·6	22·4	0·53	44·9	187
Bolivia (1968)	3·5	8·0	12·0	15·5	25·3	35·7	0·53	41·0	132
Ceylon (Sri Lanka) (1963)	4·5	9·2	13·8	20·2	33·9	18·4	0·44	32·5	140
Pakistan (1963–64)	6·5	11·0	15·5	22·0	25·0	20·0	0·37	27·0	101
South Korea (1966)	9·0	14·0	18·0	23·0	23·5	12·5	0·26	19·0	107
Group average	*5·3*	*8·6*	*12·0*	*17·5*	*31·6*	*24·9*	*0·468*	*37·2*	*147·6*
$201–300									
Malaya (1957–58)	6·5	11·2	15·7	22·6	26·2	17·8	0·36	26·6	278
Fiji (1968)	4·0	8·0	13·3	22·4	30·9	21·4	0·46	34·7	295
Ivory Coast (1959)	8·0	10·0	12·0	15·0	20·0	29·0	0·43	35·0	213
Zambia (1959)	6·3	9·6	11·1	15·9	19·6	37·5	0·48	37·1	207
Brazil (1960)	3·5	9·0	10·2	15·8	23·1	38·4	0·54	41·5	207
Ecudaor (1968)	6·3	10·1	16·1	23·2	19·6	24·6	0·38	27·5	202
El Salvador (1965)	5·5	6·5	8·8	17·8	28·4	33·0	0·53	41·4	249
Peru (1961)	4·0	4·3	8·3	15·2	19·3	48·3	0·61	48·2	237
Iraq (1956)	2·0	6·0	8·0	16·0	34·0	34·0	0·60	48·0	285
Philippines (1961)	4·3	8·4	12·0	19·5	28·3	27·5	0·48	35·8	240
Colombia (1964)	2·2	4·7	9·0	16·1	27·7	40·4	0·62	48·0	275
Group average	*4·8*	*8·0*	*11·3*	*18·1*	*25·7*	*32·0*	*0·499*	*38·5*	*244·4*
$301–500									
Gabon (1960)	2·0	6·0	7·0	14·0	24·0	47·0	0·64	51·0	368
Costa Rica (1969)	5·5	8·1	11·2	15·2	25·0	35·0	0·50	40·0	360
Jamaica (1958)	2·2	6·0	10·8	19·5	31·3	30·2	0·56	41·5	465
Surinam (1962)	10·7	11·6	14·7	20·6	27·0	15·4	0·30	23·0	424
Lebanon (1955–60)	3·0	4·2	15·8	16·0	27·0	34·0	0·55	41·0	440
Barbados (1951–52)	3·6	9·3	14·2	21·3	29·3	22·3	0·44	32·9	368
Chile (1968)	5·4	9·6	12·0	20·7	29·7	22·6	0·44	33·0	485
Mexico (1963)	3·5	6·6	11·1	19·3	30·7	28·8	0·53	39·5	441
Panama (1969)	4·9	9·4	13·8	15·2	22·2	34·5	0·48	36·7	490
Group average	*4·5*	*7·9*	*12·3*	*18·0*	*27·4*	*30·0*	*0·494*	*37·6*	*426·9*
$501–1000									
Republic of South Africa (1965)	1·9	4·2	10·2	26·4	18·0	39·4	0·58	43·7	521
Argentina (1961)	7·0	10·4	13·2	17·9	22·2	29·3	0·42	31·5	782
Trinidad and Tobago (1957–58)	3·4	9·1	14·6	24·3	26·1	22·5	0·44	32·9	704
Venezuela (1962)	4·4	9·0	16·0	22·9	23·9	23·2	0·42	30·6	904
Greece (1957)	9·0	10·3	13·3	17·9	26·5	23·0	0·38	29·5	591
Japan (1962)	4·7	10·6	15·8	22·9	31·2	14·8	0·39	28·9	838
Group average	*5·1*	*8·9*	*13·9*	*22·1*	*24·7*	*25·4*	*0·438*	*32·9*	*723·3*
$1001–2000									
Israel (1957)	6·8	13·4	18·6	21·8	28·2	11·2	0·30	21·2	1243
United Kingdom (1964)	5·1	10·2	16·6	23·9	25·0	19·0	0·38	28·1	1590
Netherlands (1962)	4·0	10·0	16·0	21·6	24·8	23·6	0·42	30·0	1400
Federal Republic of Germany (1964)	5·3	10·1	13·7	18·0	19·2	33·7	0·45	32·9	1667
France (1962)	1·9	7·6	14·0	22·8	28·7	25·0	0·50	36·5	1732
Finland (1962)	2·4	8·7	15·4	24·2	28·3	21·0	0·46	33·5	1568
Italy (1948)	6·1	10·5	14·6	20·4	24·3	24·1	0·40	28·8	1011
Puerto Rico (1963)	4·5	9·2	14·2	21·5	28·6	22·0	0·44	32·1	1101
Norway (1963)	4·5	12·1	18·5	24·4	25·1	15·4	0·35	24·9	1717
Australia (1966–67)	6·6	13·4	17·8	23·4	24·4	14·4	2·30	22·2	1823
Group average	*4·7*	*10·5*	*15·9*	*22·2*	*25·7*	*20·9*	*0·401*	*29·0*	*1485·2*
$2001 and above									
Denmark (1963)	5·0	10·8	18·8	24·2	26·3	16·9	0·37	25·4	2078
Sweden (1963)	4·4	9·6	17·4	24·6	26·4	17·6	0·39	28·6	2406
United States (1969)	5·6	12·3	17·6	23·4	26·3	14·8	0·34	24·5	3233
Group average	*5·0*	*10·9*	*17·9*	*24·1*	*26·3*	*16·4*	*0·365*	*26·2*	*2572·3*

Source: F. Paukert, *International Labour Review* (August 1973) based on data compiled by Adelman and Morris, 'An Anatomy of Income Distribution Patterns in Developing Countries'.

higher share of income received by the richest 5 per cent of income recipients – a share of 28·7 per cent compared with 19·9 per cent in the developed countries. Contrary, perhaps, to expectation, the poorest 20 per cent in developing countries receive a slightly higher share of total income than the poorest 20 per cent in developed countries – 5·3 per cent compared to 4·8 per cent.

The fact that the personal distribution of income reaches its peak of inequality at a per capita income level of around $300, while the savings ratio continues to rise beyond this level, suggests that the functional distribution of income is perhaps a more important determinant of the savings ratio than the personal distribution. Unfortunately, this aspect of the distribution of income is not well documented in the developing countries and what figures there are tend to be distorted by the large proportions of the population in self-employment. On the other hand, of the few attempts that have been made to examine the influence of the income distribution on the savings ratio, most have taken the functional distribution of income as the measure of income concentration.

A study by Modigliani attempts to relate the savings ratio across thirty-three countries to the profits–income ratio as measured by the ratio of non-wage income (including income from self-employment) to total wage and non-wage income.[1] The relation turns out to be negative which Modigliani rationalises on the grounds that many low income countries with low savings ratios will have a high profits–income ratio because of the large amount of self-employment in agriculture. Taking a sample of nineteen Western developed countries gave a positive and significant relation between the profits ratio and the savings ratio.

Houthakker has also tested the income distribution hypothesis indirectly by comparing the intercept term in equations relating personal saving per capita to personal income per capita, and private saving per capita to private income per capita for a cross-section of twenty-eight countries.[2] Houthakker finds that the intercept term is

[1] F. Modigliani, 'The Life Cycle Hypothesis of Saving and Intercountry Differences in the Savings Ratio' in *Induction, Trade and Economic Growth: Essays in Honour of Sir Roy Harrod*, ed. W. Eltis *et al.* (Oxford University Press, 1970).

[2] H. Houthakker, 'On Some Determinants of Saving in the Developed and Underdeveloped Countries'. The difference between 'private' and 'personal' saving and income is made up of corporate saving and income, respectively.

negative and significant in the private savings equation but not in the personal savings equation which suggests that corporate saving is proportionally more important in richer countries and that the distribution of income between wages and profits is a determinant of the overall savings ratio.

In conclusion, the growth of the money economy and the growing concentration of income, at least in the early stages of development, are probably the two main reasons why the savings ratio is observed to rise in relation to per capita income, both over time within countries, and across countries with radically different histories and institutional backgrounds. Without invoking these two factors it is difficult to explain the observed cross-section relation between the domestic savings ratio and the level of per capita income. The strength of the relation is quite remarkable.

The Life-Cycle Hypothesis of Saving

The strong relation between the savings ratio and per capita income across countries may be picking up the effect of income growth on saving if per capita income and the growth of income are positively correlated. Whether per capita income exerts a significant *independent* influence on the savings ratio is a matter for further empirical enquiry. First let us discuss, however, the theoretical dependence of the savings ratio on the growth of income, for which there is also a lot of empirical support.

The dependence of the savings ratio on the growth of income is known as the life-cycle hypothesis of saving. The basis of the hypothesis is that individuals and households attempt to spread out consumption evenly over their lifetime so that decisions to save are assumed to be a function not of current income but of total lifetime earnings and the stage reached in the earnings cycle. A typical pattern envisaged by the life-cycle hypothesis is dissaving in youth, positive saving in middle age and dissaving in retirement, breaking even on death (i.e. no bequests). Dissaving takes place in youth in anticipation of future earnings. Positive saving takes place in middle age in anticipation of a lower income after retirement. With this pattern of saving, consumption is more evenly spread than it would otherwise be if consumption was related to current income.

Consider now the effect of income growth on saving within this framework. Suppose first that there was zero income growth.

Assuming no bequests, the aggregate saving ratio would be zero. Out of stationary income (i.e. population growth and productivity growth zero), positive saving and dissaving would exactly offset one another. This is illustrated in Fig. 7.3 which for simplicity divides households into active and retired only. Area A = area B.

Now suppose, however, that aggregate income rises over time as a result of productivity growth. This means that the life earnings and consumption of each successive age group will be higher than the

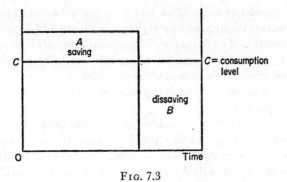

FIG. 7.3

preceding one. On the assumption that each successive age group will be aiming for a higher level of consumption in retirement, the volume of saving of the active households will exceed the dissaving of the currently retired households with a lower level of lifetime consumption. The savings ratio will tend to rise with the rate of growth of income because the higher the growth rate the greater the gap will tend to be between the dissaving of the retired people from a less prosperous generation and the consumption standards being aimed for in retirement by the current generations of working households.

Income growth is also influenced by population growth. Income growth due to population growth will affect the savings ratio according to how population growth affects the ratio of active to non-active households. In the long term the effect of population growth is to increase the ratio of active to non-active households, as compared with a declining population in which the ratio of retired to active households would be increasing. In the long run the saving ratio will tend to rise with the rate of population growth because the relative frequency of households who are actively saving will tend to increase monotonically with the rate of population growth. In the early years

of population growth, however, before the rate stabilises, saving may be impaired by the high child-dependency ratio before the children of the present generation become the workers of the next generation. If population growth is not balanced (i.e. it has not stabilised at a particular level) it is difficult to say whether that part of income growth due to population growth will raise the savings ratio or not. It depends on the balance between the increase in saving that comes about as a result of a rise in the ratio of 'active' to retired households, and the extra consumption demands made on society by a growing child-dependency ratio. This aspect of the life-cycle hypothesis of saving is best summarised by saying that saving will depend on the age structure of the population. The age structure of the population is uniquely related to population growth only if population is in balanced growth. Since retired people tend to consume more than children, however, it is probably wise to treat these two non-active groups separately.

If population is not in balanced growth, misleading results will be obtained in testing the life-cycle hypothesis if the saving ratio is regressed solely on the growth of income, without distinguishing the source of income growth. A regression of the savings ratio on the growth of income alone would only be legitimate if the same coefficient was to be expected on the two components that make up income growth, namely productivity growth and population growth. But if population growth is not balanced there is no basis for assuming that the coefficient should be the same. In this case, the test of the life-cycle hypothesis requires either that productivity growth and population growth should be entered into the analysis as separate variables, or that the savings ratio should be related simply to the rate of growth of per capita income as a crude measure of productivity growth.

Because of the lack of variability in the rate of income and productivity growth over time, it is difficult to test the life-cycle hypothesis of saving for individual countries. But inter-country differences in savings ratios can be examined to test the hypothesis. According to the hypothesis, countries with high rates of income and/or productivity growth should have higher ratios of saving to income than countries with low rates of income and/or productivity growth.

Modigliani, who has done more than any other economist to develop and test the hypothesis, finds strong support for the hypothesis taking average data for the private savings ratio for a cross-section of thirty-six developed and less developed countries over the

period of the 1950s.[1] Strong support is obtained without distinguishing income growth due to productivity growth on the one hand and population growth on the other. Modigliani's estimated equation is

$$\left(\frac{S}{Y}\right)_{private} = \underset{(1 \cdot 3)}{4 \cdot 5} + \underset{(0 \cdot 25)}{1 \cdot 42} \left(\frac{dY}{Y}\right)_{private}$$

Several other tests have been performed of the life-cycle model, notably by Houthakker[2] and Swamy.[3] Taking twenty-eight countries covering the period of the 1950s, Houthakker obtains the following results

$$\left(\frac{S}{Y}\right)_{personal} = \underset{(0 \cdot 012)}{0 \cdot 020} + \underset{(0 \cdot 28)}{1 \cdot 36} \left(\frac{dY}{Y}\right)_{personal}$$

and

$$\left(\frac{S}{Y}\right)_{domestic} = \underset{(0 \cdot 019)}{0 \cdot 046} + \underset{(0 \cdot 42)}{2 \cdot 07} \left(\frac{dY}{Y}\right)_{domestic}$$

Swamy, taking nineteen countries, obtains

$$\left(\frac{S}{Y}\right)_{personal} = constant + 1 \cdot 43 \left(\frac{dY}{Y}\right)_{personal}$$

Taking the sample of sixty-eight countries given in Appendix 1, we obtain the following result

$$\left(\frac{S}{Y}\right)_{domestic} = 14 \cdot 19 + \underset{(0 \cdot 454)}{0 \cdot 494} \left(\frac{dY}{Y}\right)_{national}$$

The regression coefficient is not significantly different from zero. When allowance is made for population growth, however, by regressing the savings ratio on the growth of per capita income, a significant relation is apparent

$$\left(\frac{S}{Y}\right)_{domestic} = 13 \cdot 22 + \underset{(0 \cdot 415)}{1 \cdot 197} \left(\frac{dY_N}{Y_N}\right)_{national}$$

[1] F. Modigliani, 'The Life-Cycle Hypothesis of Saving'. See also the references there to the evolution of his work.

[2] Houthakker, 'On Some Determinants of Saving in the Developed and Under-developed Countries'.

[3] S. Swamy, 'A Dynamic Personal Savings Function and its Long Run Implications', *Review of Economics and Statistics* (February 1968).

There is, of course, an identification problem inherent in testing the life-cycle hypothesis which arises from interdependence between growth and the savings ratio. Growth determines the savings ratio according to the life-cycle hypothesis, but growth partly depends on the savings ratio as a determinant of the rate of capital accumulation. To identify the parameters of both relations a two equation model is required which recognises the interdependence between the two variables and which can be solved using simultaneous equation techniques of estimation. Let $S/Y = \alpha_0 + \beta_0(dY/Y)$ and $dY/Y = f(I/Y)$, where (I/Y) is the investment ratio which is composed of the savings ratio plus the deficit on the balance of payments (F/Y). Thus, the model is

$$\frac{S}{Y} = \alpha_0 + \beta_0 \left(\frac{dY}{Y}\right)$$

and

$$\frac{dY}{Y} = \alpha_1 + \beta_1 \left(\frac{S}{Y}\right) + c_1 \left(\frac{F}{Y}\right)$$

The reduced form gives

$$\frac{S}{Y} = \text{constant} + \pi_0 \left(\frac{F}{Y}\right), \quad \text{where } \pi_0 = \frac{\beta_0 c_1}{1 - \beta_0 \beta_1}$$

and

$$\frac{dY}{Y} = \text{constant} + \pi_1 \left(\frac{F}{Y}\right), \quad \text{where } \pi_1 = \frac{c_1}{1 - \beta_0 \beta_1}$$

Given ordinary least squares estimates of π_0 and π_1, β_0 and β_1 can be identified, giving the true 'structural' dependence of the savings ratio on growth on the one hand and growth on the savings ratio on the other. In Modigliani's model the difference made to the coefficient estimates of taking account of the interdependence between S/Y and dY/Y is not substantial. The indirect least squares estimate of S/Y on dY/Y is $S/Y = 4.9 + 1.35(dY/Y)$ compared with the direct least squares estimate reported earlier which gave a coefficient of 1.42. Other investigators have not attempted to cope with the identification problem arising from the interdependence between savings and growth.

When the level of per capita income was considered alongside the growth rate of income as independent determinants of the savings

ratio, the following result was obtained from our sample of sixty-eight countries

$$\left(\frac{S}{Y}\right)_{\text{domestic}} = 11 \cdot 52 + \underset{(0 \cdot 381)}{0 \cdot 809} \left(\frac{dY_N}{Y_N}\right) + \underset{(0 \cdot 0010)}{0 \cdot 0045} \left(\frac{Y}{N}\right)$$

Both independent variables are statistically significant at the 95 per cent confidence level. The suggestion made earlier that the level of per capita income as a determinant of the savings ratio is a proxy for the rate of growth of income, and exerts no independent influence on the savings ratio, is therefore rejected. This conclusion contrasts with that of Modigliani whose work dismisses the level of per capita income as an explanatory variable in determining inter-country differences in the savings ratio.

When a distinction is made between the sources of income growth, the relation between the savings ratio and population growth invariably turns out to be negative, as does the relation between the savings ratio and the ratio of the non-active to the active population. This is true of the work of Modigliani, and also that of Leff, who relates the savings ratio to the proportion of the population below 14 years of age and over 65.[1] It cannot be concluded from these findings, however, that population growth is necessarily a barrier to capital formation and growth. Such a conclusion would ignore the interdependence between population growth and other growth inducing forces which in turn are favourable to capital accumulation. As I have shown elsewhere there is a strong positive relation across countries between population growth and total productivity growth, while a high rate of total productivity growth, in turn, stimulates capital accumulation.[2] Moreover, no conclusion can be drawn for population policy from the proportion of the population aged over sixty-five.

Finally it should not be overlooked that the savings ratio will also be positively related to the growth rate if the public wishes to maintain a constant proportion of money balance holdings to real income, and if we take the view, as we did earlier, that the accumulation of money balances is a stimulus to saving and complementary to the accumulation of physical capital rather than a substitute for it. McKinnon has

[1] Leff, 'Dependency Rates and Savings Rates'.
[2] A. P. Thirlwall, 'A Cross-Section Study of Population Growth and the Growth of Output and Living Standards in a Production Function Framework', *Manchester School of Economic and Social Studies* (December 1972).

called this the 'portfolio effect'.[1] The portfolio effect of growth on the savings ratio will be the more pronounced the higher the desired ratio of money balances is to income and the faster the rate of growth. The obvious intuitive explanation is that individuals find they must save more merely to maintain their existing money–income ratio. Of course, in the traditional neo-classical model, the 'portfolio effect' of growth on savings would not be regarded as a stimulus to growth because money balances act as a substitute for physical capital. In Chapter 4 we have taken the opposite view, which McKinnon also takes much more strongly, that money balances can act as a stimulus to saving and that money balance holdings and physical capital accumulation are complementary in the development process.

The effect on the equilibrium growth rate of the dependence of the savings ratio on growth (whatever its cause) is shown in Fig. 7.4 below.

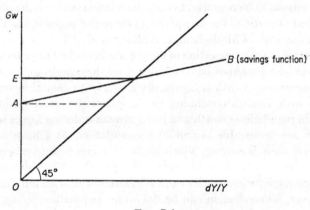

FIG. 7.4

The actual rate of growth (dY/Y) is measured on the horizontal axis, and the warranted rate (which is assumed to be below the natural rate) is measured on the vertical axis. The 45° line represents 'equilibrium' between the actual and warranted growth rates. Now suppose AB is the savings function dependent on the growth rate. Equilibrium growth is determined where AB cuts the 45° line. Clearly, the steeper the curve, that is, the greater the dependence of the savings ratio on

[1] R. I. McKinnon, *Money and Capital in Economic Development* (Washington, D.C.: The Brookings Institution, 1973).

the growth rate, the higher will be the warranted rate of growth; also, the higher the intercept of the savings function the higher the equilibrium growth rate. This dependence underlies the importance of encouraging monetisation of the economy and raising per capita income by all available means in order to increase the savings ratio. The rise in money holdings and per capita income is capable not only of stimulating saving directly, but can induce more saving once growth begins.

8

Inflation, Saving and Growth in the Open Economy

Inflation and the Balance of Payments

Policies of deficit spending financed by inflationary means can be expected to affect adversely a country's balance of payments, especially the balance of payments of developing economies which are typically very open economies with a high income elasticity of demand for imports. There are only two ways in which excess aggregate demand in any economy can be dissipated at full employment; one is by inflation, the other is through a rise in the volume of imports. If the income elasticity of demand for imports is very high, and developing countries are able to finance an import surplus, the balance of payments may take the major part of the strain of excess demand with the internal price level rising very little. In short, there are two ways in which plans to invest exceeding plans to save can result in a greater volume of total saving and investment. One is forced saving brought about by rising prices; the other is by running an import surplus. The relationship between domestic saving and investment and the foreign balance is easily seen using the national income identity

$$Y = C + I + X - M \qquad (8.1)$$

where Y is income
C is consumption
I is investment
X is exports
and M is imports.

Subtracting C and I from both sides of the equation gives

$$Y - C - I = X - M$$

or $$I - S = M - X, \qquad (8.2)$$

where $S = Y - C = $ domestic saving.

In words, equation (8.2) says that in accounting terms an excess of imports over exports is equivalent to an excess of investment over domestic saving. Or, to put it another way, a country can only spend more than it produces (invest more than it saves) if it can import more than it exports. Whether a country can import more than it exports depends, in turn, on whether it can finance the balance-of-payments deficit. There are several alternatives open to a country to finance a deficit brought about by expansionary measures at home. It can run down foreign exchange reserves, if it has any; it can attract private capital from abroad; it can borrow capital in the international money market or direct from international development agencies, or it can seek international aid in the sense of 'free' imports or foreign exchange. If the deficit cannot be financed by any of these means the country must correct the balance of payments either by internal price and income adjustments, or by policies to switch demand to home produced goods such as physical controls on imports and devaluation of the currency. Except for a successful devaluation, all the other policy measures to correct the balance of payments will defeat the purpose of the internal expansion. A devaluation can improve the balance of payments only if it increases domestic output more than it increases domestic expenditure; that is, if it increases domestic saving. This follows from equation (8.2). Only if S is raised, as a result of devaluation, will the balance of payments improve. Saving can only rise if devaluation expands output and/or discourages consumption, or if it alters the income distribution to favour saving. More often than not in developing countries devaluations are unsuccessful in achieving their objective because exports are price inelastic in demand; consumption is not discouraged, and the wealthy classes that benefit from devaluation consume a large fraction of the income gains. The inflation which arises from devaluation then erodes the competitive gains of devaluation. A more hopeful policy is a judicious mix of quotas, taxes and subsidies to regulate imports and to encourage exports. But all this presupposes that deficits cannot be financed. Those who

err on the side of caution and conservatism on the question of financing development by inflationary means are basically pessimistic about the ability to and desirability of financing deficits on the balance of payments by capital inflows. Where this pessimism is well founded there is urgent need for international action to ease the burden of borrowing. The less able a country is to finance its investment plans by importing more than it exports, the greater the domestic inflation it must be prepared to tolerate to achieve a given level of investment.

To calculate the effect of credit expansion on the balance of payments requires consideration of a number of factors. First, we need to know the direct and indirect effects of credit expansion on imports and on the capacity and willingness to export. Then we need to know what effects credit expansion are likely to have on the internal price level and on the price of exports, so that the price effects of credit expansion on exports and imports can be gauged.

The approximate effect of credit expansion, ignoring price effects, can be calculated with a knowledge of the marginal propensity to import, the income multiplier and the credit multiplier. Suppose the government of a developing country finances an investment project by borrowing from the central bank. The first set of repercussions will be that part of the expenditure will be spent directly on home goods (E_h) and a part on imports (E_M). Expenditure on home produced goods will then have multiplier effects (k) on income which induces more imports equal to $m(kE_h)$, where m is the marginal propensity to import. Imports from the initial expenditure by government will therefore be $E_M + m(kE_h)$. If the government finances its expenditure by borrowing from the central bank, however, as assumed at the beginning, part of the loan by the central bank to the government will end up as extra cash reserves in the banking system equal to the total credit (D) minus the initial expenditure on imports (E_M). According to the cash ratio and the propensity to import, the increased cash reserves of the banks permit a further expansion of credit. Suppose L is the value of the extra loans that can be made. Income rises by a further kL, and imports rise by $m(kL)$. Therefore the total rise in imports is $E_M + (E_h + L)mk$.

Using this model, Newlyn has estimated for Uganda that imports tend to rise by approximately 90 per cent of the original investment loan.[1] Similarly, Gray has estimated for Nigeria that the value of

[1] W. Newlyn, *Finance for Development* (East Africa Publishing House, 1968).

credit creation tends to be matched by an equivalent level of imports within three years.[1] Ahmad's study of deficit finance and monetary expansion in Ghana over the period 1960–5, and how increases in the money supply are split between output, prices and the balance of payments, also shows that for most of the period the balance of payments absorbed over 74 per cent of the total monetary expansion.[2]

The above analysis ignores the output effects of extra investment. The expansion of productive capacity permitted by more investment could in practice be devoted to import substitution activities or export promotion, in which case the balance of payments would not deteriorate quite so drastically as the monetary effects on imports would suggest. In general, however, given the high propensity to import and the relatively high velocity of circulation of money, it does seem that a large proportion of demand expansion to stimulate development is likely to be met by rising imports. If imports cannot be financed by more exports or foreign borrowing the only alternative is to engineer a 'successful' exchange rate depreciation, if the investment programme is to be maintained without resort to import controls which would inevitably involve domestic inflation.

The effect of internal price inflation on the balance of payments depends on whether changes in the internal price level are reflected in changes in export prices in world markets; on the rate at which other countries are inflating, and on how exports and imports respond to changes in relative prices. Since we are only discussing here policies of mild inflation, one country's price level cannot get radically out of line with another's; but assuming some change in relative prices, what will be the effect on the balance of payments? Assuming that imports and exports are responsive to changes in relative prices between domestic and foreign suppliers, the volume of imports will rise and exports will fall, and the balance of payments will deteriorate. If internal price increases are passed on into higher export prices, however, and the demand for exports is price inelastic, export proceeds will increase to meet the higher import bill. The demand for many of the exports of developing countries is relatively price in-

[1] C. S. Gray, 'Credit Creation for Nigeria's Economic Development', *Nigerian Journal of Economic and Social Studies* (November 1963).

[2] N. Ahmad, *Deficit Financing, Inflation and Capital Formation: the Ghanaian Experience 1960–65* (München: Weltforum Verlag, 1970).

elastic,[1] particularly the demand for raw materials in the short run. On the other hand, there is a growing range of semi-manufactured and light manufactured goods, the demand for which is relatively price elastic in world markets. There is fairly intense world competition in many of the new manufactured goods that developing countries are now producing in an attempt to diversify their export structure. Small deteriorations in the price competitiveness of these goods can perhaps be offset by policies of export subsidisation. An across-the-board policy of exchange depreciation will not be appropriate if a large proportion of exports are price inelastic. Exchange depreciation also tends to ossify the export structure, which may be the major factor inhibiting the growth of exports in the first place, and preventing an improvement in the balance of payments. What developing countries require above all else are exports which have a high income elasticity of demand in world markets, preferably at least equal to the income elasticity of demand for imports. If not, developing countries will have permanent balance-of-payments deficits if they try to maintain a growth of income comparable to that of other developed countries. The price elasticity of demand, and hence the rate of inflation, is of secondary importance to the income elasticity of demand for exports.

In a major study of export performance in relation to domestic inflation during the period 1953–9, Lovasy found little difference in the behaviour of exports in countries with up to 10 per cent inflation.[2] Taking countries with less than 4 per cent inflation, the volume of exports grew 35 per cent over the period; taking countries with between 4 per cent and 10 per cent inflation, exports grew by 27 per cent over the period. Within the two groups of countries there was a wider diversity of performance than between them, suggesting that price factors are not dominant in determining export performance. The same general conclusion has been reached for the industrial countries by Junz and Rhomberg.[3] Their results indicate that price competitiveness plays an identifiable, though not dominant, role in the export performance of industrial countries in markets for manu-

---

[1] Taking the developing countries as a whole. The demand for the products of any one developing country may be very elastic.

[2] G. Lovasy, 'Inflation and Exports in Primary Producing Countries', *I.M.F. Staff Papers* (March 1962).

[3] H. B. Junz and R. Rhomberg, 'Prices and Export Performance of Industrial Countries, 1953–63', *I.M.F. Staff Papers* (July 1965).

factured products. Export market shares are related to relative price changes, but the proportion of the observed variation in market shares which is explained by price factors is not very high.

Lovasy recognises a greater effect of inflation on exports from the side of domestic absorption, and argues that inflation will tend to hamper the expansion and diversification of exports by reducing the profitability of producing newer types of commodities for export, for which there is also a domestic demand. In short, there is a difference between exportable goods for which there is only a small domestic demand in relation to the supply (e.g. traditional primary product exports), and exportable goods for which there is a relatively large domestic demand which will absorb the potential exports as demand is expanded. On this point, it transpires that developing countries with mild inflation made more progress in diversifying their exports than countries with moderate and strong inflation.

It is also interesting to note that when exports were related to export prices as opposed to domestic prices (therefore taking account of changes in exchange rates) there is little systematic relation between the growth of exports and the gain in export price competitiveness, which again is indicative of the price inelasticity of exports. If the export performance of developing countries is to be fully understood attention must be paid primarily to non-price factors. The policy message is that the foreign exchange repercussions arising from the effects of inflation on the demand for exports should not be exaggerated in discussing policies of mild inflation.

It is important that a policy of domestic expansion should not impair the growth of export earnings not only because earnings from exports enable countries to buy required imports, but also because the level of domestic saving in developing countries is strongly dependent on export earnings. There are a number of reasons for this dependence. First, the propensity to save of the export sector is high. Exports, especially of primary products, tend to produce highly concentrated incomes, which raises the level of saving for any given aggregate level of income as saving theory predicts. Second, government saving relies heavily on export taxes in many developing countries. Foreign exchange earnings from exports are administratively easier to tax than more diffused wage and profit income. Taxation tends to take one of two forms. Either state-controlled marketing boards pay the producers a price less than the international price received, or the government requires that all foreign

exchange earnings be surrendered, with compensation being given in local currency at an over-valued rate. A third factor is that countries with higher rates of export growth may face less of a foreign exchange constraint on investment so that domestic saving is encouraged. The rise in export earnings causes other sectors of the economy to save more to take advantage of profitable investment opportunities. This is undoubtedly one of the major reasons why there is such a strong correlation between the growth of export earnings and the growth of output in developing countries.

Maizels has tested the savings function

$$S = a_o + b_o(Y - X) + c_o(X),$$

where Y is gross domestic product and X is export earnings.[1] In eight out of eleven countries studied Maizels finds that export earnings contribute significantly to saving. Lee has extended Maizels' analysis by taking twenty-eight countries for a longer time period.[2] Export earnings are found to be a significant determinant of domestic savings, with the coefficient on X substantially higher than on $(Y - X)$ in many cases. Chenery and Eckstein,[3] Papanek[4] and Landau[5] all obtain similar results for different samples and different time periods. In short, the hypothesis that the value of exports is an important determinant of domestic saving seems pretty robust. Since there is no reason to suppose that policies of mild inflation sustained by the majority of developing countries would jeopardise noticeably the export earnings of any of these countries, however, there is little need to qualify the argument for inflationary finance on this score.

There is still the question of imports, however, and whether or not a higher level of imports can be financed. If they cannot be financed by foreign borrowing (leaving aside the expansion of exports), there are two broad choices. Either the expansion programme must be

[1] A. Maizels, *Exports and Economic Growth of Developing Countries* (Cambridge University Press, 1968).

[2] J. K. Lee, 'Exports and the Propensity to Save in Less Developed Countries', *Economic Journal* (June 1971).

[3] H. Chenery and P. Eckstein, 'Development Alternatives for Latin America', *Journal of Political Economy* (July/August 1970, supplement).

[4] G. F. Papanek, 'Aid, Foreign Private Investment, Savings, and Growth in Less Developed Countries', *Journal of Political Economy* (January/February 1973).

[5] L. Landau, 'Determinants of Saving in Latin America', mimeographed paper, Centre for International Affairs (Harvard University).

abandoned or resort must be had to expenditure switching policies, including exchange depreciation and import substitution. If demand contraction is pursued there is no hope of inducing extra growth by expansionary means. If expenditure switching policies are pursued there is a danger that the gains from domestic expansion may be offset by losses in productive efficiency through the diversion of resources to activities which absorb a higher volume of resources for any given level of output. This may be especially true of import substitution policies if they result in unduly capital-intensive activities which subsequently operate with excess capacity.

The best guarantee that a policy of sustained expansion in developing countries will raise living standards is for the international community to design generous international assistance policies to allow the imports of the developing countries to exceed exports until a balance can be restored through the natural growth and development of the economies. Apart from increasing the volume of international assistance, one possibility is to link international monetary reform with the provision of buying power to developing countries. Except for the paranoiac fear of inflation that exists amongst the world banking community there is no reason why international money should not be created for the developing countries to buy imports from the developed countries who could hold the money in their reserves and treat it as good as gold. New international money is currently being created in the form of S.D.R.s (Special Drawing Rights on the I.M.F.), but it is not being distributed to the developing countries as aid for the purchase of development goods from the industrial countries. Three-quarters of the $9·5 billion S.D.R.s created between 1969 and 1972 were distributed to the twenty-five richest members of the I.M.F. Since the developed countries strive to achieve surpluses on their balance of payments, and developing countries lack foreign exchange to purchase imports, it would seem mutually beneficial for a much larger proportion of new S.D.R.s to be diverted to the developing nations. The S.D.R.s would end up in the reserves of the industrial nations as in the past, and real resources would have been transferred from rich to poor countries in the process. The cost to the rich countries would be no greater than any other means of converting resources into reserves. At present, the high spillover of credit expansion into imports results from two factors: the industrial structure of developing countries, which is not geared to the production of manufactured goods which people

demand as income rises; and from the high velocity of circulation of money which is a symptom of the lack of sophistication of the monetary system. The task of governments and planning authorities in developing countries must be to convince international aid-giving bodies of the viability of the expansion programme; to demonstrate that expansion and inflation can be kept under control, and to persuade them to finance deficits on the balance of payments while domestic output and exports have a chance to respond to the expansionary development programme.

The Import Surplus, Saving and Growth

Other things remaining the same, the effect of the import surplus is to raise the growth rate above what it would otherwise have been. Capital imports to finance balance of payments deficits act as a supplement to domestic saving. This is easily demonstrated using the growth formula

$$\frac{\Delta Y}{Y} \cdot \frac{I}{\Delta Y} = \frac{I}{Y} \tag{8.3}$$

where $\Delta Y/Y$ is the growth rate

$I/\Delta Y$ is the incremental capital–output ratio

and I/Y is the investment ratio.

Since from equation (8.2), $I = S + M - X$, we have

$$\frac{\Delta Y}{Y} \cdot \frac{I}{\Delta Y} = \frac{S}{Y} + \frac{M - X}{Y} \tag{8.4}$$

Assuming $I/\Delta Y$ and S/Y remain unchanged, an import surplus raises the growth rate. If all capital imports are saved and invested the growth rate will rise by the full amount of the import surplus times the productivity of capital. The import surplus may even raise the domestic savings ratio if the marginal propensity to save is greater than the average propensity to save. Import surpluses would appear to have great potential in the development process.

It is sometimes argued, however, that import surpluses financed by foreign capital inflows increase the capital–output ratio (i.e. lower the productivity of capital) and discourage domestic saving. In addition, a large fraction of capital inflows is consumed rather than

invested. The net result is that extra growth from monetary expansion financed by foreign borrowing may be negligible and could be negative. Letting $y = \Delta Y/Y$; $c = I/\Delta Y$; $s = S/Y$, and $A = (M - X)/Y$, and using equation (8.4), the growth rate in the absence of capital imports is

$$y = \frac{s}{c} \qquad (8.5)$$

Growth with capital imports (y^*) is

$$y^* = \frac{s^* + (1 - b)A}{c^*} \qquad (8.6)$$

where s^* is the new savings ratio
c^* is the new capital–output ratio
b is the propensity to consume out of capital inflows.

Growth due to capital imports is therefore

$$y^* - y = \frac{s + \Delta s + (1 - b)A}{c + \Delta c} - \frac{s}{c} \qquad (8.7)$$

If Δs is negative, Δc is positive and b is large, the effect of capital imports on growth may be negligible or even negative. Statistically, it is not possible to estimate Δs independently of b so that one of these two terms in equation (8.7) is redundant.[1] If domestic saving is regressed on capital imports, the regression coefficient will pick up both effects because of the way in which saving is defined. Because saving is defined as the difference between investment and capital

---

[1] It may be a mistake conceptually to distinguish between consumption out of capital inflows and changes in consumption plans within the country, if the source of capital imports cannot be identified. Suppose, for example, that the balance of payments deficit is financed by running down exchange reserves. How can consumption out of additional foreign resources made available be distinguished from changes in plans to save internally? Equation (8.7) is really only useful if the source of capital imports can be identified and if the saving propensities of different sectors of the economy are known. An alternative specification to equation (8.7) would be

$$y^* - y = \frac{s + (1 - b^*)A}{c + \Delta c} - \frac{s}{c},$$

where b^* is the proportion of capital imports 'consumed' (i.e. embodying the total effect on saving from an increase in capital imports).

imports, if a proportion of capital imports is consumed (i.e. $b > 0$) domestic saving will be recorded as having fallen out of a given income even in the absence of any change in the plans of residents to save (see later). We confine ourselves here to a general discussion of the relation between domestic saving and foreign capital inflows, followed by a discussion of the capital–output ratio.

Foreign Capital and Domestic Saving

Several studies have found a significant negative relation between foreign capital inflows and domestic saving. The hypothesis of a negative relation was first put forward by Haavelmo,[1] and has been tested by Rahman,[2] Griffin and Enos,[3] Chenery and Eckstein,[4] Weisskopf,[5] and Leff,[6] among others.

Using cross-country data for thirty-one developing countries in 1962, Rahman obtained the following equation

$$s = 0.14 - 0.25\,A$$
$$(t = 2.5)$$

Griffin and Enos, taking cross-section data for thirty-two developing countries for the years 1962–4, estimated the equation

$$s = 0.11 - 0.73\,A$$
$$(t = 6.6)$$

Weisskopf, taking pooled data for seventeen countries, with income and export earnings included in the equation, estimated the equation

$$S = a_o + 0.183\,(Y) - 0.227\,(F) + 0.176\,(X)$$

where F is foreign capital inflows.

[1] T. Haavelmo, 'Comment on W. Leontief's "The Rates of Long-Run Economic Growth and Capital Transfers from Developed to Underdeveloped Areas" ', Study Week on the Econometric Approach to Development Planning, Pontificae Academie Scientiarum Scrips Varia (Amsterdam: North-Holland Publishing Co., 1965).

[2] Md. A. Rahman, 'Foreign Capital and Domestic Saving: A Test of Haavelmo's Hypothesis with Cross-Country Data', *Review of Economics and Statistics* (February, 1968).

[3] K. B. Griffin and J. L. Enos, 'Foreign Assistance: Objectives and Consequences', *Economic Development and Cultural Change* (April 1970).

[4] Chenery and Eckstein, 'Development Alternatives for Latin America'.

[5] T. Weisskopf, 'The Impact of Foreign Capital Inflows on Domestic Saving in Underdeveloped Countries', *Journal of International Economics* (February, 1972).

[6] N. Leff, 'Marginal Savings Rates in the Development Process: The Brazilian Experience', *Economic Journal* (September 1968).

Chenery and Eckstein, taking time series data for sixteen Latin American countries, found the relation between domestic saving and foreign capital inflows to be negative in twelve cases.

Leff for Brazil estimated the equation (standard errors in brackets)

$$S_t = 1.78 + 0.1545 \ Y_{t-1} - 0.156 \ (F)$$
$$ \underset{(0.02)}{} \qquad \underset{(0.33)}{}$$

There are several comments that need making on the apparent inverse relation between foreign capital inflows and domestic savings before it is concluded that any programme of sustained expansion financed by foreign borrowing will be substantially defeated by a weakening of the domestic savings effort. First, an inverse relation is predictable from the accounting identities that have already been established. No necessary causal relation is implied between large capital inflows and low domestic saving in the sense that a decision has been taken by residents to save less. Given that domestic saving is equal to the excess of investment over foreign resource flows (which, in turn, are defined as equal to the deficit on the balance of payments), saving is bound to show as having fallen as long as not all foreign inflows are invested. That is, if $I - S = M - X = F$, and I rises by less than F increases, then S must fall for the identity to hold. To give a numerical example: suppose domestic saving is £1000; that foreign resource inflows (F) increase by £200, and that investment rises by only £100. Saving is now £1000 + £100 − £200 = £900. By definition, capital imports and domestic saving are negatively correlated. Without adequate theorising it cannot be assumed from the regression coefficient of saving on capital inflows that the inflow of foreign capital is the cause of low saving. It is quite possible, in fact, for the relation to be negative but for planned domestic saving to have risen. The regression coefficient relating domestic saving to capital imports cannot distinguish between changes in decisions to save on the one hand and consumption out of foreign capital inflows on the other. The fact that investment rises by only 50 per cent of capital inflows (and that saving falls by 50 per cent of capital inflows) could be the result either of more than 50 per cent of the foreign inflow being consumed coupled with a rise in the domestic savings ratio, or less than 50 per cent of the foreign inflow consumed and a reduction in plans to save. In terms of equation (8.7) it is impossible to determine Δs and b separately from a simple regression of domestic savings on

capital inflows. One must either work with b and scrap Δs,[1] or assume $b = 0$ and work with Δs. Both b and Δs cannot be determined from one regression.[2]

Having said that a negative relation between domestic saving and capital inflows may be expected for definitional reasons, there are none the less economic and institutional reasons why the relation may be negative. But the direction of causation could be either way. On the one hand, countries may decide to substitute some domestic savings for foreign capital as it becomes available. On the other hand, the poorer the country, and the lower the savings ratio, the more foreign capital the country might attract. Since foreign capital inflows are defined as the deficit on the balance of payments it is not implausible that a low savings ratio may be the 'cause' of a high volume of capital inflows.

To decide to substitute some domestic saving for foreign capital is quite natural. If foreign exchange is the dominant constraint on growth, capital inflows serve as a one-to-one substitute for domestic saving in financing investment. There will be a partial offset, however. Since investment is highly dependent on imports, domestic investment opportunities will vary closely with the availability of foreign exchange, and domestic saving will vary in response to the opportunities provided by capital inflows. The combined effect of these two forces on domestic saving will be $(\partial S/\partial F - 1)$, where $\partial S/\partial F$ is the pure foreign exchange effect on saving. As long as $\partial S/\partial F < 1$, the effect of foreign capital inflows on saving will be negative.

Even if domestic saving is the dominant constraint on growth, a negative relation between capital inflows and domestic saving is still to be expected. Any plausible utility function would suggest that a portion of any inflow of resources will be consumed so that domestic saving declines, holding income constant. No society values future consumption infinitely more than present consumption, so that some proportion of additional resources is bound to be consumed. The channels through which consumption may rise and saving fall as a result of capital inflows are numerous. Governments may decide to

---

[1] C. Kennedy and A. P. Thirlwall, 'Foreign Capital, Domestic Savings and Economic Development', *Bulletin of the Oxford Institute of Economics and Statistics* (May 1971).

[2] They are not distinct conceptually either, if the source of capital imports cannot be identified.

spend more on consumption. Foreign capital may lower private domestic saving by being offered on easy terms through development banks and other financial institutions. Through the greater abundance of capital, the incentive to save may be reduced. Capital inflows may also encourage the consumption of imports.

But it would be foolish to condemn all consumption as detrimental to the development effort. The growth rate of consumption, as well as the growth of output, needs to be an argument in the societal welfare function not only as a good in itself but also because consumption may be a necessary condition of increased output. Adequate consumption is required to maintain the health and efficiency of labour, and the availability of consumption goods can act as an incentive to increased productive effort. The types of consumption expenditures to which governments can divert more resources may be very productive indeed. Expenditure on education, health and human capital development in the widest sense are obvious examples.

So far attention has been concentrated on the partial relation between domestic saving and capital imports. The effect of capital imports on domestic saving through raising the level of output and the growth rate have been ignored. If it is assumed that the level of domestic resources remains unchanged after an amount of foreign resources becomes available, any increase in consumption will indeed be at the expense of domestic saving. But if production is expanded as a result of capital imports, increased consumption will be possible without any diminution of domestic saving. Thus, while the partial derivative of saving on foreign capital inflows may be expected to be negative given the level of income (because foreign capital and domestic saving are to a certain extent substitutes for one another), the total relation between saving and foreign capital should be positive if foreign capital raises the level of domestic income.

There is a good deal of evidence which suggests that the growth rates of countries are significantly related to the volume of external capital and especially to the level of official development assistance, as distinct from private foreign investment and other foreign capital inflows. Taking three samples of countries, Pesmazoglu[1] has estimated the relation between the growth of output (y) as the dependent variable, and the rate of growth of gross fixed investment (g_I), the

[1] J. Pesmazoglu, 'Growth, Investment and Savings Ratios: Some Long- and Medium-Term Associations by Groups of Countries', *Bulletin of the Oxford Institute of Economics and Statistics* (November 1972).

domestic savings ratio (s_d), and foreign resource inflows (s_F) as independent variables, with the following results (standard errors in brackets)

15 countries $\quad y = \quad 1\cdot54 + 0\cdot21(g_I) + 0\cdot13(s_d) + 0\cdot29(s_F)$
< \$300 p.a. $\qquad\qquad\; (0\cdot04) \qquad (0\cdot07) \qquad (0\cdot11)$

$$r^2 = 0\cdot71$$

14 countries $\quad y = -1\cdot69 + 0\cdot28(g_I) + 0\cdot22(s_d) + 0\cdot34(s_F)$
\$300–\$850 p.a. $\qquad\quad (0\cdot07) \qquad (0\cdot06) \qquad (0\cdot07)$

$$r^2 = 0\cdot91$$

14 countries $\quad y = \quad 0\cdot93 + 0\cdot22(g_I) + 0\cdot08(s_d) + 0\cdot93(s_F)$
> \$850 p.a. $\qquad\qquad\; (0\cdot12) \qquad (0\cdot05) \qquad (1\cdot18)$

$$r^2 = 0\cdot35$$

Three things are striking about the results. The first is the high proportion of the variance in growth rates explained by the total investment ratio. The second is the higher coefficient on the external savings ratio variable (s_F) than on the domestic savings ratio variable, suggesting that foreign resource inflows are more productive than domestic resources. The third striking factor is the significance of the coefficient on the capital inflows variable, especially for the middle income group of countries in the 'intermediate' stage of development. One possible explanation is that within this group of countries the foreign exchange constraint is more dominant than in either the very poor, or richer, countries, and that extra foreign resources release considerable development potential in countries at an 'intermediate' stage of development.

Papanek has also related domestic growth to foreign capital inflows, distinguishing between three types of inflow: aid (a); private foreign investment (f), and other foreign inflows (o). Taking eighty-five countries, and including the domestic savings ratio as an additional explanatory variable (s_d), he estimates the following equation (t statistics in brackets)[1]

$$y = 1\cdot5 + 0\cdot20(s_d) + 0\cdot39(a) + 0\cdot17(f) + 0\cdot19(o) \qquad r^2 = 0\cdot37$$
$$\;\;\;\;\;(6\cdot0) \qquad (5\cdot8) \quad\;\; (2\cdot5) \quad\;\; (2\cdot1)$$

The aid coefficient is highly significant, more so than the other resource inflow variables. Moreover, the coefficient estimate is

---

[1] Papanek, 'Aid, Foreign Private Investment, Savings, and Growth in Less Developed Countries'.

higher, suggesting that official development assistance is more productive than private foreign investment and other resource flows. Taking sub-samples of Asian and Mediterranean countries yields the same broad conclusions.

Given the findings in Chapter 7 that the savings ratio is dependent on the growth rate and the level of per capita income, foreign capital inflows should raise the planned level of saving indirectly through their effect on the growth rate.

In view of the positive effect of capital inflows on the domestic growth rate, and the positive effect of the growth rate on the savings ratio, the fairly large negative coefficients relating domestic saving and capital inflows reported earlier are somewhat surprising. In regressions which hold income constant a large negative coefficient would be more understandable but not in the reduced form. The results obtained are open to a number of different interpretations. Either capital imports in the samples of countries taken by the various studies were not a strong growth-inducing force and/or generated no saving, or such a large proportion of capital imports was 'consumed' that, for the definitional reasons referred to earlier, decisions to save more were disguised by accounting conventions.

Another hypothesis alluded to earlier is that the negative association between foreign capital and domestic saving is caused by a common third factor, namely low per capita income. Papanek favours this explanation. He argues:

the poorer, more slowly growing, countries are likely to receive a high proportion of grant aid and to use it to increase consumption. They are also likely to be countries with low savings rates.[1]

Aid and other resource flows often increase in times of crisis. When foreign exchange is scarce, countries naturally look for more credit and generally receive it.

Alternatively it could simply be that the causal relation is the other way round: that low saving leads to high levels of capital imports because balance of payments deficits caused by 'too much' consumption require financing.

It would be wrong, however, to leave the impression that all studies find the relation between capital imports and domestic saving to be negative. In commenting on Rahman's work, which used thirty-one countries from a fifty country sample of Chenery and

[1] Papanek, ibid.

Strout,[1] Gupta has used all fifty countries and obtains the equation (standard errors in brackets)[2]

$$s = 0\cdot1108 + 0\cdot0310(A) \qquad r^2 = 0\cdot055$$
$$(0\cdot0804)$$

The relation is insignificant but positive. Cross-classifying countries according to per capita income gives

Countries $s = 0\cdot1002 + 0\cdot3258(A)$ $r^2 = 0\cdot348$
< $125 p.a. $(0\cdot2926)$

Countries $s = 0\cdot1091 - 0\cdot0171(A)$ $r^2 = 0\cdot077$
$125–$249 p.a. $(0\cdot0611)$

Countries $s = 0\cdot1539 + 0\cdot4219(A)$ $r^2 = 0\cdot377$
> $250 $(0\cdot3281)$

The sign of the relation in two of the sub-samples of countries is also positive. On the basis of the limited evidence reported here, it would seem that the sign of the relation between foreign capital inflows and domestic saving may be quite sensitive to the sample of countries taken.

The upshot of the discussion of the relation between foreign capital inflows and domestic saving must be that a negative regression co-efficient of a particular order of magnitude cannot be taken as evidence that decisions to save in a country as a result of capital from abroad have been revised downwards to the same extent. Unless no capital imports are consumed and plans to save rise, a negative relation between capital imports and domestic saving is bound to arise from the way saving and foreign resource inflows are defined. A negative relation cannot be construed as a weakening of the development effort. It is natural for some increase in the volume of resources to be consumed; and many forms of consumption expenditure can be highly productive. Moreover, capital imports can raise saving indirectly through raising the level of output and the growth rate. Any statistical attempt to assess the causal influence of foreign capital inflows on domestic saving would need to consider whether a high volume of inflows was associated with savings which were lower

[1] H. Chenery and A. Strout, 'Foreign Assistance and Economic Development', *American Economic Review* (September 1966).

[2] K. L. Gupta, 'Foreign Capital and Domestic Savings: A Test of Haavelmo's Hypothesis with Cross-Section Data: A Comment', *Review of Economics and Statistics* (May 1970).

than would otherwise have been the case. This is virtually impossible to determine. But in any case, no studies show the *investment* ratio to have fallen as a result of capital inflows so that, unless the productivity of capital falls drastically, capital inflows must finance some additional growth.

Foreign Capital and the Capital–Output Ratio

It has been argued, however, notably by Griffin and Enos,[1] that foreign capital inflows do lower the productivity of capital, by raising the capital–output ratio, because of the tendency for international assistance to be used for prestige projects, as monuments to donor generosity, and because of a bias towards the use of international resource flows for infrastructure projects and social overhead capital. There are several comments that can be made on this view. First, there is a confusion in the argument. It is not legitimate to argue from the capital–output ratio of particular projects to the capital–output ratio for the economy as a whole, which is the ratio relevant to the model under consideration (equation 8.7). It would be quite possible for the overall capital–output ratio to fall even though projects financed by capital inflows were relatively capital intensive. This could happen in at least two ways. First, the greater availability of foreign exchange could enable a more productive use to be made of capital resources as a whole. If there is industrial excess capacity owing to a shortage of foreign exchange, the provision of capital imports permits the use of the excess capacity, lowering the capital–output ratio accordingly. Additional foreign exchange to meet 'shortages' cannot easily be acquired by devoting resources to exports or import substitutes without some cost in terms of domestic output. Capital imports also allow a change in the product mix towards more labour-intensive commodities which can reduce the overall capital–output ratio of the economy. The second point is that the particular projects undertaken could have external effects on the output of other sectors. It is true that infrastructure projects tend to have relatively high capital–output ratios, as traditionally measured,

[1] Griffin and Enos, 'Foreign Assistance: Objectives and Consequences'. See also Griffin, 'Foreign Capital, Domestic Savings and Economic Development', *Bulletin of the Oxford Institute of Economics and Statistics* (May 1970).

but the classic argument for these types of investment is that they have extensive spillover effects, yielding a high social return, and make directly productive activities more productive. The types of infrastructure projects that can yield high social returns were discussed in Chapter 6 in the section on measures to reduce the capital–output ratio.

There is no convincing evidence that countries with a high ratio of capital inflows to national income have a higher capital–output ratio than other countries, and there is no convincing evidence that the productivity of foreign resource inflows is lower than the productivity of domestic savings. On the contrary, the evidence is that foreign capital inflows are more productive than domestic resources. In the equations of Pesmazoglu and Papanek reported earlier, the coefficient relating the growth of output to foreign capital inflows is higher than the coefficient relating the growth of output to the domestic savings ratio. The results reported in Table 1.2 (in Chapter 1) warrant the same conclusion. The coefficients relating the growth of output to the investment ratio are much higher than the coefficients relating growth to the domestic savings ratio in the various samples of countries taken. Leff has argued that foreign capital imports have reduced the capital–output ratio in Brazil.[1] Indeed, Leff argues that it is because of this that a negative relation is observed between capital inflows and domestic saving. With a lower capital–output ratio, a target growth rate can be achieved with less domestic saving. The argument sounds a little far-fetched, but Leff has extensive knowledge of the Brazilian economy, and his observations must be taken as authoritative.

The question remains of whether a planned policy of inflationary finance is likely to attract the foreign capital inflows necessary to finance the import surplus, or whether inflation will discourage inflows of capital. The World Bank, which is the major multilateral lending institution to developing countries, places a heavy premium on financial stability; witness the considerable 'leverage' it has exerted in conjunction with the International Monetary Fund on economic policy in Latin America, generally with disastrous results. As we have mentioned before, however, the Latin American countries must be treated as special cases. It would be difficult for anyone to argue the case for inflationary finance that produced rates of inflation in excess of 10 per cent per annum, let alone 50 per cent. The argument

---

[1] Leff, 'Marginal Savings Rates in the Development Process'.

here is for more expansionist policies to accumulate capital and to reduce unemployment, consistent with inflation of not more than 10 per cent per annum. On the other hand, the natural creditor status of banks and the financial conservatism of banking institutions may well preclude agreement to policies involving more than, say, 5 per cent inflation. But even 5 per cent inflation would be preferable to no inflationary stimulus at all, especially as some inflation is to be expected in the natural course of growth and structural change.

There is no reason why private foreign investment should be unduly discouraged. It could well be encouraged. Inflation raises the money rate of return on investment. The only reservation that foreign investors might have is the fear that the country might indulge in currency depreciation in excess of the rate of domestic inflation which would lower the money return to the holders of the assets abroad. Also, if there is some doubt that the country can contain inflation investors may fear that the country will attempt to protect its balance of payments by imposing exchange restrictions. A mild inflation of up to 10 per cent per annum, however, should not cause undue concern.

It was suggested in Chapter 6 that the major problem in the short run of a programme of inflationary finance is likely to be containing the price of food; food being the major item of expenditure out of increases in demand. This would suggest that in the first instance capital imports might have to be used primarily for the purchase of food until the expansionary investment programme has had time to yield benefits in the form of increased agricultural output and extra foreign exchange earnings from exports. This will help to abate inflationary tendencies from the programme of expansion and assist in putting the programme on a sound footing. When the food problem is solved, the capital imports can then be used more for investment purposes. In countries such as India, probably the greatest limiting factors which have bedevilled economic development since conscious planning was adopted have been a lack of food and foreign exchange. It is these two factors above all which have limited the ability to invest without suffering 'excessive' inflation. This is not to say that using capital imports to buy food is necessarily the best strategy, or that if capital from abroad was readily available independent of the budget decisions of government it should necessarily be used for this purpose. We are not concerned here with optimal development strategy. The point to be made is that if deficit finance takes place,

and there is concern over the price of food, there may be a case for using a portion of capital imports for the purchase of food during the initial stages of the expansionary programme. Questions of the mix of foreign and domestic capital as elements in the expansion programme are outside the scope of this book.

9

Inflation and Growth: The Empirical Evidence

Despite the long history of the idea that inflation may be conducive to development, the hypothesis has never been put to a thorough, satisfactory empirical test. What evidence there is tends to be sketchy, impressionistic and inconclusive. Historical time series studies by Bhatia[1] and by Eckstein[2] give conflicting results. Bhatia attempted to examine Rostow's thesis (see Chapter 2) that the take-off stage of economic development has typically been associated with inflation by looking at the historical relation between inflation and growth in five countries – Germany, Sweden, Canada, Japan and the United Kingdom. Bhatia finds no evidence that 'take-off' in Sweden, Japan and Canada was associated with inflation. Over time, he concludes that the relation between growth and inflation has, if anything, been inverse in the United Kingdom, Germany and Japan, and significantly positive only in Sweden. Eckstein has reviewed the statistics for eight industrialised countries over nearly a century and concludes:

> periods of rapid growth occurred with and without inflation, and that periods of stagnation also saw a very wide range of price changes. Thus, as a long-run phenomenon, there is no historical association between growth and inflation.

Cross-section studies of the relation between inflation and growth also appear to be inconclusive. In an earlier study by the present author, taking fifty-one countries over the period 1958–67 no significant relation was found over the whole sample, although some interesting results emerged when the sample was split according to

[1] R. J. Bhatia, 'Inflation, Deflation and Economic Development', *I.M.F. Staff Papers* (November 1960).
[2] O. Eckstein, 'Inflation, the Wage–Price Spiral and Economic Growth' in *The Relationship of Prices to Economic Stability and Growth* (Washington: U.S. Government Printing Office, 1958).

the level of per capita income and the rate of inflation.[1] For example, for seventeen developed countries (with per capita incomes > \$800 p.a.), all of which experienced mild inflation of between 3 per cent and 8 per cent per annum, the following result was obtained: Growth $= 2.79 + 0.61$ (Inflation); $r^2 = 0.48$. For the developing countries the evidence was inconclusive, except that there appeared to be a definite negative relation between inflation and growth among countries which experienced annual rates of inflation in excess of 10 per cent. Over all countries, it was found that mild inflation tends to be associated with the highest ratio of investment to income, compared with countries with relative price stability and inflation in excess of 10 per cent. It was also found that the ratio of growth to inflation tends to be higher the more developed the country, suggesting, perhaps, that the efficiency of inflation is greater the more sophisticated the monetary system.

In a study of thirty-one developing countries Tun Wai found a positive relation between growth and inflation up to a critical inflation rate, after which growth apparently declined.[2] This is the form of relation that we hypothesised in Chapter 2 in discussing the advantages and dangers of inflation. The inflation rate which maximises the growth rate in Tun Wai's model is 12.8 per cent. The quadratic function estimated has a low level of significance, however, and Tun Wai himself did not attach much weight to the result.

Wallich in a cross-section study of forty-three countries over the period 1956–65 finds growth and inflation negatively related.[3] A rate of inflation of 1 per cent above the average appears to be associated with a growth rate of 0.04 percentage points below the average. He concludes that the depressing effect of inflation on growth works through a worsening of the quality, distribution and cost of investment.

Perhaps the most comprehensive study to date is that of Dorrance, which examines growth in relation to both inflation and the level of per capita income.[4] Dorrance puts forward the interesting idea that if

[1] A. P. Thirlwall and C. Barton, 'Inflation and Growth: The International Evidence', *Banca Nazionale del Lavoro Quarterly Review* (September 1971).

[2] U Tun Wai, 'The Relation Between Inflation and Economic Development: A Statistical Inductive Study', *I.M.F. Staff Papers* (October 1959).

[3] H. C. Wallich, 'Money and Growth; A Country Cross-Section Analysis', *Journal of Money, Credit and Banking* (May 1969).

[4] G. Dorrance, 'Inflation and Growth: The Statistical Evidence', *I.M.F. Staff Papers* (March 1966).

growth rises with the rate of inflation and then falls, and if growth rises with the level of per capita income and then falls (as suggested by the savings data in Chapter 7), we should expect the empirical evidence to conform to growth contours as drawn in Fig. 9.1 below.

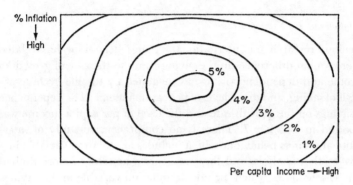

FIG. 9.1

By and large, Dorrance finds that the empirical evidence conforms to the contours, and that the data seem to support the argument for mild inflation.

In view of the paucity of cross-section studies, this chapter is devoted to a further examination of the relation between inflation and development using the data for sixty-eight countries reported in Appendix 1. In contrast to the studies reported above, however, the major emphasis will be on the relation between inflation and saving and inflation and investment, since saving and investment are the primary means through which growth is likely to be accelerated by inflation, if at all. The chapter will consist of two main sections: first, a model will be developed to test the hypothesis that inflation exerts an independent positive influence on saving, investment and growth; and secondly, the empirical results from applying the model will be discussed and the important results highlighted.

Owing to the absence of long data runs for developing countries it has not been possible to undertake time series analysis for individual countries. Even if there were long runs, however, the variation in the recorded inflation in most developing countries is likely to have been so slight as to render analysis hardly worthwhile. It cannot be stressed too often that in most developing countries inflation has been extremely mild for at least the last fifty years. The exceptions to this

statement, of course, are the countries of Latin America where inflation has been excessive and erratic. There is a growing body of literature analysing the Latin American experience, and the chapter concludes with a brief review of its conclusions such as they are.

Inflation and the Savings Ratio[1]

Previous research on international savings behaviour has related international differences in the savings ratio to the rate of growth of income and dependency ratios, as suggested by the life-cycle hypothesis of saving, and to the level of per capita income. The dependence of savings on the growth rate and the level of per capita income was reported in Chapter 7. There is no comprehensive study of international savings behaviour which includes an inflation variable in a cross-section analysis, and there are only a handful of more limited time series studies which include an inflation variable in the savings function, normally with insignificant results. In a study of six Asian countries Williamson found that the coefficient on the inflation variable was usually negative but rarely significant.[2] Only for the Philippines was the coefficient on the inflation variable found to be strongly positive. This accords with Treadgold's work on the Philippines which finds that price inflation has raised the savings ratio by the substantial erosion of real wages.[3] Landau has also included an inflation variable in a cross-section savings function for Latin America and finds the savings ratio negatively related to the rate of inflation.[4] In the highly inflationary countries of Latin America a negative relation is not unexpected for reasons that were outlined in Chapter 2, and which will be reiterated later; but what of the broad mass of countries with inflation rates of between 0 and 10 per cent?

The task is to develop and test a model that can distinguish the effect of inflation on the savings ratio from the effect of other variables

[1] The substance of this section is a modified version of my paper, 'Inflation and the Savings Ratio Across Countries', *Journal of Development Studies* (January 1974).

[2] J. G. Williamson, 'Personal Saving in Developing Nations: An Intertemporal Cross Section from Asia', *Economic Record* (June 1968).

[3] M. L. Treadgold, 'Inflation, Real Wages and the Rate of Savings in the Philippines', *The Developing Economies* (September 1970).

[4] L. Landau, 'Determinants of Saving in Latin America', Mimeographed Paper, Centre for International Affairs (Harvard University).

such as income growth and the level of per capita income. A single equation model relating the savings ratio to income growth, per capita income and inflation can be used as a first approach but there are problems of intercorrelation between the independent variables and of identification to contend with. Suppose, for instance, that inflation raises the savings ratio and the growth rate simultaneously. Not only would some of the impact of inflation be captured by the growth variable in the equation, but the very relation between the savings ratio and income growth would be in doubt. The identification problem inherent in the life-cycle hypothesis was touched on earlier in Chapter 7, but coping with this particular identification problem cannot deal with the possibility that savings and growth are simultaneously determined by inflation. The investment ratio which may be used to identify the dependence of saving on growth may itself be related to inflation.

A single equation model will also fail to capture the full impact of inflation on saving if the saving and investment ratios diverge as a result of international capital flows, which are themselves related to inflation. Suppose, for instance, that inflation opens up a balance-of-payments deficit which is financed by an inflow of foreign capital. If the inflow of foreign capital discourages domestic savings, as it is sometimes argued (see Chapter 8), or is partly consumed, but raises the growth rate, some of the variation in the savings ratio between countries which ought to be attributed to inflation will be attributed to the growth rate through the effect of inflation on the investment ratio. In addition, inflation may directly encourage private foreign investment by raising the money rate of return. If investment raises the growth rate, the effect on saving will be captured by the growth variable and not by the inflation variable in a single equation model to explain savings behaviour. But inflation was the initiating force in stimulating investment. What is required is a simultaneous equation model which recognises the interdependencies referred to in addition to the identification problem inherent in the life-cycle hypothesis of saving.

The impact of inflation on the investment ratio is best examined separately. Because investment exceeds saving by the amount of foreign resource inflows (and the relation between saving and foreign resource inflows is obscure), there may be more of a direct link between inflation and investment than between inflation and saving. And, after all, it is ultimately total saving (i.e. investment) that

matters for development, not just domestic saving alone. The effect of inflation on the investment ratio can be examined in a single equation framework without the previous worries of identification and the relation being distorted.

From the reduced form of the simultaneous equation model relating saving to inflation, the relation between inflation and growth can also be examined.

The first question to consider is the form of the function relating the savings ratio to inflation. For relatively mild rates of inflation of between, say, 0 and 10 per cent a linear approximation might do. But a linear relation would be difficult to substantiate as a general theoretical proposition. Theory suggests a quadratic of the form

$$s = a_0 + b_0(dP/P) + c_0(dP/P)^2; \; b_0 > 0, \, c_0 < 0$$

with the savings ratio(s) reaching a maximum at some 'optimum' rate of inflation, $(dP/P)^*$, beyond which the ratio declines where the yield from the redistribution effects of inflation is offset by a decline in voluntary saving. Since inflation is a tax on money it is natural to expect people to avoid the tax if it becomes burdensome in relation to the convenience of holding money. This is notwithstanding the real balance effect on saving which comes about as a result of the public's desire to restore the real value of its cash holdings during inflation. As inflation becomes more and more severe people may be expected to economise on holdings of cash for transactions purposes. Thus, as the rate of inflation rises, voluntary saving may be expected to fall, and a point will come when the decline in voluntary saving begins to outweigh any favourable effects on saving that result from income redistribution. What we have in mind is a profile of saving in relation to inflation as shown in Fig. 9.2.

OR shows the rise in the savings ratio that may result from income redistribution. VV gives the relation between the 'voluntary' savings ratio and inflation. VS shows the change in the total domestic savings ratio as a combination of the other two functions. It reaches a maximum where the negative slope of VV exceeds the positive slope of OR. The simple two-sector model developed in Chapter 6 is a linear model (in a cross-section context) which seeks to approximate the slope of OR, and is designed to give some a priori estimate of what the slope of the observable relation (VZ) is likely to be up to some arbitrarily decided maximum inflation rate (e.g. OP). Since the model does not incorporate the anticipated decline in voluntary saving, the coefficient

estimate of the model is likely to be an overestimate of the observed relation. The quadratic function mentioned earlier seeks to estimate the total relation (VS). From the empirical estimates, with a measure of inflation introduced non-linearly into the savings equation, we can see whether a rough empirical estimate for the 'optimum' rate of inflation can be obtained. Some observers have suggested inflation

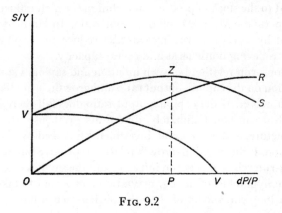

FIG. 9.2

rates of between 5 per cent and 10 per cent for maximising the savings ratio, but such speculations have not usually been based on econometric evidence.[1]

It is often argued that the positive effect of mild inflation on saving can only be short run because ultimately inflation will be anticipated by the private sector in general, and wage-earners in particular, so that the redistribution effects of inflation are ultimately zero. Apart from the fact that the 'short run' may be a long period of time, there is also the possibility of an indirect effect of inflation on saving through a fall in the capital–output ratio, and the effect of faster growth on saving through the life-cycle hypothesis of saving. The relation between inflation and saving via the growth rate, through the link between inflation and the long-term capital–output ratio, is much more tenuous and much less certain than the short-term effects of inflation on saving, but overall there is a strong presumption that the productivity of capital will be raised, or could be if the inflation is government financed, for the reasons discussed in Chapter 6. Presumably one of the main purposes of government financed expenditure is to alter the structure of investment and production to yield

[1] e.g. Harberger 'Some Notes on Inflation in Latin America'.

returns to society higher than the private returns forgone. If the investment expenditure is on research and development, which improves the stock of knowledge, the inflationary finance will have exerted a permanent favourable influence on the sustainable rate of capital accumulation. In the private sector, increased investment may embody skills and technology which are irreversible in the sense that they add to the stock of production techniques which influence more or less permanently the capital–output ratio. Inflationary policies financed by foreign borrowing can also reduce the capital–output ratio by relieving bottlenecks and excess capacity.

The long-run relation between inflation and saving, via the effect of inflation on the capital–output ratio and growth, is not likely to be linear, however. If the capital–output ratio does fall there is a limit to which it can fall. Ultimately, diminishing returns must set in to infrastructure, and other social, investments financed by higher rates of inflation. If the inflation–growth relation is positive but non-linear, the long-run relation between inflation and the savings ratio, via the life-cycle hypothesis of saving, may also be expected to take on this form. A long-run model of the relation between inflation and the savings ratio may be thought of as predicting roughly the same form of relationship as the short-term model. This is convenient because an analysis of a cross-section of countries is likely to contain a mixture of long-run and short-run influences. Moreover, without knowing how 'long' is the 'short run' it would be impossible to distinguish empirically between the short- and long-run models. In the subsequent empirical analysis, therefore, the distinction between the short and long run is forgotten, and the general hypothesis is tested that mild inflation raises the domestic savings ratio and that 'excessive' inflation lowers it.

The Linear Model

It seemed worthwhile in the first instance to test the simple hypothesis that

$$S/Y = f(dY/Y, dP/P, Y/N) \tag{9.1}$$

or, using the alternative formulation of the life-cycle model (assuming population is not in balanced growth)

$$S/Y = g(dY_N/Y_N, dP/P, Y/N) \tag{9.2}$$

where S/Y is the domestic savings ratio

dY/Y is the percentage rate of growth of total income

dY_N/Y_N is the percentage rate of growth of per capita income

dP/P is the percentage rate of inflation

and Y/N is per capita income in \$U.S.

The expectation is that $f_1' > 0$; $f_2' > 0$; $f_3' > 0$; $g_1' > 0$. The savings equations can be estimated with different combinations of the independent variables. The data relate to average values of the variables for sixty-eight countries over the period 1958–68 (see Appendix 1). The equations will be estimated for three main samples – developing countries, developed countries and all countries combined – and for several samples of the developing countries, grouped according to 'continents' and per capita income, recognising that developing countries as a whole are a very heterogeneous group. A division of the sample according to the type of inflation is ideally required, but unfortunately it is virtually impossible to say what any given rate of inflation in a country is primarily due to. But as we recognised earlier there is likely to be some variation in savings behaviour at the same rate of inflation according to the type of inflation. A 5 per cent cost inflation can be expected to produce different results from a 5 per cent demand inflation. In all equations per capita income is treated as an exogenous variable. This is justified on the grounds that per capita income stands as a proxy for the broader characteristics of a country than simply its capacity to save out of income.

It has been argued, however, that the full impact of inflation on the savings ratio may not be captured using a single equation model because inflation may affect foreign capital inflows which on the one hand may 'discourage' domestic saving but on the other hand may raise domestic saving by raising the growth rate. In general, inflation-induced growth may raise the savings ratio, but the rise in the savings ratio will be attributed to growth and not to inflation in a single equation model. To obtain an estimate of the 'true' effect of inflation on saving a simultaneous equation model is required from which structural estimates can be made by indirect least squares from the reduced form of the system. The model developed contains three structural relations[1]

---

[1] dY/Y can be replaced by dY_N/Y_N on the alternative version of the life-cycle hypothesis. The model is estimated using both formulations.

$$S/Y \ = S(dY/Y, dP/P)$$

$$dY/Y = G(I/Y) \qquad (9.3)$$

$$I/Y \ = I(dY/Y \ dP/P \ Y/N)$$

where S/Y dY/Y and I/Y are endogeneous and dP/P and Y/N are assumed to be predetermined. In linear estimating form we have

$$S/Y \ = a_0 + b_0(dY/Y) + c_0(dP/P) + u$$

$$dY/Y = a_1 + b_1(I/Y) + v \qquad (9.4)$$

$$I/Y \ = a_2 + b_2(dY/Y) + c_2(dP/P) + d_2(Y/N) + z$$

where u, v and z are stochastic error terms with constant variance.

The model requires little discussion. The effects of inflation on saving via the growth rate are captured by relating the growth rate to the investment ratio and the investment ratio to the inflation rate. The investment ratio and the savings ratio differ to the extent of foreign capital inflows or outflows. Solving the model in terms of the exogeneous variables, dP/P and Y/N, gives the following reduced form equations (omitting error terms)

$$S/Y \ = \pi_0 + \left[\frac{b_0(b_1c_2)}{\Delta} + c_0\right](dP/P) + \left[\frac{b_0(b_1d_2)}{\Delta}\right](Y/N)$$

$$dY/Y = \pi_1 + \frac{(b_1c_2)}{\Delta}(dP/P) + \frac{(b_1d_2)}{\Delta}(Y/N) \qquad (9.5)$$

$$I/Y \ = \pi_2 + \frac{(b_2 + c_2)}{\Delta}(dP/P) + \frac{(b_2 + d_2)}{\Delta}(Y/N)$$

where $\Delta = 1 - b_1b_2$.

The reduced form of the system is useful for three purposes. First, we can look at the full impact of inflation on the savings ratio by comparing the coefficient on dP/P in the reduced form with the coefficient on dP/P in the single equation model. Secondly we can examine the growth–inflation relation. This will be particularly useful when the inflation variable is entered non-linearly because 'optimal' rates of inflation in relation to growth can then be looked at as well as optimal rates of inflation in relation to the savings ratio. The growth–inflation relation will be considered in a separate section later. Thirdly, the model can be solved to obtain estimates of the structural coefficients, b_0 and c_0.

The detailed results of testing the single equation and simultaneous equation models are reported in Appendix 2. Here the major findings will be highlighted. The samples of countries analysed separately consist of a mixture of sixty-one developed and developing countries; eighteen developed countries; thirty-seven developing countries; twenty-one countries with per capita incomes between $200 and $799 p.a.; sixteen countries with per capita incomes of less than $200 p.a.; fifteen countries of Latin America, and seven African countries. None of the samples includes countries with inflation rates in excess of 10 per cent per annum.

By way of summary, it may be said from the outset that none of the results is very encouraging for the hypothesis that inflation raises the domestic savings ratio independently of other variables. The inflation variable generally has the hypothesised positive sign, but in most samples the coefficient is statistically insignificant at the 95 per cent confidence level. It looks as if the effects of inflation are dissipated mainly in the form of higher capital imports, leaving the relation between inflation and domestic saving weak. It will be shown later, in fact, that there is a much stronger association between the investment ratio and inflation than between the domestic savings ratio and inflation. If the proportion of capital imports that is 'consumed' could be appropriated back to domestic saving (see Chapter 8) a much stronger relation between inflation and domestic saving might emerge from the statistics. None the less, let us highlight some of the interesting results that emerge from the different samples of countries taken. All bracketed terms are standard errors of the coefficients.

Taking all sixty-one observations, with the rate of inflation as the only independent variable in the savings function, gave the equation

$$S/Y = 16{\cdot}450 + 0{\cdot}237(dP/P)$$
$$\phantom{S/Y = 16{\cdot}450 + 0{\cdot}}{\scriptstyle(0{\cdot}472)}$$

The coefficient is positive but the standard error of the coefficient is clearly too large for any statistical significance to be attached to it.

Considering inflation in conjunction with the level and growth of per capita income gave the following equation

$$S/Y = 11{\cdot}861 + 0{\cdot}700(dY_N/Y_N) + 0{\cdot}110(dP/P) + 0{\cdot}0043(Y/N)$$
$$\phantom{S/Y = 11{\cdot}861}{\scriptstyle(0{\cdot}406)}\phantom{+ 0{\cdot}700(dY_N/Y_N)}{\scriptstyle(0{\cdot}420)}\phantom{+ 0{\cdot}110(dP/P)}{\scriptstyle(0{\cdot}0010)}$$

Only the per capita income variable is significant. The coefficient on the life-cycle variable is insignificant compared with the results

obtained in Chapter 7, probably because of the intercorrelation between the independent variables.

Taking the reduced form of the simultaneous equation model makes little difference to the results. The size of the savings–inflation coefficient rises from 0·110 to 0·162, but it is still insignificant at conventional levels of significance. In view of this there seemed little point in making indirect least squares estimates of the structural parameters of the savings equation in the simultaneous model.The per capita income variable retains its strong significance in the re-duced form. Indeed in all the savings functions estimated, using different combinations of independent variables, the per capita income variable always shows up as a strong determinant of the sav-ings ratio. This merely goes to support what was reported in Chapter 7 using a different model specification.

When the sample of countries was split into developed and de-veloping countries, using \$800 per capita as the arbitrary criterion for division, the results for the separate groups reveal some interesting contrasts. While the sign on the inflation variable is positive in the developed countries, it is negative in the developing countries. The sign on the per capita income variable, on the other hand, is negative in developed countries and positive in the developing countries. None of the coefficients is statistically significant at the 95 per cent level of confidence, however.

When the developing country group is split into two, using \$200 per capita as the criterion for division, further interesting contrasts emerge. While the coefficient on the inflation variable is consistently negative in the very poor countries, it is consistently positive in the middle-income range of countries. But in neither case does the relation differ significantly from zero.

Lastly, the inflation hypothesis in a linear model was considered in the context of two continents, Africa and Latin America. The results for Latin America are especially interesting. Inflation exerts a statistically significant negative effect on the savings ratio in the life-cycle model holding per capita income constant. Taking the two alternative versions of the life-cycle hypothesis we have

$$S/Y = 16 \cdot 189 - 1 \cdot 588(dY/Y) - 0 \cdot 391(dP/P) + 0 \cdot 0202(Y/N)$$
$$ (0 \cdot 592) (0 \cdot 128) (0 \cdot 0066)$$

and

$$S/Y = 10 \cdot 426 - 1 \cdot 142(dY_N/Y_N) - 0 \cdot 262(dP/P) + 0 \cdot 0190(Y/N)$$
$$ (0 \cdot 481) (0 \cdot 103) (0 \cdot 0068)$$

Landau has also found a negative relation between inflation and the savings ratio in Latin America.[1] Two explanations suggest themselves. One is that within the sample of countries, inflation has been so excessive as to discourage saving in the ways outlined earlier in the book. A second possibility is that inflation in Latin America has been primarily structural in origin, but policy has been implemented as if the inflation was of the demand variety, which has depressed income and saving while leaving the rate of inflation largely untouched. Without knowing more precisely the origins of inflation, the latter explanation is no more than speculation at this stage. The Latin American experience is examined in more detail at the end of the chapter.

For the small sample of African countries the inflation variable is also negative but not significantly different from zero. The major determinant of differences in the savings ratio between African countries appears to be the level of per capita income, as the equation below indicates

$$S/Y = -1 \cdot 039 + 1 \cdot 740(dY/Y) - 0 \cdot 172(dP/P) + 0 \cdot 064(Y/N)$$
$$ (1 \cdot 513) (0 \cdot 717) (0 \cdot 028)$$

The Non-Linear Model

The hypothesis is that up to a certain rate of inflation the savings ratio increases with the rate of inflation but beyond this point the effects of inflation on saving through redistribution effects are offset by a decline in voluntary saving. To test this hypothesis it is difficult to know what function to fit to the data *a priori*. Observation of the crude scatter diagrams for the various samples of countries gives very little guidance. The obvious first approach is to fit a quadratic function in dP/P. In the non-linear model, therefore, $(dP/P)^2$ is added to all the equations which contain dP/P in the linear model, with the expectation that the coefficient on $(dP/P)^2$ is < 0. $(dP/P)^2$ becomes an additional predetermined variable in the model. Provided the coefficient on the variable $(dP/P)^2$ is negative, the model can be used to estimate the rate of inflation that maximises the savings ratio.

The results of estimating the non-linear model are outlined in full in Appendix 2. The number of observations used in each sample in the non-linear model is generally larger than in the linear model because the countries with high rates of inflation are retained in the sample.

[1] Landau, 'Determinants of Saving in Latin America'.

Hence, the samples and results are not strictly comparable but some general remarks may be made. First, the quadratic form appears to approximate the data better than the linear model. In all samples, except two, the sign of the coefficient on dP/P is positive and on $(dP/P)^2$ negative. In the linear model, it will be remembered, the sign of the coefficient on dP/P was negative for the developing countries. The standard errors of the coefficients are affected by the intercorrelation between (dP/P) and $(dP/P)^2$ but this is unavoidable. The most that can be extracted from the results are some loose profiles of saving in relation to inflation of the type discussed theoretically. In all the samples of countries, except for the African countries and countries with per capita incomes below \$200 p.a., the second-order conditions for a maximum are satisfied so that point estimates can be made of the 'optimum' rate of inflation, and confidence limits around the estimates obtained. It may also be noted that the coefficient on dP/P in some samples is close to that predicted by the two-sector model in Chapter 6.

To obtain point estimates of the rates of inflation which maximise the savings ratio, we differentiate the chosen equations with respect to dP/P and set them equal to zero. From the estimating equation

$$S/Y = \alpha + \beta(dP/P) - \gamma(dP/P)^2$$

we have

$$\frac{\partial(S/Y)}{\partial(dP/P)} = \beta - 2\gamma(dP/P) = 0$$

Hence, the 'optimum' rate of inflation is $\dfrac{\beta}{2\gamma}$.

To narrow down the range of equations that could be taken, attention is confined firstly to the equations in the single equation model which include only dP/P and $(dP/P)^2$ as independent variables, and secondly to the reduced form equations which include per capita income as an independent variable in addition. The results and the significance of the point estimates are shown in Table 9.1. The estimates obtained taking all observations, and the developed countries alone, do not appear unreasonable, and accord with off-the-cuff remarks of casual empiricists, but in both cases two standard deviations around the estimates do not exclude zero as a possibility. The estimates of the optimum rate of inflation for the developing countries are higher and

significant at the 95 per cent confidence level. But the range in which the point estimates lie is very wide. For the Latin American countries, where the point estimates are roughly the same as for the developing countries as a whole, the estimates are not significantly different from zero.

Taking the results of the linear and non-linear models as a whole one is forced to the overall conclusion that, on the available evidence, the relation between mild inflation and the domestic savings ratio is positive but comparatively weak. Ignoring measurement errors, which is a real possibility in any research of this nature, at least four possible explanations can be advanced for the weak relation. First, countries adjust much more quickly to inflation than was argued earlier, so that the redistribution effects of inflation are slight. Second, countries react differently to inflation which simple control variables like the level of per capita income cannot possibly take account of. In this connection a clear distinction needs to be made between policies of inflationary finance and their manifestation in the form of rising prices. The same rate of inflation may be associated with different degrees of monetary expansion due to differences in the supply response of the economy; consequently, the same inflation rate may produce a differential savings response. Strictly speaking, to find a weak relation between the savings ratio and the inflation rate cannot damage the argument against inflation-induced growth without knowledge of the supply response. Third, the origins of inflation may differ between countries. Inflations which arise from excess demand are more likely to be accompanied by increased saving than inflations which are structural in origin or cost-induced. In this respect, it may be significant that the inflation–saving relation seems to be closer across developed countries than across developing countries. In the developing countries, the rate of structural inflation may be expected to be higher than in the developed countries, and to be subject to wide variation between them. Finally, as suggested at the outset, the inflation–saving relation may be distorted by the balance of payments effects of inflation resulting in capital imports which, if 'consumed', will be recorded as a reduction in domestic saving, since domestic saving is defined as domestic investment minus capital imports. What this suggests is that a closer relation is to be expected between the investment ratio and inflation than between the domestic savings ratio and inflation. This expectation is confirmed as will be seen below.

Table 9.1
'Optimum' Rates of Inflation

Sample (no. of observations)	'Optimum' inflation rate to maximise saving	0·95 Confidence interval[1]	Range of inflation experienced	Mean rate of inflation
All observations (68)	9% 7%	Estimates not significant at 0·95 level	0·2% to 100%	6·4%
Developed countries (18)	6% 6%	Estimates not significant at 0·95 level	2·0% to 8·7%	3·4%
Less developed countries (43)	28% 23%	15% to 41%	0·2% to 100%	8·0%
Countries with per capita incomes $200–$799 (27)	20% 19%	4% to 36%	0·2% to 40·9%	6·8%
Countries with per capita incomes < $200 (17)	Second order conditions not satisfied	—	—	—
Latin America (19)	27% 24%	Estimates not significant at 0·95 level	0·2% to 40·9%	9·2%
Africa (8)	Second order conditions not satisfied	—	—	—

[1] From the quadratic $Y = \alpha + \beta X + \gamma X^2$, the variance of the point estimate of

$$\frac{\partial Y}{\partial X}\left(= \frac{\beta}{2\gamma} \right)$$

is

$$\frac{1}{(2\gamma_0)^4}\left((2\gamma_0)^2 \operatorname{var} \hat{\beta} + \beta_0{}^2 \operatorname{var} \hat{\gamma} - 4\gamma_0\, \beta_0 \operatorname{cov}(\hat{\beta}\,\hat{\gamma}) + (\operatorname{var} \hat{\beta})(\operatorname{var} \hat{\gamma}) + \operatorname{cov}(\hat{\beta}\,\hat{\gamma})^2 \right)$$

Inflation and the Investment Ratio

The arguments advanced in support of a positive relation between mild demand inflation and the savings ratio can also be used in support of a positive relation between inflation and the investment ratio. Apart from the fact that inflation may result from plans to invest exceeding plans to save, and that investment is bound to rise with inflation if inflation worsens the trade deficit which is financed by capital inflows, inflation may also be expected to enhance the profitability of investment by raising the money rate of return and reducing the real rate of interest. The prospect of high returns may also attract additional capital investment from abroad. If the inflation is induced by government, the interest rate is likely to be kept low by an appropriate expansion of the money supply, otherwise the purpose of inflationary finance would be defeated. There is a good deal of evidence that private investment and inflation are positively correlated, even in highly inflationary countries. Ternent finds a positive association between inflation and private investment in Brazil 1948–64.[1] Lim concludes that in South Korea inflation has been conducive to investment, and finds no evidence of 'inefficiency' in the investment process which inflation is said to breed.[2]

There are other case studies, however, which show that the expansion of government investment programmes has discouraged private investment, and where excessive inflation has shifted the composition of investment away from fixed capital formation towards investment in inventories and other more liquid assets. Ahmad finds in his study of deficit finance in Ghana over the period 1960–5 that deficit finance, and a rising proportion of government investment to total investment, was accompanied by a falling off in private investment as a result of uncertainty and shortages of foreign exchange.[3] The growth rate also apparently declined slightly owing to the changing structure of investment in favour of public enterprise. State enterprises were tending to work below capacity because of shortages of skills and spare parts.

[1] J. Ternent, *Inflation and Private Investment in Latin America*, unpublished doctoral dissertation, University of Oregon (March 1967).

[2] Y. Lim, 'Inflation and Capital Formation: Post-War Korea', *Economia Internazionale* (May 1971).

[3] N. Ahmad, *Deficit Financing, Inflation and Capital Formation: The Ghanaian Experience 1960–65* (München: Weltforum Verlag, 1970).

The argument is also sometimes advanced that inflation will discourage productive investment by widening the gap in returns between investments which have high social benefits and investments which have high private benefits, e.g. investment in inventories, luxury housing, foreign assets and so forth. Inflation increases the desire for liquidity because it increases the frequency of unforeseen opportunities for advantageous purchases. This desire for liquidity tends to manifest itself in the purchase of short-term physical assets, which absorb society's resources, and which are relatively unproductive compared to investment in long-term physical capital or financial assets. There are two main asset switches to be expected: one out of long-term physical assets, such as investments in plant and machinery, the other out of illiquid money assets. Inventories are probably the most desirable asset in highly inflationary circumstances, giving liquidity and real value certainty. Dorrance has suggested that in Colombia, Mexico, Brazil and Chile there is clear evidence of an association between inflation and the rate of inventory accumulation.[1] Shaalan has also found in a study of eight high-inflation countries in Latin America that inflation, at least in the short run, tends to bias the composition of investment towards inventories.[2] Over the long period, however, continuous inflation has not been associated with undue bias towards investment in inventories. Presumably in the long term inflation becomes anticipated, interest rates adjust, and monetary assets and long-term physical assets lose some of their relative unattractiveness resulting from uncertainty.

The weight of empirical evidence indicates that if inflation accelerates beyond a certain point, investment in fixed capital may be discouraged as the future becomes uncertain as to whether inflation will accelerate still further or will be brought under strict control. Unless a fairly stable rate of inflation is anticipated fixed investment in plant and machinery may suffer at the expense of investment in more liquid short-term physical assets and investment overseas. As with the savings ratio, the interesting question is whether an 'optimum' rate of inflation in relation to fixed investment can be discerned empirically.

[1] G. Dorrance, 'The Effect of Inflation on Economic Development', *I.M.F. Staff Papers* (March 1963).

[2] A. S. Shaalan, 'The Impact of Inflation on the Composition of Private Domestic Investment', *I.M.F. Staff Papers* (July 1962).

In the linear model, the investment ratio function may be specified as

$$I/Y = h(dY/Y, dP/P, Y/N) \qquad (9.6)$$

and in the non-linear model

$$I/Y = r(dY/Y, dP/P, (dP/P)^2, Y/N) \qquad (9.7)$$

There is no need for a simultaneous equation approach to an estimation of the parameters of the model, for the reasons already outlined. As reported earlier, a much stronger association is apparent between inflation and the investment ratio than between inflation and the savings ratio which suggests, as anticipated, that the domestic savings–inflation relation may be upset by the effects of inflation on the balance of payments which neither the single equation nor reduced form models can adequately take account of because the disturbance partly arises from accounting conventions.

The inflation variable shows up more strongly in the investment equations in the sense that the coefficient relating the investment ratio to the rate of inflation tends to be higher and its standard error lower than in the savings equations. However, the growth of income and the level of per capita income still seem to be of predominant importance. In the sample of sixty-one countries we estimate

$$I/Y = 13 \cdot 64 + \underset{(0 \cdot 291)}{1 \cdot 449(dY_N/Y_N)} + \underset{(0 \cdot 285)}{0 \cdot 184(dP/P)} + \underset{(0 \cdot 0007)}{0 \cdot 0025(Y/N)}$$

When the sample of countries is split into developed and developing, using $800 per capita as the criterion for division, the inflation variable is positive and significant at the 90 per cent confidence level in the case of the developed countries. In the developing countries the sign of the coefficient is negative. Per capita income is significant in determining the investment ratio in developing countries, as well as in determining the savings ratio, which is suggestive that per capita income may be a common cause of both domestic saving and capital imports as argued by Papanek in the context of the debate over whether it is capital imports that lower domestic saving, or low saving that produces high ratios of capital imports to income (see Chapter 8).

When the developing country group is split into two, using $200 per capita as the criterion for division, the investment equations again yield more satisfactory results than the savings equations. The relation between the investment ratio and the rate of inflation alone in the

countries with per capita incomes between \$200 and \$799 is estimated as

$$I/Y = 16 \cdot 728 + 1 \cdot 460(dP/P)$$
$${\scriptstyle(0 \cdot 852)}$$

and including the growth and level of per capita income as independent variables gives

$$I/Y = 13.190 + 0 \cdot 343(dY_N/Y_N) + 1 \cdot 049(dP/P) + 0 \cdot 0100(Y/N)$$
$${\scriptstyle(0 \cdot 607)}{\scriptstyle(0 \cdot 856)}{\scriptstyle(0 \cdot 0082)}$$

In Latin America and Africa the investment equations reveal the same adverse impact of inflation on the investment ratio as on the savings ratio. But the relation is no longer statistically significant in the Latin American case.

The results of testing the non-linear model are poor. The quadratic formulation is not to be preferred to the linear model. This result, however, is quite consistent with the improvement registered when the quadratic function was applied to the savings data. If inflation raises investment through capital imports, and domestic saving and capital imports are negatively related, we should expect investment and saving both to rise together at first, but then, as inflation worsens the balance of payments, for investment to continue to rise while domestic saving falls. This is what the evidence seems to indicate. The hypothesis that high rates of inflation react unfavourably on a country's investment ratio is rejected here.

In view of the reasonably encouraging results from relating the investment ratio to the rate of inflation, perhaps future work ought to concentrate more on the relation between *total* savings and inflation than on domestic savings and inflation alone, in recognition of the important role that capital imports can play in the development process. Because of the way domestic saving is defined, the relation between the rate of inflation and the domestic savings ratio is bound to be distorted in the presence of capital imports. In any case, total saving is a more relevant concept than domestic saving alone.

Inflation and Growth

The results of relating the growth of income to the rate of inflation in the reduced form of the simultaneous equation model developed earlier are as inconclusive as those of the studies mentioned at the beginning of the chapter. In the linear model, taking sixty-one

countries, growth is positively related to inflation but not significantly so. In no other sample of countries is the sign of the coefficient on the inflation variable positive. Some of the factors upsetting the inflation–saving relation will also upset the inflation–growth relation, especially the possibility of differential supply response to inflationary policies in different countries. In addition, the relation between growth and the rate of inflation may be disturbed by the fact that the relative price of investment and consumption goods differs between countries so that the same sacrifice of domestic consumption buys a different quantity of investment goods. Thus a given amount of inflation producing the same surplus for investment has less impact on growth the higher the relative price of investment goods. In other words, the capital–output ratio is higher. If it were possible, it would be desirable for this factor to be taken into account in undertaking cross-section studies of inflation and growth.

There is also the effect of inflation on the terms of trade to consider. If the terms of trade differ between countries, the same consumption sacrifice at home means a differential ability to purchase investment goods from abroad. How much less investment is bought depends on the proportion of total investment goods bought from abroad.

The quadratic specification of the growth–inflation relation fits the data no better except in the case of the developed countries where the coefficient estimates are strikingly significant. Fitting the function $dY/Y = f(dP/P, (dP/P)^2)$ by ordinary least squares gave the following result

$$dY/Y = -0.042 + \underset{(0.983)}{2.329(dP/P)} - \underset{(0.095)}{0.206(dP/P)^2}$$

and with per capita income also included as an explanatory variable

$$dY/Y = 1.402 + \underset{(0.754)}{1.844(dP/P)} - \underset{(0.075)}{0.161(dP/P)^2} - \underset{(0.0004)}{0.0003(Y/N)}$$

Since the relation between the investment ratio and inflation is very weak for the developed countries the inference must be that there is a strong negative association between inflation and the capital–output ratio. Such a relation is to be expected if the cause of inflation is demand pressing on capacity output. The 'optimum' rate of inflation to maximise growth implied by the above equations is 6 per cent, which is of the same order of magnitude for maximisation of the savings ratio, as reported in Table 9.1. The point estimates are statistically significant at the 95 per cent confidence level.

For those who believe that most developing countries have been over-cautious in financing capital formation by inflationary means, and have sacrificed growth and employment as a result, the results reported here might seem disappointing on the surface. A sharp distinction needs making, however, between policies of inflationary finance and the process of inflation itself. In many respects, the more successful the policy of inflation-induced expansion, the less the inflation rate will be. A lack of association between inflation and growth may be more a reflection of the differential response of countries to inflationary policies than indicative that inflationary policies are abortive of growth. Ideally, a measure of inflation-induced growth is required which is independent of the symptoms of excess demand. This could be obtained at the government level from the size of the budget deficit, but it would be difficult to obtain information in the private sector on divergences between plans to invest and plans to save unless some measure of credit availability was used.

It must also be borne in mind that results from a cross-section of countries are only a valid guide to behaviour within countries to the extent that the countries approximate to the cross-section model. The case for more expansionist policies within any individual country, on the hypothesis that more real capital formation can be financed, is certainly not destroyed by the cross-section evidence; the more so, bearing in mind the mild inflation rates recorded by most developing countries outside Latin America during the sample period, which probably represent minimum structural rates of inflation and not excess demand. What is badly needed are long runs of time series data for individual countries so that the significance of inflation (or, better still, inflationary policies) can be examined in the context of individual countries. It is no accident that to date the most well documented area of the world is Latin America, which has been unique in its inflationary experience among developing countries. Most other developing countries really have very little inflationary experience to analyse. This chapter concludes with a brief assessment of the Latin American experience.

The Special Case of Latin America

It was noted earlier that there appears to be a definite negative relation between inflation and growth in Latin America taking a

cross-section of fifteen countries over the period 1958–68. Before jumping to the conclusion that Latin American experience provides evidence that inflation is detrimental to growth, however, two factors must be borne in mind. The first is that the rates of inflation experienced in Latin America have been uniquely high, and it would be difficult to condone such rates even if economic theory predicted output gains. But economic theory does not. Throughout the book care has been taken to distinguish between mild inflation on the one hand and 'excessive' inflation on the other which can discourage voluntary saving and affect adversely the structure of investment most favourable to growth. The second point, and the more fundamental one in the Latin American context, is that not all economists are agreed that it is rapid inflation that has been the cause of slow growth. Rather, it is the pursuit of orthodox economic policies of demand management in the high-inflation countries that have depressed growth, while leaving the rate of inflation largely unchecked, because excess demand has not been the primary cause of inflation in the first place. The primary sources of inflation have been 'structural', it is argued, which are inherent in the process of structural change and which are therefore not amenable to demand management. On this interpretation inflation in Latin America has been a necessary condition for growth in the sense of being an inevitable concomitant of development. Inflation has been necessary for growth rather than a stimulus to it, but it has not been detrimental to growth. Three questions naturally arise. What are the 'structural' factors referred to? If structural factors have been the primary cause of inflation, why have these factors manifested themselves so severely in this part of the world? Thirdly, what is the evidence that inflation has been a necessary condition for growth in Latin American countries, which is a view implicit in the structuralist school of thought?

While it would be misleading to treat the Latin American countries as homogeneous, and to express a common 'structuralist' viewpoint applicable to all countries, certain themes consistently recur in the writings of those who adhere to a structural explanation of inflation. First, the process of development itself is one of structural change involving shifts in demand and supply from one sector to another according to the income elasticity of demand for products and the elasticity of supply of products with respect to price. If factors of production are relatively immobile, however, and supplies inelastic, shortages will develop and prices rise in those sectors where demand is

expanding rapidly. Price increases can then be transmitted to other sectors according to the input–output relations of the economy. Price increases lead to wage demands, initiating a wage–price spiral. The faster the rate of growth, the greater the degree of structural change and the greater the degree of inflation generated by structural bottlenecks. In the structuralist writing particular emphasis has been paid to the inelasticity of food supply as a primary source of inflationary pressure, which has initiated a wage–price spiral in the urban sector.

A second structural factor stressed has been the incapacity to import goods required for development purposes, because of the slow growth of export proceeds, which has necessitated policies of high-cost import substitution and exchange-rate devaluation, both of which have been inflationary. It should be clear that if in the process of structural change the demand for manufactured goods rises relative to the growth of output as a whole, and manufactured goods require a fixed proportion of imports to produce them, imports must rise faster than the growth of output. But, in the absence of foreign capital inflows, imports can only rise faster than the volume of output if export proceeds rise faster than output. In general, however, export proceeds have not kept pace with foreign exchange requirements owing to deterioration in the terms of trade, the low price elasticity of demand for exports, erratic variations in supply and the loss of markets from the substitution of synthetic products for raw materials.

A third factor stressed by the structural school is the inelasticity of tax revenue with respect to income growth, which has meant that tax revenue has not been forthcoming in adequate quantities to finance necessary public expenditure to sustain the desired growth rate. This has necessitated large and growing budget deficits leading to an excessive expansion of the money supply. Expansion of the money supply has become an inflationary force but for structural reasons in the sense that without the monetary expansion growth would be impaired. In a financial system where there are few non-bank sources of finance, and where the banking system is forced to finance government budget deficits, expanding the money supply also expands credit to the private sector of the economy adding to the inflationary pressure. This also means, of course, that in periods of financial stringency controlling the money supply may entail that supply is cut back by more than demand; hence the coexistence of inflation and

stagnation. Morley[1] explains the coexistence of inflation and stagnation in Brazil during most of the nineteen-sixties in these terms, and
Maynard and Van Rijckeghem[2] suggest that Argentina has suffered
in the same way.

Why these structural features of a developing economy should be
present in a more acute form in Latin America than in other developing regions of the world is not entirely clear. One class of reasons may
lay in the lack of preparedness for industrialisation, bad planning, and
a more restrictive social structure than elsewhere. Prior to the steep
decline in primary product prices in the nineteen-thirties, inflationary
tendencies in Latin America were mild. Exports were relatively
healthy; population growth was low because of high death rates, and
the supply of agricultural output was sufficient to meet domestic needs
without prices rising. In these circumstances there were no strong
pressures or incentives to effect changes in the land tenure and fiscal
systems, or to diversify exports – changes which have subsequently
become necessary in the face of industrialisation and rapid structural
change. Latin America can therefore be said to have entered its
industrialisation phase with a regressive and inelastic tax structure,
institutional bottlenecks in the agricultural sector and an export trade
heavily dependent on a handful of commodities. The effects of
structural rigidities and structural bottlenecks became exacerbated
by more rapid population growth as the death rate declined. Agriculture could not absorb the population increase, which therefore
overflowed into the cities, and which demanded food which the
agricultural sector could not provide. Inevitably, food prices rose,
stimulating wage demands and frequently leading to political up-
heaval as well. The necessity to import food then worsened the balance
of payments. Seers,[3] in his model of inflation and growth based on the
Latin American experience, considers the slow growth of exports to
pay for imports and the rapid rise in population, coupled with rapidly
rising economic aspirations, to be the major reasons why Latin

[1] A. Morley, 'Inflation and Stagnation in Brazil', *Economic Development
and Cultural Change* (January 1971).

[2] G. Maynard and W. Van Rijckeghem, 'Stabilisation Policy in an Inflationary Economy: An Analysis of the Argentina Case' in *Development
Policy: Theory and Practice*, ed. G. Papanek (Harvard University Press, 1968).

[3] D. Seers, 'A Theory of Inflation and Growth in Underdeveloped
Economies based on the Experience of Latin America', *Oxford Economic
Papers* (June 1963).

America has experienced more inflationary pressures than other developing regions.

But what truth is there in the arguments that food supplies have been inelastic, that export proceeds have lagged and that public deficits have been necessary to maintain the growth of output because of the inability to raise tax revenue? Are these factors common to all Latin American countries that have experienced high rates of inflation, or do the countries differ considerably in their experience?

The food-supply hypothesis has been examined exhaustively by Edel for eight countries since 1951 – Argentina, Brazil, Chile, Colombia, Mexico, Peru, Uruguay and Venezuela.[1] The proposition is tested that food production has lagged behind the required rate of growth which has pushed up food prices, caused balance-of-payments difficulties, and has led to overall economic stagnation. Given the rate of population growth, and the income elasticity of demand for food, Edel calculates that the rate of growth of food supply has lagged behind in five of the eight countries examined, namely Argentina, Chile, Peru, Colombia and Uruguay, but not in Mexico, Brazil and Venezuela. The cause of slow growth has been primarily the low price elasticity of supply. Edel concludes that agricultural stagnation has been a major source of inflationary pressure in Latin America. Food shortages have triggered off inflationary cycles and disrupted programmes of economic stabilisation.

There has been no comprehensive study, embracing a wide cross-section of countries, of the significance of the other elements in the structuralists' argument. The case histories of some individual countries have been fairly well documented, however, and a certain amount can be learnt from these.

In his analysis of the Chilean inflation Sunkel takes a structuralist approach.[2] As such, he condemns the orthodox stabilisation policies instituted by Chile as disastrous for economic growth and long-run development. Sunkel distinguishes three main categories of inflationary pressure: basic or structural inflationary pressures, exogenous inflationary pressures and cumulative inflationary pressures induced by inflation itself. The basic inflationary pressures relate to the structural factors already discussed. In Chile these have consisted of stag-

---

[1] M. Edel, *Food Supply and Inflation in Latin America* (Praeger, 1969).

[2] O. Sunkel, 'Chilean Inflation: An Unorthodox Approach', *International Economic Papers*, vol. x (1960).

nant food supply (also claimed by Edel), inability to diversify exports, inadequate capital formation and rigidities in the tax system. From 1940 to 1952, when prices rose steadily at an average annual rate of 18 per cent, agricultural output per head declined by 16 per cent. Exogenous inflationary pressures refer to such factors as rising import prices and political disturbances. Cumulative inflationary pressures refer to those mechanisms that propagate inflation once it is under way. In the Chilean case, the propagative mechanisms have consisted of political and social clashes between the government and the private sector on the one hand, and between social groups on the other, for an increased command over the country's real resources. Inflation has also been propagated by policies designed to cure it. Price controls to curb inflation have often diverted real capital formation from the production of basic goods and essential services to activities making very little contribution to productive capacity. Public investment expenditure has also tended to be cut because of growing current expenditure and inelastic tax revenue which has aggravated production bottlenecks and accentuated structural inflationary pressures.

Stabilisation measures were formally introduced in 1956 and 1957 after an eighty-fold rise in the wholesale price index from 1939, and a doubling of the price level in 1955 alone. The stabilisation measures consisted of restrictive monetary policy; curbs on wage and salary increases; cut-backs in public investment expenditure; devaluation and import controls; and the granting of favourable prices for agricultural commodities. But the stabilisation programme did not eliminate the various inflationary pressures; it merely curbed the propagation mechanisms producing stagnation and a regressive shift in the income distribution. The International Monetary Fund (I.M.F.), which has instituted stabilisation programmes in several countries of Latin America, has apparently been indifferent to the unemployment and the loss of output which has resulted from the pursuit of orthodox policy. In its 1950 report on the process of inflation in Chile it argued that a credit restriction to be effective must force businessmen to sell goods at prices lower than they had anticipated, if necessary at a loss. It must also make it financially impossible for businessmen to increase wage rates, and it must cause a certain minimum amount of unemployment.

Sunkel advocates a stabilisation programme which concentrates on eradicating the rigidities in the supply of goods, especially in the

agricultural and export sectors, and which increases the built-in flexibility of taxes.

A basically structuralist interpretation has also been offered by Eshag and Thorp of the post-war inflation in Argentina, particularly in the light of the experience of the country during the five year stabilisation programme initiated by the International Monetary Fund in 1959.[1] Over the period of the programme, industrial production was stagnant and the cost-of-living index rose by about 400 per cent, a rate of inflation higher than that experienced in any previous five year period. The external balance was also more precarious at the end of the stabilisation period than at the beginning. Devaluation and the pricing policies pursued had virtually no impact on agricultural production or export earnings from primary products. Eshag and Thorp conclude that the experience of the country during the five year stabilisation programme throws considerable doubt on the validity of the I.M.F. philosophy that inflationary pressures generated in the process of development can be tackled by orthodox policies. Eshag and Thorp trace the origin of the post-war inflation in Argentina to balance-of-payments problems caused by a deterioration in the terms of trade and the incapacity of exports to finance the purchase of imports necessary for development. Policies of price incentives were initiated to encourage agricultural production and exports, but they had little impact because of the restrictive nature of the land tenure system. All that happened was that the price incentives raised retail prices and instigated a wage–price spiral. Restrictive monetary and fiscal policy was then introduced which caused excess capacity and more inflation.

The essence of the I.M.F. stabilisation programme instituted in 1959 was completely orthodox. There was to be strict monetary and fiscal policy. All consumer subsidies and price controls were to be ended, and direct controls on trade and payments removed. A controlled floating-exchange rate was introduced, which promptly depreciated by 30 per cent in the first year. As a result of the currency depreciation and the abandonment of price controls and subsidies, the cost of living doubled in 1959, while the gross domestic product fell by 5 per cent and manufacturing production by even more. A vigorous wage–price spiral was triggered off. The automatic response

[1] E. Eshag and R. Thorp, 'Economic and Social Consequences of Orthodox Policies in Argentina in the Post-War Years', *Bulletin of the Oxford University Institute of Economics and Statistics* (February 1965).

of the I.M.F. was to pursue orthodox demand management policies even more rigorously. Production picked up somewhat in 1960 and 1961, largely due to the inflow of foreign capital, but then stagnated again in 1962 and 1963 following demand management policies to control the balance of payments which deteriorated as a result of the revival in production in 1961.

Maynard and Rijckeghem[1] have developed a useful model of the Argentinian economy to throw light on the *modus operandi* through which stabilisation policies in Argentina have produced the results they have. They lay the blame on credit restrictions which have tended to curtail output more than demand by forcing firms to dismiss labour and to cut back output through lack of liquidity to finance current production at continually rising costs. Their suggested stabilisation programme consisted of two main policies: the prevention of wages rising faster than prices, and the control of the money supply such as to maintain production in the private sector, but which at the same time would control demand by restricting public sector deficits.[2] In the view of Maynard and Rijckeghem, public sector deficits have been a major source of inflation, but deficits would not have been necessary had tax revenue been more elastic with respect to income. They claim that credit restriction has itself harmed tax revenue because firms have found it more profitable not to pay tax to maintain liquidity, and to pay the fine for tax avoidance instead.

A new stabilisation policy was introduced with some success with the advent of the military government in 1966. In 1967 inflation was 23 per cent and growth 1 per cent; in 1968 inflation was 12 per cent and growth 9 per cent; in 1969 inflation was 7 per cent and growth 6 per cent; in 1970 inflation was 14 per cent and growth 5 per cent. The stabilisation programme followed closely the types of recommendations made by Maynard and Rijckeghem. Wage rate increases were kept below price rises and bank credit was allowed to expand to maintain firm liquidity but the money supply was cut to a fraction of the increase in bank credit. The policy lasted as long as there were no major food shortages raising the price of agricultural goods. In 1970, however, the policy largely broke down as a result of increases in the price of beef.

[1] Maynard and Rijckeghem, 'Stabilisation Policy in an Inflationary Economy'.

[2] In effect, the policy would amount to controlling the money supply to keep it from expanding faster than bank credit.

The post-war economic history of Argentina would appear to be a classic example of the structuralist point that demand management policies are ultimately irrelevant in the presence of structural weaknesses in the economy. Inflation must be a necessary condition of growth until the structural weaknesses are remedied by structural cures. The basic weaknesses of the Argentine economy have been the poor performance of the export sector and the slow growth of agricultural productivity, both of which may be ascribed to undue emphasis on the industrial sector in development planning. Growth has been far too unbalanced.

Peru provides another case study where the vicissitudes of the internal economy have been dominated by the balance of payments, and where orthodox policies to stabilise the economy could not hope to be successful without depressing output. Fortunately for the stabilisation policy in Peru, however, it coincided with an upsurge in export receipts which makes it look as if the stabilisation policy was successful. In fact, Peru's success has been in spite of, not because of, stabilisation policies.

Following the stabilisation measures to control inflation in 1959, the economy made considerable progress during the next five years. The revival in exports which took place, however, had little to do with the stabilisation policies, but resulted from the revival of world demand for Peruvian products. The prices of cotton, copper and sugar rose, and the average price rise of all major exports was 40 per cent over the period 1949–65. Over the same period the volume of exports rose 60 per cent. As a result of the growth of export earnings, imports were allowed to grow and tax revenue increased, allowing public investment to expand without large budget deficits being incurred. Owing to the fortuitous external circumstances which mitigated the inflationary pressures in the economy, Peru was also able to pursue a successful wage policy which further assisted exports, compared to many other Latin American countries where orthodox economic policies initiated a wage–price spiral.[1]

In contrast to Chile, Argentina and Peru, there seems to be some consensus that in Brazil the causes of inflation have not been primarily structural in origin, but rather excessive monetary expansion and incompetent planning and economic policy-making in general,

[1] For a concise analysis of the Peruvian case see R. Thorp, 'Inflation and Orthodox Economic Policies in Peru', *Bulletin of the Oxford Institute of Economics and Statistics* (August 1967).

resulting in excess capacity at home and balance-of-payments difficulties abroad. Brazil has had the highest average inflation rate of any country in Latin America in the post-war period. In his meticulous study of inflation and development in Brazil, Kahil has examined the structuralist thesis and rejects it.[1] He finds no evidence of food shortage (which concurs with Edel's findings), no serious rigidities in the supplies of factors of production and that Brazil's balance-of-payments difficulties cannot be considered an independent cause of inflation. Rather, the deficits on the balance of payments have been caused by faulty policies and inflation itself.

The basic causes of inflation have been growing public deficits, the rapid expansion of bank credit, exaggerated increases in the legal minimum wage and the lack of a proper development policy. The cause of credit expansion has been political, argues Kahil; to win the allegiance of the urban masses. Inflation was the only way to 'anonymously' redistribute income and jobs to the urban masses, whose allegiance the government sought. In the early post-war years there was little necessity to control inflation because it was accompanied by substantial real growth, and the redistributive effects of inflation were relatively mild. It was not until 1958 when a severe wage–price spiral developed that the distributional consequences became severe and apparent. Even so there was reluctance to stabilise. In 1964 the government crumbled at the hands of the military.

Some of the 'inflationary' policies encouraged capital formation; others not. Quantitative import restrictions from 1948 to 1953, the results of which led to inflationary pressures subsequently, acted as a strong stimulus to investment in the industrial sector by favouring capital goods. But the considerable incentives to the import of capital goods that were offered also led to considerable waste and inefficiency. Investments were made without regard to complementarities in production, which increased the country's reliance on imports. More important, investment in capital goods out of domestic resources was discouraged. Non-essential goods, subject to import restrictions, became more profitable to produce domestically. To keep domestic capacity fully employed required large inflows of foreign resources which never came. The consequence was a steady increase in inflationary pressure. Because of the import policies pursued, the development of the industrial sector became unbalanced with a

[1] R. Kahil, *Inflation and Economic Development in Brazil 1946–1963* (Oxford University Press, 1972).

neglect of overhead capital and a heavy concentration on the production of 'non-essential' goods. In the late 1950s the legacy of industrial imbalance forced Brazil into the position of choosing between unemployment and chronic deficits on the balance of payments. The view has been expressed by Furtado that:

> it would be going too far to say that inflation was necessary for industrialisation . . . but the fact remains that industrialisation, as it actually happened, was certainly helped along by inflation. Inflation was not extraneous to the industrialisation process but removed obstacles from its path . . . the cause of inflation was not economic development itself but the lack of a proper development policy.[1]

Kahil finds no evidence that inflation financed more real investment in Brazil. Shifts in the income distribution brought about by inflation apparently combined, after 1955, to exert a strong downward pressure on the country's savings ratio. Investment itself was discouraged by price control policies and by excess capacity in the capital goods industries as a result of the misguided import control policies discussed earlier. Also, because of the decline in the terms of trade after 1954 a given consumption sacrifice at home was able to purchase less investment goods. The ability to purchase investment goods from abroad with a given volume of consumption goods sacrificed was 30 per cent less in 1963 than in 1954.

At the same time, Kahil contends that inflation redistributed resources to relatively inefficient activities within the private sector, in addition to redistributing resources to the public sector. As a result of inflation, the public sector's share of gross fixed capital formation rose from 18 per cent in 1945 to 43 per cent in 1960. And with negative real interest rates in the private sector it became profitable to purchase land, buildings and so forth, and to leave them idle, and to enlarge plant and machinery with little thought for its effectiveness and economic usefulness. These are all dangers of excessive inflation that were discussed in Chapter 2.

Kahil concludes that Sir Arthur Lewis's dictum that 'inflation which is due to the creation of money for the purpose of accelerating capital formation results in accelerated capital formation' is not valid for Brazil. All that deficit financed development programmes

---

[1] C. Furtado, 'Industrialisation and Inflation', *International Economic Papers*, no. 12 (1967).

achieved was to transfer command over capital resources from the relatively efficient private sector of the economy to the relatively inefficient public sector. The tendency for inflation to accelerate induced a wasteful use of resources within each sector because of the profit illusions it created and the disruptions it caused in the fiscal and banking systems.

The conclusion that emerges from this limited number of brief case studies is that it would be misleading to tar every Latin American economy with the same brush, and to treat the causes and consequences of inflation as identical in all cases. What does emerge fairly strongly, however, is that whether inflation was initiated by monetary or structural factors, the two sets of forces tend to become inextricably linked once inflation is under way. When cost and demand factors feed each other, inflation becomes necessary for growth. It is difficult, however, to find any firm evidence that monetary expansion and inflation have been a direct stimulus to growth in Latin America in the sense of providing additional resources for development which have been used productively for that purpose, and which would not otherwise have been available. Given the rates of inflation experienced, however, this should occasion no surprise. The arguments for mild inflation do not carry over to inflation rates approaching 50 per cent. The Latin American countries provide case studies of the dangers of inflation and point to the vital necessity of a sound agricultural base before launching an expansionary programme of industrialisation and employment creation by inflationary means.

Conclusion

The conclusions of an analysis in which the theory is often ambiguous in its predictions and the empirical evidence is inconclusive must necessarily be tentative. But some of the main points can be brought together. There is no doubt from the recorded statistics that the inflationary experience of most developing countries outside Latin America over the two decades of the 1950s and 1960s has been mild absolutely and relative to the recent inflationary experience of the world economy (at the time of writing). Consistent with this fact is evidence of a great deal of financial conservatism. The purpose of the book has been to redress the bias in the development literature against inflationary finance as a means of accelerating the rate of growth of output and employment. The case rests on two implicit

assumptions. The first is that conventional taxation and capital imports cannot be relied on to provide sufficient resources to meet development needs, and that inflationary finance can provide a useful supplement. The second is that the benefits of a policy of controlled inflation are likely to outweigh the costs. Because inflation is a tax on money, monetary expansion in excess of the growth of output can redistribute resources to governments who can use the proceeds of the inflation tax to raise the rate of capital formation and to alter the capital intensity of production by investing resources in labour-using techniques. High-yielding labour-intensive projects will not only raise the growth rate but also possess the potential to improve the income distribution as well. These are the important potential benefits of inflationary finance.

Leaving aside the possibility that the expansionary policy may be poorly administered, which can hardly be blamed on the policy itself, the major danger of inflationary finance undoubtedly comes from its repercussions on the price of food. This is probably the main reason why governments have been so cautious in embarking on policies of deficit finance. There are two solutions to the problems of rising food prices. One is to devote a large proportion of deficit finance expenditure to quick and high-yielding labour-intensive projects in the agricultural sector. The second is to use a portion of capital inflows for the purchase of food. The former solution is by far the more appealing if there are enough quick and high-yielding projects to rely on. The policy would create very little additional inflationary pressure and would raise the level of employment at the same time. What this amounts to is a plea, which is commonplace these days, for a greater volume of investment resources to be devoted to the agricultural sector in developing economies, but as part of a general expansionist policy. The alternative policy of expanding investment in the industrial sector and using capital imports to buy food is not so appealing, unless it is thought desirable to foster the development of indigenous capital goods industries embodying a technology more suitable to the needs of developing countries than the technology embodied in imported capital goods. What the optimal strategy is will depend on comparative advantage and the prices of foreign exchange and domestic factors of production.

The traditional methods of financing development are by taxation and capital imports. Our implicit assumption has been not only that tax revenue and capital imports cannot be relied on to provide

sufficient resources for investment, but that even if the tax system could be improved and capital imports increased, inflationary finance could still provide a useful additional supplement to development finance, the benefits of which would outweigh the costs as long as the warranted growth rate lay below the natural rate. For as long as the warranted growth rate lies below the natural rate there will be unemployed labour. The traditional argument against inflation is that it redistributes income from the poor to the rich and is therefore inegalitarian. It is true that the functional distribution of income will tend to alter in favour of profits, but it does not follow that wage-earners will be worse off absolutely or that the size distribution of personal income will become more unequal. As we showed in Chapter 2, a redistribution of income to profits is quite compatible with a rise in the real wage rate. More important still, inflationary finance has the potential to provide work for people who previously would not have figured in the size distribution of personal income because they were unemployed. Another argument against inflation is that it imposes welfare losses on the community by discouraging the holding of real money balances which are costless to produce. But the comparison to be made is not between inflation and no inflation, but between the welfare losses of inflationary finance compared with the welfare losses of other means of finance such as conventional taxation. The conventional tax system involves enormous administrative costs.

Throughout the book care has been taken to distinguish demand inflation from other types of inflation which may be features of the development process. The distinction is not only important theoretically but is also important to bear in mind in interpreting the empirical evidence. A certain amount of inflation is to be expected in the process of growth and structural change. To suppress structural inflation would be to suppress growth. Similarly cost inflation may have to be validated as the price of growth. But neither structural inflation nor cost inflation is a direct growth stimulus. Because the extent of structural and cost inflation may vary from country to country, cross-section analysis of the relation between inflation and growth may obscure the true stimulus that demand inflation may give to growth.

Finally, it should be stressed that we are not advocating here policies of irresponsible monetary expansion which may lead to inflation getting out of hand. What we are advocating are rates of

demand inflation of between 3 and 5 per cent, which, superimposed on a rate of structural inflation of between 1 and 5 per cent, might give a range of inflation of between 4 and 10 per cent. In principle, there is no reason why it should be more difficult to stabilise inflation at a rate between 4 and 10 per cent than at a rate of less than 4 per cent. Provided there is positive productivity growth, real living standards can rise without profits being impaired, and governments have a steady supply of revenue. A policy of mild inflation is not as unattractive as it sometimes made out to be.

Appendix 1

Data on Savings, Investment, Per Capita Income, Growth and Inflation

DEVELOPING COUNTRIES	(1) S/Y	(2) I/Y	(3) Y/N	(4) $\dfrac{dY_N}{Y_N}$	(5) $\dfrac{dY}{Y}$	(6) $\dfrac{dP}{P}$
Argentina	20	20	599	1·1	2·8	27·4
Barbados	9	25	325[e]	6·0	7·1	1·8[s]
Bolivia	8	16	116	1·8	4·7	7·9
Brazil	16	17	210[e]	2·2	5·6	40·9[t]
Cambodia	13[a]	17	100	1·3[h]	3·8[h]	3·7
Ceylon	13	16	125	1·8	4·3	1·5
Chile	12	14	325[f]	1·6	4·2	22·4
Colombia	18	20	245	1·5[i]	4·4[i]	10·6
Costa Rica	16	21	340	0·4	4·7	1·9
Cyprus	12	21	536	3·9	5·0	0·9
Dominican R.	12	16	219	—0·5	3·0	1·1
Ecuador	12	15	176	1·5	4·7	3·1
El Salvador	12	12	226	2·3[j]	6·3[j]	0·3
Fiji	22	20	235	3·1	3·9	1·6
Ghana	14	14	170	0	2·7	6·9
Greece	15	24	500	5·3	5·8	1·9[t]
Guatemala	9	12	256	1·8	4·9	0·2
Guyana	20	24	227	—0·2[r]	2·5[r]	2·2
Honduras	12	16	200	1·5	5·0	2·0
Indonesia	6	8	84	0	2·3	100·0
Iran	16	17	150	4·6[j]	7·6[j]	3·1
Ireland	14	18	644	4·0	4·2	3·1
Jamaica	17	24	364	3·1	5·3	2·9[t]
Kenya	17[b]	15	88	2·7[b]	5·0[b]	1·9

Developing Countries (contd.)	(1) S/Y	(2) I/Y	(3) Y/N	(4) $\dfrac{dY_N}{Y_N}$	(5) $\dfrac{dY}{Y}$	(6) $\dfrac{dP}{P}$
Malaysia	18	17	224^g	$3{\cdot}0^m$	$6{\cdot}2^m$	$1{\cdot}0^t$
Malta	16	25	420	$3{\cdot}6$	$3{\cdot}5$	$1{\cdot}2$
Mauritius	18	16	210^e	$0{\cdot}8$	$4{\cdot}0$	$1{\cdot}5$
Mexico	13	16	391	$2{\cdot}6^i$	$6{\cdot}2^i$	$2{\cdot}6$
Morocco	14	15	171	$0{\cdot}5$	$2{\cdot}2$	$2{\cdot}5$
Nicaragua	13	17	275^g	$3{\cdot}0$	$6{\cdot}4$	$1{\cdot}0$
Nigeria	10	13	58	$3{\cdot}4^m$	$5{\cdot}5^m$	$2{\cdot}7^n$
Pakistan	11	14	92	$1{\cdot}0$	$3{\cdot}7$	$5{\cdot}1$
Paraguay	10	14	158	$1{\cdot}0$	$3{\cdot}7$	$5{\cdot}1$
Philippines	13	19	222	$1{\cdot}6$	$5{\cdot}0$	$4{\cdot}4^i$
Portugal	13	18	375	$4{\cdot}8$	$5{\cdot}7$	$3{\cdot}4$
Puerto Rico	4	28	896	$7{\cdot}1^n$	$9{\cdot}0^n$	$2{\cdot}7$
Sierra Leone	9^c	12^c	93	$2{\cdot}0^p$	$3{\cdot}6^p$	$3{\cdot}4$
Spain	21	23	484	$5{\cdot}0$	$6{\cdot}0$	$4{\cdot}5$
Sudan	11	13	90^e	$1{\cdot}5^g$	$4{\cdot}1^g$	$1{\cdot}7$
Taiwan	16	20	170	$5{\cdot}9$	$9{\cdot}4$	$5{\cdot}1$
Thailand	19	21	110	$4{\cdot}6$	$8{\cdot}0$	$2{\cdot}1$
Trinidad and Tobago	16	25	526	$2{\cdot}4$	$5{\cdot}5$	$3{\cdot}0$
Turkey	12	15	250	$2{\cdot}6$	$5{\cdot}1$	$7{\cdot}9$
U.A.R.	10^d	16^d	133^e	$2{\cdot}9^i$	$5{\cdot}7^i$	$3{\cdot}0$
Uruguay	12	12	545	$-1{\cdot}1$	$0{\cdot}2$	$37{\cdot}7$
Venezuela	24	25	715	$1{\cdot}8$	$5{\cdot}2$	$0{\cdot}8^i$
S. Vietnam	0	10	262	$2{\cdot}1^r$	$4{\cdot}4^r$	$14{\cdot}3$
Zambia	27	27	173	$5{\cdot}0$	$8{\cdot}1$	$4{\cdot}1$

Developed Countries	(1) S/Y	(2) I/Y	(3) Y/N	(4) $\dfrac{dY_N}{Y_N}$	(5) $\dfrac{dY}{Y}$	(6) $\dfrac{dP}{P}$
Australia	25	25	1557	$2{\cdot}8$	$4{\cdot}9$	$2{\cdot}5$
Austria	25	24	866	$3{\cdot}8$	$4{\cdot}4$	$3{\cdot}1$
Belgium	20	20	1316	$3{\cdot}6$	$3{\cdot}8$	$2{\cdot}5$
Canada	23	23	2488	$2{\cdot}7$	$4{\cdot}7$	$2{\cdot}1$
Denmark	20	19	1424	$4{\cdot}2$	$4{\cdot}9$	$5{\cdot}3$
Finland	27	26	1034	$4{\cdot}1$	$4{\cdot}9$	$4{\cdot}5^i$
France	24	24	1390	$4{\cdot}2$	$5{\cdot}3$	$3{\cdot}4$
W. Germany	28	25	1209	$4{\cdot}1$	$5{\cdot}0$	$2{\cdot}5$
Iceland	25	29	1500^e	$2{\cdot}1^i$	$4{\cdot}2^i$	$8{\cdot}7$

DEVELOPED COUNTRIES (contd.)	(1) S/Y	(2) I/Y	(3) Y/N	(4) $\dfrac{dY_N}{Y_N}$	(5) $\dfrac{dY}{Y}$	(6) $\dfrac{dP}{P}$
Israel	9	25	894	5·0	8·5	5·1
Italy	22	22	823	4·8	5·3	3·3
Japan	35	35	705	9·4	10·4	4·9
Netherlands	26	25	1149	4·0	5·3	3·0
New Zealand	24	24	1338	2·0	3·9	3·0u
Norway	28	30	1339	4·2	5·0	3·4
S. Africa	20	24	432	3·0	5·7	2·2
Sweden	24	24	2148	3·9	4·5	3·5
Switzerland	26	26	1745	2·8	4·5	2·8
U.K.	18	17	1232	2·6	3·2	3·0
U.S.A.	18	18	3490	3·2	4·5	2·0

KEY

$a = $ 1962–6; $b = $ 1964–8; $c = $ 1963–6; $d = $ 1963–8; $e = $ av. of 1958 and 1967; $f = $ av. of 1963 and 1968; $g = $ av. of 1958 and 1966; $h = $1959–66; $i = $ 1958–67; $j = $ 1959–67; $k = $ 1960–5; $m = $ 1958–66; $n = $ 1961–8; $p = $ 1963–6; $q = $ 1962–4; $r = $ 1960–6; $s = $ 1958–65; $t = $ 1959–68; $u = $ 1960–8.

Column 1 refers to the average ratio of domestic saving to national income over the period 1958–68 unless otherwise stated.

Column 2 refers to the average ratio of total (including stocks) gross domestic investment to national income over the period 1958–68 unless otherwise stated.

Column 3 refers to per capita national income in $U.S. and is an average of the figures for the two years 1958 and 1968, unless otherwise stated.

Column 4 refers to the percentage rate of growth of real per capita income per annum in $U.S. 1958–68, unless otherwise stated.

Column 5 refers to the percentage rate of growth of total real income per annum in $U.S. 1958–68 unless otherwise stated.

Column 6 refers to the annual average percentage rate of increase in the consumer price index 1958–68 unless otherwise stated.

All the data were obtained from the *U.N. National Accounts Statistics*, vol. 2 (1969) and the *U.N. Statistical Yearbook 1969*.

Appendix 2

Regression Results of the Relation between Saving and Inflation and Investment and Inflation

Linear Model

	Constant	dY/Y	dY_N/Y_N	dP/P	Y/N	r^2
		ALL OBSERVATIONS (61)				
Savings						
Single equation						
$S/Y =$	16·450			+0·237		0·004
				(0·468)		
$S/Y =$	15,331	+0·222		+0·226		0·007
		(0·514)		(0·472)		
$S/Y =$	13·491		+1·051	+0·151		0·091
			(0·446)	(0·452)		
$S/Y =$	11·632	+0·382		+0·142	+0·0048	0·267
		(0·407)		(0·409)	(0·0010)	
$S/Y =$	11·861		+0·700	+0·110	+0·0043	0·295
			(0·406)	(0·420)	(0·0010)	
Reduced form						
$S/Y =$	13·597			+0·162	+0·0047	0·258
				(0·407)	(0·0010)	
$dY/Y =$	5·132			+0·051	—0·0002	0·095
				(0·120)	(0·0003)	
$dY_N/Y_N =$	2·742			—0·036	+0·0005	0·131
				(0·015)	(0·0003)	
$I/Y =$	18·270			—0·109	+0·0034	0·278
				(0·061)	(0·0008)	

	Constant	dY/Y	dY_N/Y_N	dP/P	Y/N	r^2
Investment						
$I/Y =$	19·223			+0·343		0·014
				(0·376)		
$I/Y =$	13·253	+1·189		+0·285		0·154
		(0·383)		(0·351)		
$I/Y =$	14·578		+1·651	+0·207		0·342
			(0·306)	(0·311)		
$I/Y =$	10·531	+1·307		+0·223	+0·0035	0·372
		(0·334)		(0·306)	(0·0008)	
$I/Y =$	13·643		+1·449	+0·184	+0·0025	0·445
			(0·291)	(0·285)	(0·0007)	

DEVELOPED COUNTRIES (18)

Savings						
Single equation						
$S/Y =$	22·299			+0·355		0·030
				(0·502)		
$S/Y =$	13·819	+1·761		+0·432		0·146
		(1·234)		(0·490)		
$S/Y =$	19·237		+0·840	+0·403		0·076
			(0·947)	(0·509)		
$S/Y =$	15·806	+1·577		+0·383	—0·0006	0·164
		(1·307)		(0·509)	(0·0011)	
$S/Y =$	21·251		+0·661	+0·342	—0·0008	0·103
			(1·029)	(0·527)	(0·0012)	
Reduced form						
$S/Y =$	24·013			+0·291	—0·001	0·077
				(0·591)	(0·875)	
$dY/Y =$	5·201			—0·058	—0·0002	0·075
				(0·099)	(0·0002)	
$dY_N/Y_N =$	4·172			—0·077	—0·0003	0·080
				(0·130)	(0·0002)	
$I/Y =$	22·885			+0·702	—0·0011	0·172
				(0·522)	(0·0011)	
Investment						
$I/Y =$	21·002			+0·722		0·123
				(0·515)		
$I/Y =$	10·038	+2·277		+0·871		0·290
		(1·213)		(0·481)		
$I/Y =$	20·580		+0·115	+0·778		0·124
			(1·022)	(0·535)		
$I/Y =$	11·966	+2·099		+0·824	—0·0006	0·304
		(1·284)		(0·500)	(0·0011)	
$I/Y =$	23·468		—0·139	+0·691	—0·0011	0·173
			(1·065)	(0·546)	(0·0012)	

	Constant	dY/Y	dY_N/Y_N	dP/P	Y/N	r^2

LESS DEVELOPED COUNTRIES (37)

Savings
Single equation

	Constant	dY/Y	dY_N/Y_N	dP/P	Y/N	r^2
$S/Y =$	4·901			—0·442 (0·287)		0·063
$S/Y =$	14·426	+0·092 (0·359)		—0·437 (0·292)		0·065
$S/Y =$	14·585		+0·116 (0·334)	—0·432 (0·292)		0·066
$S/Y =$	13·667	+0·078 (0·362)		—0·389 (0·302)	+0·0028 (0·0039)	0·079
$S/Y =$	13·994		+0·038 (0·357)	—0·391 (0·301)	+0·0027 (0·0042)	0·078

Reduced form

	Constant	dY/Y	dY_N/Y_N	dP/P	Y/N	r^2
$S/Y =$	14·055			—0·392 (0·297)	+0·0029 (0·0039)	0·078
$dY/Y =$	4·952			—0·044 (0·142)	+0·0005 (0·0018)	0·007
$dY_N/Y_N =$	1·577			—0·018 (0·144)	+0·0039 (0·0019)	0·119
$I/Y =$	13·811			—0·058 (0·294)	+0·0160 (0·0038)	0·353

Investment

	Constant	dY/Y	dY_N/Y_N	dP/P	Y/N	r^2
$I/Y =$	18·494			—0·337 (0·346)		0·026
$I/Y =$	15·880	+0·509 (0·425)		—0·309 (0·345)		0·065
$I/Y =$	15·904		+0·952 (0·369)	—0·255 (0·323)		0·185
$I/Y =$	11·677	+0·430 (0·351)		—0·039 (0·292)	+0·015 (0·003)	0·381
$I/Y =$	12·927		+0·560 (0·340)	—0·048 (0·287)	+0·013 (0·004)	0·402

	Constant	dY/Y	dY_N/Y_N	dP/P	Y/N	r^2

COUNTRIES WITH PER CAPITA INCOME $200–$799 p.a. (21)

Savings
Single equation

	Constant	dY/Y	dY_N/Y_N	dP/P	Y/N	r^2
$S/Y =$	13·785			+0·510 (0·756)		0·023
$S/Y =$	19·535	−1·143 (0·634)		+0·517 (0·714)		0·172
$S/Y =$	14·816		−0·444 (0·473)	+0·584 (0·762)		0·069
$S/Y =$	19·676	−1·133 (0·657)		+0·541 (0·767)	−0·0006 (0·0062)	0·173
$S/Y =$	14·512		−0·511 (0·578)	+0·537 (0·814)	+0·0016 (0·0078)	0·071

Reduced form

	Constant	dY/Y	dY_N/Y_N	dP/P	Y/N	r^2
$S/Y =$	14·350			+0·583 (0·808)	−0·0020 (0·0065)	0·028
$dY/Y =$	4·696			−0·036 (0·274)	+0·0012 (0·0022)	0·016
$dY_N/Y_N =$	0·317			−0·090 (0·331)	+0·0073 (0·0026)	0·299
$I/Y =$	13.299			+1·018 (0·838)	+0·0125 (0·0068)	0·271

Investment

	Constant	dY/Y	dY_N/Y_N	dP/P	Y/N	r^2
$I/Y =$	16·728			+1·460 (0·852)		0·133
$I/Y =$	18·040	−0·260 (0·774)		+1·461 (0·873)		0·139
$I/Y =$	15·004		+0·742 (0·518)	+1·335 (0·834)		0·222
$I/Y =$	15·346	−0·435 (0·731)		+1·002 (0·854)	+0·0130 (0·0069)	0·286
$I/Y =$	13·190		+0·343 (0·607)	+1·049 (0·856)	+0·0100 (0·0082)	0·284

	Constant	dY/Y	dY_N/Y_N	dP/P	Y/N	r^2

COUNTRIES WITH PER CAPITA INCOME < $200 p.a. (16)

Savings
  Single equation

$S/Y =$	14·775			—0·568		0·114
				(0·423)		
$S/Y =$	10·781	+0·745		—0·479		0·327
		(0·367)		(0·355)		
$S/Y =$	12·371		+0·806	—0·414		0·282
			(0·461)	(0·404)		
$S/Y =$	8·217	+0·704		—0·639	+0·0268	0·418
		(0·357)		(0·390)	(0·0194)	
$S/Y =$	9·239		+0·807	—0·587	+0·0301	0·399
			(0·439)	(0·401)	(0·0197)	

  Reduced form

$S/Y =$	11·654			—0·721	+0·0300	0·230
				(0·427)	(0·0214)	
$dY/Y =$	4·877			—0·145	+0·0045	0·019
				(0·300)	(0·0150)	
$dY_N/Y_N =$	2·990			—0·190	—0·0000	0·047
				(0·247)	(0·0124)	
$I/Y =$	13·422			—0·147	+0·0209	0·095
				(0·345)	(0·0179)	

Investment

$I/Y =$	15·598			—0·026		0·000
				(0·347)		
$I/Y =$	10·578	+0·937		+0·084		0·563
		(0·228)		(0·239)		
$I/Y =$	12·543		+1·024	+0·168		0·455
			(0·310)	(0·272)		
$I/Y =$	8·976	+0·911		—0·015	+0·0167	0·623
		(0·221)		(0·242)	(0·0121)	
$I/Y =$	10·356		+1·025	+0·047	+0·0210	0·550
			(0·293)	(0·268)	(0·0131)	

	Constant	dY/Y	dY_N/Y_N	dP/P	Y/N	r^2
			LATIN AMERICA (15)			

Savings
Single equation

	Constant	dY/Y	dY_N/Y_N	dP/P	Y/N	r^2
$S/Y =$	12·917			—0·037		0·011
				(0·098)		
$S/Y =$	17·996	—0·950		—0·167		0·136
		(0·722)		(0·137)		
$S/Y =$	14·445		—0·723	—0·098		0·127
			(0·572)	(0·107)		
$S/Y =$	16·189	—1·588		—0·391	+0·0202	0·533
		(0·592)		(0·128)	(0·0066)	
$S/Y =$	10·426		—1·142	—0·262	+0·0190	0·490
			(0·481)	(0·103)	(0·0068)	

Reduced form

	Constant	dY/Y	dY_N/Y_N	dP/P	Y/N	r^2
$S/Y =$	9·308			—0·132	+0·0140	0·228
				(0·103)	(0·0076)	
$dY/Y =$	4·332			—0·162	+0·0039	0·557
				(0·041)	(0·0030)	
$dY_N/Y_N =$	0·978			—0·113	+0·0044	0·277
				(0·052)	(0·0038)	
$I/Y =$	12·612			—0·312	+0·0226	0·359
				(0·138)	(0·0101)	

Investment

	Constant	dY/Y	dY_N/Y_N	dP/P	Y/N	r^2
$I/Y =$	18·441			—0·159		0·094
				(0·137)		
$I/Y =$	17·255	+0·222		—0·129		0·097
		(1·080)		(0·205)		
$I/Y =$	16·604		+0·869	—0·086		0·172
			(0·816)	(0·152)		
$I/Y =$	15·038	—0·559		—0·403	+0·024	0·376
		(1·001)		(0·216)	(0·001)	
$I/Y =$	12·209		+0·411	—0·265	+0·020	0·375
			(0·779)	(0·168)	(0·011)	

	Constant	dY/Y	dY_N/Y_N	dP/P	Y/N	r^2
			AFRICA (7)			

Savings
 Single equation

	Constant	dY/Y	dY_N/Y_N	dP/P	Y/N	r^2
$S/Y =$	14·201			—0·311		0·028
				(0·816)		
$S/Y =$	16·999	—0·591		—0·483		0·060
		(1·610)		(1·012)		
$S/Y =$	17·771		—1·487	—0·737		0·254
			(1·349)	(0·887)		
$S/Y =$	—1·039	+1·740		—0·172	+0·064	0·658
		(1·513)		(0·717)	(0·028)	
$S/Y =$	1·348		+1·909	—0·197	+0·075	0·590
			(2·453)	(0·833)	(0·048)	

Reduced form

	Constant	dY/Y	dY_N/Y_N	dP/P	Y/N	r^2
$S/Y =$	9·549			—0·554	+0·042	0·508
				(0·660)	(0·021)	
$dY/Y =$	6·085			—0·219	—0·012	0·568
				(0·210)	(0·006)	
$dY_N/Y_N =$	4·295			—0·187	+0·017	0·820
				(0·141)	(0·004)	
$I/Y =$	12·411			—0·293	+0·019	0·653
				(0·227)	(0·007)	

Investment

	Constant	dY/Y	dY_N/Y_N	dP/P	Y/N	r^2
$I/Y =$	14·536			—0·182		0·057
				(0·329)		
$I/Y =$	16·513	—0·418		—0·303		0·152
		(0·627)		(0·394)		
$I/Y =$	16·240		—0·709	—0·385		0·364
			(0·510)	(0·335)		
$I/Y =$	9·211	+0·525		—0·178	+0·026	0·735
		(0·545)		(0·258)	(0·010)	
$I/Y =$	9·250		+0·735	—0·155	+0·032	0·727
			(0·821)	(0·279)	(0·016)	

Non-Linear Model

	Constant	dY/Y	dY_N/Y_N	dP/P	$(dP/P)^2$	Y/N	r^2
Savings			ALL OBSERVATIONS (68)				
Single equation							
$S/Y =$	17·432			+0·017 (0·158)	−0·0009 (0·0017)		0·057
$S/Y =$	14·189	+0·612 (0·473)		+0·024 (0·161)	−0·0012 (0·0017)		0·081
$S/Y =$	12·856	+1·437 (0·407)		+0·087 (0·149)	−0·0015 (0·0016)		0·214
$S/Y =$	9·749	+0·820 (0·397)		+0·072 (0·134)	−0·0013 (0·0014)	+0·0051 (0·0009)	0·370
$S/Y =$	11·118		+1·096 (0·362)	+0·091 (0·129)	−0·0014 (0·0014)	+0·0043 (0·0009)	0·413
Reduced form							
$S/Y =$	14·222			+0·014 (0·135)	−0·0010 (0·0014)	+0·0049 (0·0009)	0·326
$dY/Y =$	5·447			−0·070 (0·042)	+0·0003 (0·0004)	−0·0002 (0·0003)	0·109
$dY_N/Y_N =$	2·883			−0·073 (0·044)	+0·0004 (0·0005)	+0·0006 (0·0003)	0·141
$I/Y =$	17·715			−0·047 (0·112)	−0·0005 (0·0012)	+0·0034 (0·0008)	0·293
Investment							
$I/Y =$	20·378			−0·093 (0·131)	−0·0003 (0·0014)		0·105
$I/Y =$	14·489	+1·113 (0·371)		−0·016 (0·126)	−0·0007 (0·0013)		0·218
$I/Y =$	15·144		+1·643 (0·305)	+0·026 (0·111)	−0·0010 (0·0012)		0·390
$I/Y =$	11·354	+1·260 (0·325)		+0·017 (0·110)	−0·0008 (0·0012)	+0·0036 (0·0007)	0·417
$I/Y =$	14·128		+1·444 (0·289)	+0·028 (0·103)	−0·0030 (0·0011)	+0·0025 (0·0007)	0·484

	Constant	dY/Y	dY_N/Y_N	dP/P	$(dP/P)^2$	Y/N	r^2
Savings			DEVELOPED COUNTRIES (18)				
Single equation							
$S/Y =$	18·467			+2·216 (2·558)	−0·179 (0·241)		0·044
$S/Y =$	11·403	+1·659 (1·276)		+1·839 (2·517)	−0·135 (0·238)		0·165
$S/Y =$	18·254		+0·632 (1·293)	+1·236 (3·301)	−0·081 (0·318)		0·080
$S/Y =$	13·450	+1·547 (1·350)		+1·470 (2·776)	−0·103 (0·260)	−0·0004 (0·0012)	0·174
$S/Y =$	20·780		+0·585 (1·327)	+0·678 (3·511)	−0·032 (0·336)	−0·0007 (0·0013)	0·104
Reduced form							
$S/Y =$	21·088			+1·557 (2·806)	−0·120 (0·262)	−0·0008 (0·0012)	0·091
$dY/Y =$	1·402			+1·844 (0·745)	−0·161 (0·075)	−0·0003 (0·0004)	0·314
$dY_N/Y_N =$	0·526			+1·501 (0·582)	−0·150 (0·054)	−0·0000 (0·0002)	0·404
$I/Y =$	26·710			−0·953 (2·850)	+0·157 (0·266)	−0·0013 (0·0012)	0·192
Investment							
$I/Y =$	22·249			+0·166 (2·664)	+0·058 (0·251)		0·126
$I/Y =$	12·173	+2·367 (1·256)		−0·371 (2·479)	+0·120 (0·234)		0·303
$I/Y =$	22·101		+0·437 (1·353)	−0·510 (3·456)	+0·125 (0·332)		0·132
$I/Y =$	16·083	+2·152 (1·309)		−1·075 (2·692)	+0·181 (0·252)	−0·0009 (0·0012)	0·331
$I/Y =$	26·522		+0·355 (1·354)	−1·487 (3·583)	+0·211 (0·343)	−0·0013 (0·0013)	0·196

	Constant	dY/Y	dY_N/Y_N	dP/P	$(dP/P)^2$	Y/N	r^2

LESS DEVELOPED COUNTRIES (43)

Savings

Single equation

	Constant	dY/Y	dY_N/Y_N	dP/P	$(dP/P)^2$	Y/N	r^2
$S/Y =$	13·570			+0·084 (0·090)	−0·0015 (0·0009)		0·116
$S/Y =$	12·889	+0·131 (0·343)		+0·094 (0·095)	−0·0016 (0·0010)		0·119
$S/Y =$	13·126		+0·166 (0·337)	+0·096 (0·094)	−0·0016 (0·0010)		0·121
$S/Y =$	11·652	+0·165 (0·341)		+0·061 (0·098)	−0·0012 (0·0010)	+0·0047 (0·0036)	0·157
$S/Y =$	12·391		+0·071 (0·345)	+0·056 (0·100)	−0·0012 (0·0010)	+0·0043 (0·0037)	0·152

Reduced form

	Constant	dY/Y	dY_N/Y_N	dP/P	$(dP/P)^2$	Y/N	r^2
$S/Y =$	12·540			+0·050 (0·094)	−0·0011 (0·0010)	+0·0045 (0·0035)	0·151
$dY/Y =$	5·361			−0·070 (0·044)	+0·0004 (0·0004)	−0·0008 (0·0016)	0·155
$dY_N/Y_N =$	2·092			−0·098 (0·044)	+0·0006 (0·0004)	+0·0025 (0·0016)	0·175
$I/Y =$	14·714			−0·155 (0·092)	+0·0007 (0·0010)	+0·0136 (0·0035)	0·383

Investment

	Constant	dY/Y	dY_N/Y_N	dP/P	$(dP/P)^2$	Y/N	r^2
$I/Y =$	17·782			−0·052 (0·102)	−0·0004 (0·0011)		0·146
$I/Y =$	15·038	+0·529 (0·380)		−0·011 (0·105)	−0·0007 (0·0011)		0·186
$I/Y =$	15·195		+0·971 (0·351)	+0·016 (0·098)	−0·0008 (0·0010)		0·286
$I/Y =$	11·326	+0·631 (0·320)		−0·110 (0·092)	+0·0005 (0·0009)	+0·0141 (0·0034)	0·440
$I/Y =$	13·220		+0·713 (0·319)	−0·091 (0·092)	+0·0002 (0·0009)	+0·0117 (0·0034)	0·454

	Constant	dY/Y	dY_N/Y_N	dP/P	$(dP/P)^2$	Y/N	r^2

COUNTRIES WITH PER CAPITA INCOMES $200-$799 p.a. (27)

Savings

Single equation

	Constant	dY/Y	dY_N/Y_N	dP/P	$(dP/P)^2$	Y/N	r^2
$S/Y =$	14·461			+0·285 (0·290)	−0·0073 (0·0075)		0·038
$S/Y =$	16·404	−0·366 (0·551)		+0·243 (0·300)	−0·0068 (0·0077)		0·057
$S/Y =$	14·613		−0·053 (0·445)	+0·281 (0·297)	−0·0073 (0·0077)		0·039
$S/Y =$	16·305	−0·363 (0·566)		+0·240 (0·314)	−0·0067 (0·0080)	+0·0002 (0·0056)	0·057
$S/Y =$	14·376		−0·087 (0·495)	+0·265 (0·318)	−0·0070 (0·0081)	+0·0010 (0·0062)	0·040

Reduced form

	Constant	dY/Y	dY_N/Y_N	dP/P	$(dP/P)^2$	Y/N	r^2
$S/Y =$	14·265			+0·276 (0·305)	−0·0071 (0·0079)	+0·0006 (0·0055)	0·039
$dY/Y =$	5·606			−0·100 (0·113)	+0·0011 (0·0029)	−0·0009 (0·0020)	0·214
$dY_N/Y_N =$	1·269			−0·126 (0·131)	+0·0016 (0·0034)	+0·0049 (0·0024)	0·262
$I/Y =$	15·878			−0·023 (0·318)	−0·0029 (0·0082)	+0·0110 (0·0058)	0·229

Investment

	Constant	dY/Y	dY_N/Y_N	dP/P	$(dP/P)^2$	Y/N	r^2
$I/Y =$	19·332			+0·124 (0·324)	−0·0063 (0·0084)		0·109
$I/Y =$	17·905	+0·269 (0·621)		+0·155 (0·337)	−0·0067 (0·0086)		0·117
$I/Y =$	16·651		+0·949 (0·458)	+0·181 (0·305)	−0·0064 (0·0079)		0·249
$I/Y =$	13·759	+0·377 (0·590)		+0·014 (0·328)	−0·0034 (0·0083)	+0·0113 (0·0059)	0·243
$I/Y =$	14·972		+0·713 (0·494)	+0·066 (0·317)	−0·0041 (0·0081)	+0·0074 (0·0061)	0·296

	Constant	dY/Y	dY_N/Y_N	dP/P	$(dP/P)^2$	Y/N	r^2
		COUNTRIES WITH PER CAPITA INCOMES < $200 p.a. (17)					

Savings

Single equation

	Constant	dY/Y	dY_N/Y_N	dP/P	$(dP/P)^2$	Y/N	r^2
$S/Y =$	14·861			−0·615	+0·0052		0·310
				(0·463)	(0·0040)		
$S/Y =$	10·585	+0·746		−0·522	+0·0045		0·477
		(0·367)		(0·421)	(0·0040)		
$S/Y =$	12·439		+0·807	−0·451	+0·0038		0·442
			(0·461)	(0·442)	(0·0042)		
$S/Y =$	8·312	+0·705		−0·701	+0·0063	+0·0270	0·549
		(0·356)		(0·427)	(0·0041)	(0·0194)	
$S/Y =$	9·328		+0·808	−0·645	+0·0058	+0·0303	0·533
			(0·439)	(0·439)	(0·0042)	(0·0197)	

Reduced form

	Constant	dY/Y	dY_N/Y_N	dP/P	$(dP/P)^2$	Y/N	r^2
$S/Y =$	11·762			−0·809	+0·0072	+0·0302	0·402
				(0·468)	(0·0045)	(0·0214)	
$dY/Y =$	4·890			−0·153	+0·0012	+0·0045	0·118
				(0·329)	(0·0032)	(0·0151)	
$dY_N/Y_N =$	3·010			−0·203	+0·0017	−0·0001	0·150
				(0·272)	(0·0026)	(0·0124)	
$I/Y =$	13·437			−0·157	+0·0008	+0·0210	0·435
				(0·392)	(0·0038)	(0·0180)	

Investment

	Constant	dY/Y	dY_N/Y_N	dP/P	$(dP/P)^2$	Y/N	r^2
$I/Y =$	15·590			−0·022	−0·0005		0·375
				(0·380)	(0·0036)		
$I/Y =$		+0·936		+0·094	−0·0014		0·727
		(0·228)		(0·262)	(0·0025)		
$I/Y =$	12·520		+1·023	+0·186	−0·0023		0·659
			(0·310)	(0·298)	(0·0028)		
$I/Y =$	8·981	+0·991		−0·016	−0·0002	+0·016	0·765
		(0·221)		(0·265)	(0·0025)	(0·012)	
$I/Y =$	10·355		+1·024	+0·050	−0·0009	+0·021	0·719
			(0·293)	(0·294)	(0·0028)	(0·013)	

	Constant	dY/Y	dY_N/Y_N	dP/P	$(dP/P)^2$	Y/N	r^2
			LATIN AMERICA (19)				

Savings

Single equation

	Constant	dY/Y	dY_N/Y_N	dP/P	$(dP/P)^2$	Y/N	r^2
$S/Y =$	12·545			+0·210	−0·0038		0·066
				(0·291)	(0·0075)		
$S/Y =$	14·154	−0·299		+0·165	−0·0031		0·080
		(0·627)		(0·313)	(0·0078)		
$S/Y =$	13·442		−0·439	+0·186	−0·0036		0·099
			(0·593)	(0·297)	(0·0076)		
$S/Y =$	11·244	−0·212		+0·091	−0·0020	+0·0097	0·191
		(0·611)		(0·309)	(0·0076)	(0·0070)	
$S/Y =$	10·955		−0·503	+0·090	−0·0022	+0·0104	0·227
			(0·570)	(0·292)	(0·0073)	(0·0068)	

Reduced form

	Constant	dY/Y	dY_N/Y_N	dP/P	$(dP/P)^2$	Y/N	r^2
$S/Y =$	10·039			+0·120	−0·0025	+0·0099	0·184
				(0·288)	(0·0073)	(0·0067)	
$dY/Y =$	5·677			−0·140	+0·0022	−0·0011	0·253
				(0·125)	(0·0031)	(0·0029)	
$dY_N/Y_N =$	1·818			−0·061	+0·0006	+0·0008	0·081
				(0·131)	(0·0033)	(0·0030)	
$I/Y =$	14·501			−0·046	−0·002	−0·013	0·201
				(0·350)	(0·008)	(0·008)	

Investment

	Constant	dY/Y	dY_N/Y_N	dP/P	$(dP/P)^2$	Y/N	r^2
$I/Y =$	17·937			+0·075	−0·0039		0·054
				(0·361)	(0·0092)		
$I/Y =$	15·465	+0·459		+0·144	−0·0050		0·076
		(0·772)		(0·386)	(0·0096)		
$I/Y =$	16·024		+0·936	+0·125	−0·0044		0·153
			(0·706)	(0·355)	(0·0090)		
$I/Y =$	11·166	+0·587		+0·035	−0·0034	+0·014	0·236
		(0·731)		(0·369)	(0·0091)	(0·008)	
$I/Y =$	12·942		+0·857	+0·005	−0·0026	+0·012	0·283
			(0·675)	(0·346)	(0·0087)	(0·008)	

	Constant	dY/Y	dY_N/Y_N	dP/P	$(dP/P)^2$	Y/N	r^2

Savings

AFRICA (7)

Single equation

	Constant	dY/Y	dY_N/Y_N	dP/P	$(dP/P)^2$	Y/N	r^2
$S/Y =$	26·713			−8·206 (3·969)	+0·921 (0·457)		0·517
$S/Y =$	29·073	−0·517 (1·298)		−8·301 (4·472)	+0·914 (0·514)		0·542
$S/Y =$	26·458		−0·508 (1·424)	−7·420 (4·998)	+0·812 (0·599)		0·537
$S/Y =$	9·568	+1·127 (1·941)		−3·889 (5·865)	+0·424 (0·664)	+0·046 (0·041)	0·716
$S/Y =$	10·762		+2·306 (2·186)	−5·909 (4·269)	+0·686 (0·505)	+0·066 (0·043)	0·787

Reduced form

	Constant	dY/Y	dY_N/Y_N	dP/P	$(dP/P)^2$	Y/N	r^2
$S/Y =$	19·514			−5·741 (4·346)	+0·615 (0·510)	+0·027 (0·023)	0·668
$dY/Y =$	8·818			−1·642 (1·464)	+0·168 (0·171)	−0·016 (0·008)	0·673
$dY_N/Y_N =$	3·795			+0·073 (1·126)	−0·030 (0·132)	−0·016 (0·006)	0·823
$I/Y =$	14·975			−1·623 (1·645)	+0·158 (0·193)	+0·015 (0·009)	0·717

Investment

	Constant	dY/Y	dY_N/Y_N	dP/P	$(dP/P)^2$	Y/N	r^2
$I/Y =$	19·026			−3·015 (1·764)	+0·330 (0·203)		0·433
$I/Y =$	20·810	−0·391 (0·547)		−3·086 (1·885)	+0·325 (0·216)		0·515
$I/Y =$	18·815		−0·419 (0·599)	−2·367 (2·103)	+0·240 (0·252)		0·512
$I/Y =$	11·507	+0·393 (0·744)		−0·982 (2·249)	+0·091 (0·254)	+0·022 (0·016)	0·751
$I/Y =$	11·778		+0·842 (0·843)	−1·689 (1·648)	+0·184 (0·195)	+0·029 (0·016)	0·811

Name Index

Subject Index

agricultural areas: and money market 118; opportunities for investment 143

balance of payments 31, 112, 140, 174, 197, 203, 213, 217, 218, 223, 224, 226–30; and credit expansion 180; and inflation 178–86

banking system 102, 104, 110–15, 137, 222; branch banking 114; deposits 110, 111, 139; development banks 115–17; fractional reserve banking 110, 113, 133–5, 138–9; issue of currency 113; provision of credit 111, 229; stabilisation role 113–14

borrowing, methods of 14

budget: deficit 220, 222, 228; surplus 68

capital: accumulation 5–8, 79–84, 86, 90, 102, 110, 141, 174, 175, 197; allocation of 102; deepening 92; formation 110, 160, 215, 220, 225, 229, 230, 232; imports 209, 213, 217, 218; market 102, 104, 118; physical 81–2, 175, 176; productivity 139–40; taxes 154–6; under-utilisation 145–8

see also foreign capital

capital-intensive techniques 148–56

capital–labour ratio 2, 90–2, 148

capital–output ratio 2–3, 9, 65, 67–9, 71, 74–6, 78, 139, 145, 148, 152–4, 160, 186, 205, 206, 219; and foreign capital 195; and inflation 158–9; empirical

evidence 156–9; investment and multiplier 141–4; reduction of 140–1

capital-scarcity 68, 72, 88, 150

capitalist spending 95

cash balances 43, 81, 83, 129

consumption 27, 190, 191; and money 82–4; expenditure 191, 194; growth rate 191; ratio 17

cost inflation xi, 30, 61, 207, 213, 233; pure cost models 44–6

credit: availability 220; controls 113, 225, 227; creation 86, 101, 110–11; expansion 229

credit-financed growth 134–40

Currency Board system 112

debt instruments 110–11

deficit financing and spending 12–14, 62, 99, 113, 141, 180, 181, 197–8, 215, 224, 229, 232

deflationary spiral 106 n.

demand and supply investment 67

demand inflation xi, xii, 22, 30, 34, 37, 58, 62, 122, 207, 211, 215, 233, 234; pure demand models 38–44

demand management policies 61, 146, 221, 227, 228

deposit facilities and banking 110, 111, 139

depression and unemployment 71

devaluation 179, 225, 226

developed countries: inflationary experience 34, 213, 217; warranted and natural growth rates 70

developing countries: banking systems 112–15; branch banking 114; capital scarcity 68, 72, 88; development banks 115–17;